D1714740

SAMUEL, SAUL AND JESUS

SOUTH FLORIDA STUDIES IN THE HISTORY OF JUDAISM

Edited by
Jacob Neusner
William Scott Green, James Strange
Darrell J. Fasching, Sara Mandell

Number 105
SAMUEL, SAUL AND JESUS
Three Early Palestinian Jewish
Christian Gospel Haggadoth

by
Roger David Aus

SAMUEL, SAUL AND JESUS
Three Early Palestinian Jewish Christian Gospel Haggadoth

by

Roger David Aus

Scholars Press
Atlanta, Georgia

SAMUEL, SAUL AND JESUS
Three Early Palestinian Jewish Christian Gospel Haggadoth

Publication of this book was made possible by a grant from the Tisch Family Foundation, New York City. The University of South Florida acknowledges with thanks this important support for its scholarly projects.

Library of Congress Cataloging in Publication Data
Aus, Roger, 1940-
　　Samuel, Saul, and Jesus / by Roger David Aus.
　　　　p.　cm.　— (South Florida studies in the history of Judaism　; no. 105)
　　Includes bibliographical references and index.
　　ISBN 1-55540-969-5
　　1. Bible. N.T. Gospels—Criticism, interpretation, etc.
2. Jesus Christ—Temple visit at age twelve. 3. Samuel (Biblical judge) in the new Testament. 4. Jesus Christ—Preaching at Nazareth. 5. Saul, King of Israel, in the New Testament. 6. Jesus Christ—Crucifixion. 7. Aggada. I. Title. II. Series.
BS2555.2.A94　1994
226'.06—dc20　　　　　　　　　　94-9894
　　　　　　　　　　　　　　　　CIP

Printed in the United States of America
on acid-free paper

Dedication

To

Samuel Brevig (b. 1874, d. 1937),
my maternal grandfather,
named after a great Israelite,

and

Jonathan, son number three
("Aller guten Dinge sind drei"),
named after the beloved son of Saul

* * *

"Haggadoth ... attract the heart of man like wine."
(*Sifre Deut.* Ha jazinu 317 on Deut 32:14)

"If you wish to know Him who spoke and the world
came into being, study haggadah, for from it you will
thus know Him ... and cleave to His ways."

(*Sifre Deut.* JEqeb 49 on Deut 11:22)

Table of Contents

CHAPTER TWO

CHAPTER THREE

Preface

Already in the Hebrew Bible Samuel was ranked on the same level as Moses (Jer 15:1). Judaic tradition then greatly embellished this figure, who anointed Israel's first king, Saul. In the middle of the first century C.E., for example, Philo of Alexandria called Samuel "the greatest of kings and prophets" (*Ebr.* 143). Judaic lore also emphasized the seer's intercession for others, adumbrated in 1 Sam 12:17-18 and Ps 99:6. Yet Samuel's relevance to the "New" Testament has not been properly recognized up to now. Although there are articles in the *Theological Dictionary of the New Testament* on Aaron and Balaam, for example, none exists on Samuel. The three chapters of the present volume aim to partly alleviate this deficit.

Chapter One interprets the narrative of the twelve-year-old Jesus in the Temple (Luke 2:41-51a) in light of Judaic traditions regarding the child and boy Samuel in the Temple (1 Samuel 1-3). After analyzing fifteen similarities between the two stories, I propose that a Palestinian Jewish Christian author, probably writing in Aramaic, based his material primarily on Judaic Samuel traditions.

Chapter Two deals with Jesus' rejection at Nazareth (Mark 6:1-6a), and Judaic traditions concerning the rejection of the anointed one Saul by the prophet Samuel and others. I point out twelve similarities between the two narratives and conclude that here, too, a Palestinian Jewish Christian author, probably writing in Aramaic, derived his motifs and terminology from Judaic lore concerning Samuel and Saul.

In other essays I have dealt with two specific aspects of Jesus' trial and crucifixion.[1] Here in Chapter Three I describe the Judaic background of the three prodigia at the crucifixion: an earthquake and saints rising

---

[1]Cf. "The Release of Barabbas (Mark 15:6-15 par.; John 18:39-40), and Judaic Traditions on the Book of Esther," and "The Death of One for All in John 11:45-54 in Light of Judaic Traditions," in *Barabbas and Esther and Other Studies in the Judaic Illumination of Earliest Christianity* (USFSHJ 54; Atlanta: Scholars Press, 1992) 1-27 and 29-63, respectively.

from the dead (Matt 27:51b-53), the sun's eclipse (Mark 15:33 par.), and the tearing or rending of the Temple curtain (Mark 15:38 par.). Connected to this complex is Jesus' promise to the repentant criminal crucified with him, that he will be with him in Paradise today (Luke 23:43). It is based on Judaic tradition regarding Samuel's words to Saul in 1 Sam 28:19. Finally, on the basis of the latter, I propose that a very early Palestinian Jewish Christian christology viewed Jesus' soul (not his body) as already ascending to God at the time of his death on the Cross. It is connected to the strange episode of Matt 27:51b-53. Stranger yet is the fact that such remnants have survived at all. The mainstream view, based primarily on Hos 6:2, was that Jesus rose from the dead only three days later, on Easter Sunday.

The argumentation and conclusions reached in the above studies are new in their present form. I have not encountered them in the secondary literature available to me on the three narrative complexes. I myself reached these conclusions only after considering the Judaic sources on which they are based for a number of years. Wherever possible I have sought to ascertain the earliest elements in the history of a particular Judaic tradition. Sometimes, however, a striking motif or philological parallel has only survived, for example, in a relatively late rabbinic source. Each such similarity must then be evaluated on its own terms.

The large number of Judaic sources employed here are enumerated with a full bibliography at the end of this volume. In the text only the standard abbreviations are given. While an index of the biblical and post-biblical passages cited would be simply too voluminous, an index of modern authors has been included. It helps to indicate where my own conclusions agree with, or more often differ from, those of contemporary scholarship.

None of the pericopes analyzed here is historical, although I do not deny, for example, that Jesus may have made pilgrimages to the Jerusalem Temple with his family, and some residents of Nazareth may have later rejected their native son as the Messiah. Nevertheless, the specific narratives of the twelve-year-old Jesus and Jesus' rejection at Nazareth, as now found in the gospels, were constructed decades later by Palestinian Jewish Christians on the basis of "Old" Testament and Judaic models in order to express *religious truths*. This was typical of Judaic haggadah,[2] and I point out relevant parallels in the respective

---

[2]Cf. the statement by M. Herr in the art. "Aggadah" in *EJ* (1971) 2.355: "the *aggadah* does contain truth which is greater than that of historical and philological reality, and more important than that of the natural sciences." For other Jewish Christian examples of haggadic narratives which express religious truths, see *Water into Wine, and the Beheading of John the Baptist.* Early Jewish-Christian

chapters.   One example is the three-hour solar eclipse at Jesus'
crucifixion, which is astronomically impossible. For the first Christians,
all Jews, it expressed however the religious truth that God was in
mourning for His only Son. He therefore followed the human mourning
custom of extinguishing the household lamp on such an occasion. No
early Palestinian Jewish Christian took this solar eclipse literally. Rather,
its religious meaning was primary. Unfortunately, lack of familiarity
with Judaic sources, customs, and the nature of haggadah,[3] has led to a
debate on the historicity of specific gospel passages which is false in its
premises. Constructed narratives can nevertheless be true in a religious
sense.

I would hope that the three chapters of this volume may contribute
to a deeper appreciation by non-Jewish Christians, and by interested
Jews, of the immensely creative energy of the earliest Palestinian Jewish
Christians. They employed, for example, biblical and Judaic traditions
on Samuel and Saul to describe in a masterful way new situations in the
life of him whom they now considered to be the Messiah, the Son of God.
Both their literary and their theological artistry should be admired for
what they are.

My thanks go to Professor Étan Levine of Haifa for reading a first
draft of Chapter Two, and to Dr. Niko Oswald of Berlin in regard to
some Hebrew and Aramaic expressions. Because of an eye operation, I
am grateful to my son Martin and the Reverend Ralph Zorn for help in
proofreading. Finally, I would sincerely like to thank Professor Jacob
Neusner for accepting this volume in the series *South Florida Studies in the
History of Judaism*. May it encourage other students of the New
Testament to become better acquainted with Judaic sources, and to
undertake similar studies. I can confirm that this can be a fascinating
treasure hunt.

Roger David Aus
April 1993
Berlin, Germany

Interpretation of Esther 1 in John 2:1-11 and Mark 6:17-29 (BJS 150; Atlanta:
Scholars Press, 1988), and the chapter "Die Weihnachtsgeschichte im Lichte
jüdischer Traditionen vom Mose-Kind und Hirten-Messias (Lukas 2, 1-20)" in
Weihnachtsgeschichte, Barmherziger Samariter, Verlorener Sohn. Studien zu ihrem
jüdischen Hintergrund (ANTZ 2; Berlin: Institut Kirche und Judentum, 1988) 11-
58.
[3]On the haggadah/aggadah, cf. also the remarks by M. Herr and the excerpt from
the *Encyclopaedia Hebraica* in the art. "Aggadah" in *EJ* (1971) 2.354-366.

Max Liebermann, "The Twelve-Year-Old Jesus in the Temple," 1879.
Courtesy of the Hamburger Kunsthalle; black-and-white photo by Elke Walford.

1

The Child Jesus in the Temple (Luke 2:41-51a), and Judaic Traditions on the Child Samuel in the Temple (1 Samuel 1-3)

Introduction

For the first eighteen years of my life I encountered Heinrich Hofmann's portrayal of "The Boy Jesus in the Temple" daily. It hung in the living room of our homes in Jamestown and Fargo, North Dakota, U.S.A. In Berlin I later became well acquainted with Max Liebermann's masterful 1879 rendering of the same subject.[1] President and honorary president of the Prussian Academy of Arts from 1920-32, as a Jew Liebermann was forced to leave the Academy by the National Socialists (Nazis) in 1933. He had already been given a solid taste of this Anti-Semitism when his picture was first displayed at the international exhibition of art in Munich in 1879. Very shortly thereafter Christian Bavarian legislators publicly called it "blasphemous," although the entire jury considered it the best picture which had been painted in Munich in fifty years.[2]

One aspect of Liebermann's presentation of the twelve-year-old child Jesus in the Jerusalem Temple is noteworthy here. Luke 2:46 relates that his parents found Jesus "sitting among the teachers, listening to them and asking them questions" (RSV). Liebermann has all five of the scholars he portrays listen very carefully to the child Jesus, who gestures

---

[1]Cf. the illustrated brochure "Hamburger Kunsthalle. Der zwölfjährige Jesus im Tempel, von Max Liebermann," ed. H. Leppien (Kulturstiftung der Länder, no date, ca. 1989).
[2]*Ibid.* 6, 20-21.

with his hands before his chest. The two sages closest to him are both sitting wrapped in their prayer shawls. Yet Jesus, in contrast to the gospel account, is standing.[3]

This artistic liberty, taken by the master Jewish artist Liebermann, is similar to the artistic liberty an early Palestinian Jewish Christian took when he created the scene of the twelve-year-old Jesus in the Temple in light of Judaic traditions on the child/boy Samuel in the Temple. The following six sections substantiate this proposal.

I
Peculiarities in the Pericope Luke 2:41-51a

It is general scholarly consensus that the song of thanksgiving in Luke 1:46-55, the "Magnificat," recited by Jesus' mother Mary, is modeled on the song in 1 Sam 2:1-10, recited by Samuel's mother Hannah.[4]

Joseph and Mary's "presentation" of their firstborn son Jesus in the Temple in Jerusalem, coupled with a sacrifice (Luke 2:22b-24), also recalls Elkanah and Hannah's presentation of their firstborn son Samuel in the Temple at Shiloh, coupled with a sacrifice (1 Sam 1:24-25, 27b).

In addition, in Luke 2:36-38 a prophetess named Hannah ("Αννα), eighty-four years old, worships in the Jerusalem Temple, also by fasting and prayer. She thanks God, speaking of him (the Messiah) to all who expect the redemption of Jerusalem. In Judaic tradition the mother of Samuel, in the Septuagint "Αννα, is also considered to be very old when her prayer for offspring is granted.[5] This is in fulfillment of her intense

---

[3]H. Hofmann also has the child Jesus and the Temple teachers standing. Contrast the sitting Jesus in Rembrandt's etching of 1654 (reproduced in *ibid.*, 18).

[4]Cf. already E. Burrows, *The Gospel of the Infancy and Other Biblical Essays* (London: Burns, Oates & Washbourne, 1940) 10. See also G. Caird, "The First and Second Books of Samuel" in *IB* 2 (1953) 882, as well as H. Stoebe, *Das erste Buch Samuelis* (KAT 8,1; Gütersloh: Mohn, 1973) 103. The continuation of this tradition is found in the song of "Anna," at the birth of her daughter Mary, in "The Protevangelium of James" 6:2 (Hennecke and Schneemelcher, *New Testament Apocrypha* 1.377-378). The whole section is based on 1 Samuel 1-2, as shown in the footnotes.

[5]In *Midr. Samuel* 4/1 (Hebrew in Buber, *Midrash Samuel* 54-55; German in Wünsche, *Aus Israels Lehrhallen* 5.28), R. Simeon b. Laqish, a second generation Palestinian Amora (Strack and Stemberger, *Introduction* 95), says this fulfillment took place when she was 100, as with Abraham, or at 90, as with Sarah. R. Yoḥanan (b. Nappaḥa), also a second generation Palestinian Amora and brother-in-law of R. Simeon b. Laqish *(ibid.,)*, says Hannah was "remembered at the age of 130, as Jochebed (the mother of Israel's first redeemer, Moses) was. In *Pesiq. R.* 43/5 (Friedmann 181; Braude 763) and *Eliyyahu Rabbah* 18 (Hebrew in Friedmann

praying in the Temple of Shiloh (1 Sam 1:10-16, 26-27). She thanks God in 1 Sam 2:1-10, also in regard to the future messianic king (v 10).[6] In Judaic tradition Hannah is also considered a prophetess.[7]

The figure of Hannah in 1 Samuel 2 is combined here in Luke 2:36-38 with that of "the women who served at the entrance to the tent of meeting" (at the Temple in Shiloh): 1 Sam 2:22. The Targum of this verse says they came to "pray" there,[8] as in Luke 2:37. In the parallel tradition, the Septuagint of Exod 38:8 has these same women "fast," also as in Luke 2:37. Targum Yerushalmi I on the verse adds that they "praise and give thanks" (to God) at this time.[9]

Finally, the two verses which frame the narrative of the twelve-year-old Jesus in the Temple in Luke 2:41-51a,[10] vv 40 and 52, describing the growth of Jesus as a child and boy, are clearly reminiscent of the description of the boy Samuel in 1 Sam 2:21b, 26 and 3:19a. Indeed, with the exception of the addition of "wisdom" and of "God" for "the Lord," Luke 2:52, for example, agrees very closely with the Hebrew of 1 Sam 2:26.

All of these factors in chapters one and two of the Third Gospel make it very probable that Luke 2:41-51a is also somehow related to the narrative of Elkanah, Hannah, and their child/boy Samuel in 1 Samuel 1-3 in Judaic tradition.[11] Before I make a number of these comparisons in section II, it will be helpful to point out eight peculiarities in Luke 2:41-51a.

1) In v 41 Jesus' parents are described as going to Jerusalem every year at the festival/feast of "Passover." The emphasis on this

---

99; Braude and Kapstein 259), Hannah had been childless for nineteen and one half years before conceiving Samuel.

[6]Cf. for example *Midr. Sam.* 5/17 on 1 Sam 2:10's "horn" as that of the messianic King (Buber, *Midrash Samuel* 64; Wünsche, *Aus Israels Lehrhallen* 5.43).

[7]Cf. *b. Meg.* 14a (Soncino 82-83), where in regard to 1 Sam 2:1 she is one of the seven prophetesses of Israel. See also *Seder 'Olam* 21 (Milikowsky Hebrew 355, English 510), as well as Philo, *Som.* 1.254.

[8]Cf. the Aramaic in Sperber, *The Bible in Aramaic* 2.98-99, and the English in Harrington and Saldarini, *Targum Jonathan of the Former Prophets* 107. See also *Tg. Onq.* Exod 38:8 (Drazin, *Targum Onkelos to Exodus* 336-337), *Tg. Yer.* I (Rieder, *Targum Jonathan* 1.141; Etheridge, *The Targums* 570), and *Targum Neofiti* on the same verse (Díez Macho, *Neophyti 1*, 2.255 and 526), as well as *Midr. Sam.* 7/4 on 1 Sam 2:22 (Wünsche, *Aus Israels Lehrhallen* 5.49, with n. 2).

[9]Aramaic in Rieder, *Targum Jonathan* 1.141. For these sources, cf. Str-B 2.141.

[10]For the exact extent of the pericope, see the discussion below in section IV.

[11]I do not here espouse joint authorship of these sections, although it should not be excluded. My purpose is simply to show that Palestinian Jewish Christians (see below) also described other incidents now found in the Lucan birth narrative, in addition to 2:41-51a, in light of Judaic traditions on 1 Samuel 1-2.

particular festival remains unexplained in regard to the other two pilgrimage festivals of Weeks and Booths (Exod 23:14-17; 34:18-24; Leviticus 23; Deuteronomy 16), just as important.

2) In v 42, "according to the custom of the feast" is puzzling. The RSV therefore adds "the feast" to the beginning of v 43: "and when the feast was ended." Yet in this case, "of the feast" in Greek would normally come after "And when they had completed the days," and not before "and."

3) In v 43 the narrator relates that Jesus' parents didn't notice that he remained in Jerusalem when they started to return (to Nazareth). This highly unusual lack of parental care, contrasted to that in v 48b, points to the artificial plot of the whole incident.

4) In v 44 the term συνοδία, "company" (RSV),[12] occurs, singular in the entire NT.

5) In v 46 Jesus' parents, having returned to Jerusalem and sought him for three days, find him sitting in the Temple among the teachers (of the Torah), listening to them and asking them questions. No mention is made of where the lad has slept and eaten for four days, which also shows the artificiality of the plot. This question and similar ones are irrelevant to the narrator.

6) In v 48 the expression ὀδυνώμενοι is difficult. In the sense of mental and spiritual pain, the term only occurs in the NT here and in Acts 20:38.

7) In v 49 Jesus' response to his mother suddenly becomes plural: "Why were *you* seeking me?" In addition, the meaning of the Greek phrase ὅτι ἐν τοῖς τοῦ πατρός μου δεῖ εἶναι με is open to numerous interpretations. Not only Jesus' parents had difficulty in understanding it (v 50). Scholars today also seek to establish its probable meaning.

8) Finally, the term τὸ ῥῆμα in v 50 is translated in the RSV as "the saying." This recalls the Hebrew noun דבר, both "word" and "matter,"[13] which also may point to a Semitic original.

These eight observations point to the pericope of Luke 2:41-51a as a constructed story with numerous philological and logical peculiarities. In addition, the question must be raised as to whether it derives from a Semitic original, based on earlier Judaic interpretation of Samuel as a

---

[12]BAGD 791 explains it as: "caravan, group of travelers."

[13]Cf. Jastrow 278 and BDB 182-184. In Luke 2:50, the verb "he spoke" would have the same Semitic root. In v 51b, τὰ ῥήματα means "things." As I point out in section IV below, however, it is of Lucan origin, deriving from 2:19.

child and boy in 1 Samuel 1-3. The following sections seek to illuminate the peculiarities in philology and plot in the narrative of the twelve-year-old Jesus in the Temple, to argue for a Semitic original, to define the extent, content, age, purpose, genre and historicity of the original narrative, and to point out many similarities between the boy Jesus and the child/boy Samuel in Judaic tradition. To the latter I shall now turn.

II
Similarities Between the Twelve-Year-Old Jesus and the Child/Boy Samuel in Judaic Tradition

A large number of similarities in expressions and motifs exist between the narrative of the twelve-year-old Jesus in the Temple, and Judaic traditions regarding the child/boy Samuel in the Temple in 1 Samuel 1-3. While the reader may differ with an individual argument, cumulatively the similarities I now analyze present a strong case for the Palestinian Jewish Christian author of Luke 2:41-51a as dependent on Palestinian Judaic Samuel traditions.[14]

1. A Parental Pilgrimage.

A.

Luke 2:41 relates that Jesus' parents went annually to Jerusalem for the feast/festival of Passover. The technical term for "going on a pilgrimage" is found in v 42, "to go up" (ἀναβαίνομαι). It corresponds to the Hebrew עלי, עלה, Aramaic עלי, עלא: "to go up (to Jerusalem and the Temple for the festival)." The more complete form is the verb plus לרגל, "to go up by foot." The term עולי רגלים or עולי רינלאין עולי רינלין means "pilgrims."[15]

It is important to note that although the Torah prescribed only males' going up to Jerusalem at the three pilgrimage festivals (Exod 23:17; 34:23;

---

[14]For many of these Judaic sources, cf. Ginzberg, *The Legends of the Jews* 4.57-60, with the relevant notes in 6.215-220, to whom I am frequently indebted. See also J. Lauterbach, "Samuel. In Rabbinical Literature" in *JE* (1905) 2.7, as well as A. Rubens, "Samuel. In the Aggadah" in *EJ* (1971) 14.783-84. For recent bibliography on Luke 2:41-52, cf. F. Bovon, *Das Evangelium nach Lukas (Lk 1,1-9,50)* (EKKNT III/1; Zurich: Benziger; Neukirchen-Vluyn: Neukirchener, 1989) 151; G. Wagner, *An Exegetical Bibliography of the New Testament. Luke and Acts* (Macon, Georgia: Mercer University, 1985) 45-47; J. Fitzmyer, *The Gospel According to Luke I-IX* (AB 28; Garden City, New York: Doubleday, 1981) 447-48; and R. Brown, *The Birth of the Messiah. A Commentary on the Infancy Narratives in Matthew and Luke* (Garden City, New York: Doubleday, 1979) 496.

[15]Jastrow 1081, d), and 1082. A comprehensive treatment of pilgrimage in biblical and Judaic sources is found in S. Safrai, *Die Wallfahrt im Zeitalter des Zweiten Tempels* (Forschungen zum jüdisch-christlichen Dialog 3; Neukirchen: Neukirchener, 1981).

Deut 16:16), here Mary accompanies Joseph, and they take their twelve-year-old son along. Her presence was not required by Scripture at such a pilgrimage. Like other women, she came along voluntarily.[16] Her participation here makes her appear particularly devout. Yet Mary went along because Hannah went along on pilgrimages to the Temple with her husband Elkanah. In addition, the fact that *both* parents search for Jesus in the caravan and in Jerusalem heightens the dramatic tension. Also, by Mary's posing the question of 2:48, the author provides himself with a means of contrasting Jesus' father and his Father. This would have been more difficult to present if Joseph had been alone and himself had asked a similar question.

Other expressions in 2:41-51a also point to a pilgrimage. The "company" or "caravan" of pilgrims from Nazareth (v 51; cf. v 39), including Joseph and Mary's "relatives and acquaintances" in v 44, will be analyzed below in section five. Here, however, it should be noted that one Hebrew and Aramaic expression for "parents," corresponding to the γονεῖς of Luke 2:41 and 43, is שְׁיָרָה/שְׁיִירָא.[17] This is important in regard to the Semitic original of 2:41-51a I propose below in section III, especially as a word play with "caravan" and "remaining behind, being left behind."

The result of the pilgrimage to the Temple in Jerusalem by Jesus' parents is that they leave their twelve-year-old son there by mistake. The pilgrimage is the literary device used by the author to get Jesus from Nazareth into the Jerusalem Temple precincts, where he can display his great understanding of the Torah and also point to his special relationship to his Father.

B.

For the period of the Second Temple, numerous pilgrimage psalms are attested.[18] Already for the time of the First Temple, various fragments of such psalms are found in the prophets.[19] Yet *the* scriptural passage which proves the existence of pilgrimages before the sixth century B.C.E. exile of many Israelites to Babylonia is the narrative of Elkanah and Hannah with their child Samuel, in 1 Samuel 1-3.[20] I shall relate other relevant Judaic interpretation of these chapters below. Here only the pilgrimage aspects of the Hebrew text by itself should be noted.

---

[16]Cf. *m. Ḥag.* 1:1 (Danby 211) and many other early rabbinic texts cited by P. Billerbeck in Str-B 2.141-142. Only a small number also obligated women to appear at the three pilgrimage festivals.

[17]Cf. Jastrow 1562. Another, more frequent term, is הוֹרִים (Jastrow 340).

[18]Cf. the references cited in Safrai, *Die Wallfahrt* 17.

[19]*Ibid.* 8, n. 42.

[20]*Ibid.* 7-8.

1 Sam 1:3 remarks that Elkanah used to "go up" year by year (with his first wife Peninnah, including her sons and daughters - v 4) from his native city to worship and to sacrifice to the Lord (in the Temple - v 9) at Shiloh. This occurred annually (v 7, with "going up"). Once Elkanah and his entire household, without pregnant Hannah, "went up" to offer to the Lord the yearly sacrifice and to pay his vow (v 21). However, after Hannah had weaned her child Samuel, she herself "took him up," with offerings, to the house of the Lord in Shiloh (v 24). There both parents brought the child to the priest Eli (v 25), left him there in the Temple (v 28), and returned home (2:11). In contrast to Jesus' parents, they *intentionally* left Samuel in the Temple. Later the parents "went up" annually to Shiloh, also providing their boy with clothing (2:19).

This great emphasis on the annual "going up" of the parents of the child/boy Samuel to the Temple in Shiloh, and their leaving him there, provided the scriptural basis for a Palestinian Jewish Christian, who described Jesus' parents as "going up" annually to the Temple in Jerusalem, and once (mistakenly) leaving him there in Luke 2:41-51a.

Various aspects of this pilgrimage of Jesus' parents to the Jerusalem Temple, with their twelve-year-old son, will now be elucidated in light of Judaic tradition on 1 Samuel 1-3.

2. An Annual Pilgrimage.

A.

Luke 2:41 states that Jesus' parents "used to go" to Jerusalem "annually" at the feast/festival of Passover. The first Greek expression is the imperfect of πορεύομαι. It corresponds to the Hebrew היו הולכים. The verb היה, הוה, הוי with the present participle of another verb frequently means "used to."[21]

The second Greek expression, κατ᾽ ἔτος, "annually, yearly, each year, every year," is only found here in the entire NT. One of the peculiarities of Luke 2:41-51a, as noted above in the Introduction, is that Jesus' parents are represented here as making an "annual" pilgrimage to Jerusalem (only) at Passover. The other pilgrim festivals, Weeks and Booths, are not mentioned, although they were just as binding as Passover. Again, the reason for this peculiar usage of "annually" is found in 1 Samuel 1-2.

---

[21]Cf. Jastrow 338. A good example is *Eliyyahu Rabbah* 8(9) in Friedmann 47, Braude and Kapstein 150. Commenting on 1 Sam 1:3, the midrash says Elkanah "used to go on pilgrimage" (היה א' עולה) four times a year (to Shiloh). See also P. McCarter, Jr., *I Samuel* (AB 8; Garden City, New York: Doubleday, 1980) 49 on 1 Sam 1:3: "This man used to go up...."

B.

The only occurrence of κατ᾽ ἔτος in the Septuagint is 2 Macc 11:3, where Lysias (cf. 1 Macc 3:32-33) intends to "put up the high priesthood for sale 'every year.'" Josephus employs the expression, however, eight times,[22] and also has the variants ἀνὰ πᾶν ἔτος,[23] κατὰ πᾶν ἔτος,[24] and καθ᾽ ἔκαστον ἔτος[25]. The association of "annually" and the pilgrimage festivals is found in *Ant.* 18.95: "This was the procedure at the three festivals 'each year' (ἑκάστου ἔτους) and on the fast day [Day of Atonement]."[26]

Yet the origin of the term κατ᾽ ἔτος in Luke 2:41 lies in the "annual" pilgrimage of Samuel's parents Elkanah and Hannah to the Temple in Shiloh. 1 Sam 1:3 relates of Elkanah that he used to go up "year by year" (מימים ימימה) from his city to worship and sacrifice at Shiloh. This motif is repeated in 1:7 (שנה בשנה), with the house of the Lord; 1:21 with the "yearly" sacrifice (הימים); and 2:19, which repeats the expressions found in 1:3 and 21.

The Septuagint translates none of these occurrences in 1 Samuel 1-2 by κατ᾽ ἔτος. 1 Kgdms 1:3, for example, repeats the clumsy Hebrew phrase: ἐξ ἡμερῶν εἰς ἡμέρας. This shows that the Palestinian Jewish Christian author of Luke 2:41-51a, basing his narrative in part on the biblical account in Hebrew of the annual pilgrimage of the child Samuel's parents to the Temple in Shiloh, was not influenced by the Septuagint at this point.

The Targum has "annually" (שנא בשנא) only in 1 Sam 1:7.[27] It, or an earlier form of it, does not appear to have influenced the author either. He was working independently here.

The peculiar emphasis of Jesus' parents' making a pilgrimage "annually" to Jerusalem at the festival of Passover (and at no other time), thus probably derives from the "annual pilgrimage of the child/boy Samuel's parents to the Temple in Shiloh.

3.   The Festival.

A.

Luke 2:41 relates that Jesus' parents used to go annually to Jerusalem at the "festival/feast" (ἑορτή) of Passover. Verse 42 repeats the term in

---

[22]Cf. *Ant.* 4.69; 8.57,141,160,396; 12.169; 13.55 and 20.211.
[23]In *Bell.* 7.218.
[24]In *Ant.* 9.238; 12.92,412; and 18.377.
[25]In *Ant.* 1.96 and 11.63.
[26]English translation in the LCL edition of Josephus by L. Feldman. This variant is also found in *Ant.* 4.240.
[27]Cf. Sperber, *The Bible in Aramaic* 2.94.

the difficult phrase "according to the usage of the festival/feast," where some versions and commentators prefer to associate the latter term with the following verse. The RSV, for example, has: "and they went up according to custom; and when the feast was ended...." This emphasis, through repetition, on a "festival/feast" also derives from Judaic tradition on 1 Samuel 1-2.

B.

The Targum, certainly representing popular tradition here, changes the inexplicit Hebrew "from day to days" in 1:3 to "from the time of festival to festival" (מועד), and in 1:21 the sacrifice "of days" to "of the festival" (מועדא). In 2:19 the Targum also has for "from days to days" "from the time of festival to festival" (מועדא), and for the sacrifice "of days" "of the festival" (מועדא).[28] (On the "festival" of Passover in *Pseudo-Philo* regarding Elkanah and Hannah's pilgrimage to the Temple in Shiloh, including the מועדה of Exod 13:10, see the next section, four, on "Passover.")

In the Septuagint, ἑορτή translates the Hebrew מועד twenty-nine times, and מועדה once. The emphasis on the "festival/feast" in Luke 2:41-42 derives from Judaic tradition, still reflected in the present version of the Targum of 1 Samuel 1-2 regarding the pilgrimage of the child/boy Samuel's parents to the Temple. There they went up to "the festival/feast" and offered a "festival" sacrifice. Later, when the Semitic original of Luke 2:41-51a was translated into Greek in Greek-speaking Jewish Christian circles, the term מועד/מועדא was correctly rendered by ἑορτή, a translation well attested already in the Septuagint.

4. Passover.

A.

Luke 2:41 notes that Jesus' parents used to go (on a pilgrimage) annually to Jerusalem at the festival/feast of Passover. It is justifiable to ask why they regularly made their pilgrimage just then, and not at the festival of Weeks or Booths, or at all three. Again, the author of Luke 2:41-51a here shows his dependence on Judaic tradition regarding the specific festival at which Samuel's parents used to go up to the Temple in Shiloh.

B.

In regard to 1 Sam 1:3, where Elkanah went up annually from his city to worship and sacrifice to the Lord at Shiloh, *Pseudo-Philo* in 50:2 relates that this occurred with his wives Hannah and Peninnah on "the

---

[28]*Ibid.*, 2.94-98. English in Harrington and Saldarini, *Targum Jonathan of the Former Prophets* 103-107.

good day of Passover."[29] This is a Hebraism for יום טוב, "good day," which means "festival."[30] The pilgrimage of Elkanah and his wives to the Temple thus took place at the festival of Passover in this Palestinian work from about the time of Jesus, originally composed in Hebrew.[31] It is based on the comparison of the phrase in 1 Sam 1:3, מימים ימימה, with the same phrase in Exod 13:10, connected to the "appointed time" or festival/feast (מועדה) of Unleavened Bread = Passover.[32]

This very early tradition is still mirrored in a late Jewish source. In *Aggadat Bereshit* 29, the expression "from days to days" of 1 Sam 1:3 is commented upon by the expositor's saying: "This is Passover," for which Exod 13:10 is cited.[33]

Finally, 1 Sam 1:24 says that at the time Hannah weaned her son Samuel, she took him up (on a pilgrimage) to the house of the Lord in Shiloh, where she and her husband sacrificed (v 25).

Tannaitic tradition relates that weaning took place at twenty-four months.[34] Rabbinic tradition is united in maintaining that Hannah also

---

[29]Cf. the English by D. Harrington in *OTP* 2.364.

[30]Jastrow 569. Cf. the Latin *die bono pasche* in Harrington, Pseudo-Philon, *Les Antiquités Bibliques* 1.328, as well as the commentary in 2.213. Ginzberg in *The Legends* 6.216, n.9, first called attention to this.

[31]Cf. *OTP* 2.298-300.

[32]Cf. the art. "Feasts and Fasts" C.2a by J. Rylaarsdam in *IDB* 2.263, as well as his "Passover and Unleavened Bread" in 3.663-668. On this same principle of comparison, see also *Pseudo-Philo* 48:3, referring to Judg 21:19 (*OTP* 2.362).

[33]Cf. Buber, *Aggadat Bereshit* 60. Ginzberg, *The Legends* 6.216, n.9, mistakenly has chapter 19 instead of 29. Pseudo-Jerome on 1 Sam 1:3 states that Elkanah went up to the house of the Lord at the three festivals of Passover, Pentecost (Weeks) and Tabernacles (Booths). Cf. this work, perhaps by a converted Jew from the ninth century C.E., in *Pseudo-Jerome. Questions on the Book of Samuel*, ed. A. Saltman 13, with the Latin text on p. 66. The passage is also found in Migne, *PL* 23.1393. In the same chapter (2), Pseudo-Jerome alludes to Elkanah's going up to Shiloh with "his house" in 1 Sam 1:21, also on the pilgrimage festivals *(ibid.)*. He cites Exod 23:14 and Deut 16:16 for this. Saltman's view of "Pseudo-Jerome's valueless and pointless inventions" (23) is greatly exaggerated. The author definitely had access to Judaic material on 1 Samuel 1. A singular tradition in *Midr. Sam.* 1/8 has R. Joshua b. Levi, a first generation Palestinian Amora (Strack and Stemberger, *Introduction* 92-93), interpret the "day" of 1 Sam 1:4 as the (final, fiftieth) day of the festival of Weeks, Pentecost (Buber, *Midrash Samuel* 46; Wünsche, *Aus Israels Lehrhallen* 5.13, with n.1).

[34]Cf. for example *t. Nid.* 2:1-6 (Neusner 6.208-209, where it is the "normal" time; R. Eliezer [b. Hyrcanus, a second generation Tanna-Strack and Stemberger, *Introduction* 77] in 2:3 maintains twenty-four months but not longer); *m. Giṭ.* 7:6 (Danby 316); *t. Giṭ.* 5:6 (Neusner 3.230-231); *Lam. Rab.* 1:1 §11 (Soncino 7.78, with n.1); and J. Preuss, *Biblisch-talmudische Medizin* (New York: KTAV, 1971) 471.

weaned her son Samuel at this time.[35] The second generation Tanna R. Eliezer b. Hyrcanus[36] states that Hannah conceived, that is, the Lord "remembered" her (1 Sam 1:19) at New Year's since the same term occurs in association with New Year's in Lev 23:24.[37] Early Judaic tradition maintained that God brings His glory upon, and reveals the new age to, a seven month child like Isaac.[38] The sixth generation Babylonian Amora Mar Zutra[39] states in this regard that Sarah bore Isaac in the seventh month, before its completion. He derives this from 1 Sam 1:20, where Hannah conceived and bore Samuel at six months and two days, the minimum number of cycles (תקופות) being two, and days (ימים) two.[40]

R. Eliezer b. Hyrcanus says Isaac was born at Passover. Like his mother Sarah, Hannah, too, was "visited" on New Year's.[41] Although not explicitly stated, this must mean that Samuel was also born, like Isaac, at Passover. Since he was weaned exactly twenty-four months later, Elkanah and Hannah's pilgrimage with their child Samuel to the Temple in Shiloh in 1 Sam 1:24 also took place at Passover.

The same pilgrimage festival was attended by Jesus' parents, who went up with him from Nazareth to the Temple in Jerusalem, precisely at Passover.

---

[35]Cf. the very early writing *Pseudo-Philo* 51:1 (*OTP* 2.365), as well as *Num. Rab.* Bemidbar 3/8 on Num 3:15 (Soncino 5.82), and *y. Ber.* 4:1 (Neusner/Zahavy 1.158) by R. Yose b. R. Bun, a fifth generation Palestinian Amora (Strack and Stemberger, *Introduction* 106). Parallels to the latter are found in *y. Bikk.* 2:1,64c (Neusner 10.160), *y. Taᶜan.* 4:1,67c (Neusner 18.239), and *Midr. Sam.* 3/3 on 1 Sam 1:20-22 (Wünsche, *Aus Israels Lehrhallen* 5.23).

[36]Cf. n. 34.

[37]Cf. *b. Roš Haš.* 10b-11a (Soncino 39-41). See also *b. Ber.* 29a (Soncino 176) and *Yeb.* 64b (Soncino 430). One tradition has Gen 21:1, with the Lord's "visiting" Sarah (and her conceiving and bearing Isaac in v 2), as the Torah reading for New Year's in the early Palestinian triennial lectionary system. The haftarah or prophetic reading on this occasion is the story of Hannah (in 1 Samuel 1-2). See *b. Meg.* 31a (Soncino 188), as well as *Pesiq. R.* 43 (Braude 754, n. 1), and the art. "Triennial Cycle" in *EJ* (1971) 15.1387.

[38]Cf. *Pseudo-Philo* 23:8 (*OTP* 2.333). In *The Legends* 6.217, n. 13, Ginzberg cites *Midrash Haggadol* to the extent that "all prophets were seven-month children."

[39]Strack and Stemberger, *Introduction* 108.

[40]Cf. *b. Roš. Haš.* 11a (Soncino 41, with n. 10).

[41]Cf. *b. Roš. Haš.* 10b (Soncino 39), where R. Joshua (b. Hananya), also a second generation Tanna (Strack and Stemberger, *Introduction* 77-78), agrees with him. In *Tanhuma* Vayera 17 on Gen 21:1 (Singermann 136-137) it is stated that Isaac was born in the seventh month, "in the night of Passover." Some rabbinic authorities here read Hannah as one of the four barren women "visited" at New Year's.

5. Returning Home from a Pilgrimage, and Completing Days.

A.

Luke 2:42 states that when Jesus was twelve years old, they (his parents and he) went up (pres. ptc.) according to the usage of the feast/festival. Verse 43 continues with the aorist active participle of τελειόω: "And when they had 'completed' the days (of the festival), they 'returned' (ὑποστρέφω); yet the child/boy Jesus remained in Jerusalem, and his parents didn't know it."

I suggest that the phrases "completing days" and "returning" are due to the influence of 1 Sam 1:19-20 on the Palestinian Jewish Christian author of Luke 2:41-51a.

B.

1 Sam 1:19 states that when Samuel's parents had finished their pilgrimage to the Temple in Shiloh, they "returned" (וַיָּשֻׁבוּ) and went home to Ramah. This is very similar to the motif of Jesus' parents' "returning" to their home town of Nazareth after making their pilgrimage to the Temple in Jerusalem (Luke 2:43).

In the Septuagint, the verb ὑποστρέφω,   when it has a Hebrew equivalent, translates שוב sixteen times, and three other verbs only once each. 1 Kgdms 1:19 cannot have influenced the author of Luke 2:41-51a in v 43, for it reflects a different tradition: "and they go their way. And Elkanah entered his house at Armathaim...." This indicates that the Palestinian Jewish Christian author of the narrative of the twelve-year-old Jesus was rather dependent on what is still found in the MT: "they returned." The Targum is the same: ותבו.[42]

Secondly, the next verse, 1 Sam 1:20, states: "And it happened at the coming round/circuits (תְּקֻפֹות) of days that..." The rare noun תְּקוּפָה here implies "completion."[43] This is exactly how the Targum translates this unusual phrase: "And it happened at the time of 'the completion of days'..." (משלם יומיא)[44]. The noun here, מְשְׁלַם, means "completion, end."[45] The Hebrew root שלם is translated a number of times in the Septuagint by τελέω, τελειόω and τέλειος.[46] This makes it probable that the Palestinian Jewish Christian author of Luke 2:41-51a borrowed not only the motif of Jesus' parents' "returning" home in v 43 from the Hebrew or Aramaic of 1 Sam 1:19. He also was influenced by a Semitic Judaic tradition of "the

---

[42]Cf. Sperber 2.95.

[43]Cf. BDB 880, as well as נקף II 2 (BDB 669). The noun occurs only four other times in the MT.

[44]Sperber 2.95; cf. Harrington and Saldarini, *Targum Jonathan of the Former Prophets* 104.

[45]Jastrow 856.

[46]Cf. the concordance of Hatch-Redpath, 1342-1343.

completion of days" found in the Hebrew of 1 Sam 1:20, and explicitly in the Targum of the verse, when he described Joseph, Mary and Jesus as having "completed the days" (of the feast/festival) in Luke 2:43. This cannot have come from the Septuagint, which has at 1 Kgdms 1:20, "And it came to pass at the time of days...," with no mention of "completing" them.

The above two phrases in Luke 2:43, "returning" home from a pilgrimage to the Temple, and "completing days," are thus probably more evidence for the Palestinian Jewish Christian author of Luke 2:41-51a as dependent on 1 Samuel 1-3 and on Semitic Judaic traditions regarding this narrative of the childhood and youth of Samuel.

6. A Caravan.

A.

Luke 2:44 says that when Jesus' parents began their return to Nazareth from their annual Passover pilgrimage to the Temple in Jerusalem, "they thought he was in the 'caravan' (συνοδία)." This is the only occurrence of the term in the NT.[47] Joseph and Mary are pictured as having joined a caravan together with their relatives and acquaintances (also in v 44) in order to make the pilgrimage. Here, too, the imagery most probably derives from Elkanah and Hannah's pilgrimage with their child Samuel to the Temple in Shiloh, as seen through Palestinian Jewish Christian eyes.

B.

In *t. Pesaḥ.* 1:4 the phrase occurs: "Those joining a caravan...thirty days before Passover...." The Hebrew for the first part is היוצאין בשיירה.[48] The members of a caravan are called "those traveling in a caravan" in *t. B. Meṣ.* 7:13: הולכי שיירא.[49] A description of pilgrims traveling in a caravan in Judaic sources, as wwell as of the three main routes taken by Galilean pilgrims to Jerusalem, is given by Safrai.[50]

---

[47]Cf. BAGD 791: "caravan, group of travelers." LSJ 1720 II cites for "party of travellers, caravan" Strabo's "Geography" 4.6.6 and 11.14.4 from the first century B.C.E. and the first century C.E. In Josephus' *Ant.* 6.243 and *Bell.* 2.587 the term means "escort" or "accomplices." The Greek term occurs as a rare loan word in Hebrew סינודיא, in the sense of "escort." See Krauss, *Griechische und Lateinische Lehnwörter* 2.390. In LXX Neh 7:5 and 64 it means "company."

[48]Cf. Zuckermandel/Liebermann 155. In *The Tosefta* 2.115 Neusner translates: "People leaving on a caravan...." See the same expression in *b. Pesaḥ.* 6a (Soncino 23 – "he who sets out in a [caravan] company"), *B. Bat.* 146b (Soncino 633), and *Ḥul.* 75b (Soncino 418), as well as *m. Giṭ.* 6:5 (Albeck 3.291).

[49]Cf. Neusner, *The Tosefta* 4.114; Zuckermandel/Liebermann 387.

[50]Cf. his *Die Wallfahrt* 121-127, 133-141, and 54-63.

P. Billerbeck correctly notes that the Hebrew שְׁיָרה, Aramaic שְׁיָרָא is "the most common designation for a company of travelers or a caravan in rabbinic sources."[51] In the United Bible Societies' Hebrew New Testament, Luke 2:44 is also translated as "they thought he was found 'in the caravan' (בַּשְּׁיָרה).[52]

I suggest that this term, either in Aramaic or Hebrew, lies behind the συνοδία of Luke 2:44. It provides a fine word play with the expression "parents" in vv 41 and 43, as noted in section one above: שירה/שיירא. The same is true for Jesus' "remaining behind" in v 43, to be analyzed below in section III.

To my knowledge, none of Elkanah's pilgrimages to the Temple in Shiloh, including those undertaken with Hannah and Samuel, is labeled a "caravan," as above. Nevertheless, Elkanah is *the* example in the MT and in Judaic sources for making a pilgrimage there, as I will illustrate in the next section, seven. This most probably caused the Palestinian Jewish Christian author of Luke 2:41-51a to borrow many motifs from the pilgrimages of Elkanah and his family. He then employed a Semitic term well known to him in the first century C.E. to describe the pilgrimage company as a "caravan." This also added to the narrative's artistic appeal through its word play with "parents" and "to remain behind," something much appreciated by his first Palestinian Jewish Christian hearers.

7.   Relatives and Acquaintances.

A.

Luke 2:44 relates that when Jesus' parents returned to Nazareth in Galilee from their pilgrimage to the Temple in Jerusalem, they thought he was in their caravan. Having gone "a day's journey," they sought him among their "relatives" (οἱ συγγενεῖς) and "acquaintances" (οἱ γνωστοί). These expressions also derive from the pilgrimages of Elkanah, together with Hannah and the child Samuel, to the Temple in Shiloh, and from general pilgrimage terminology.

B.

It took three days of fast walking from Jerusalem to southern Galilee, some 100 kilometers or 60 miles, by the most direct route through

---

[51]Str-B 2.148. It occurs five times in the Mishnah: *'Erub.* 1:8 and twice in 1:10, *Giṭ.* 6:5 and *Ṭ. Yom* 4:5.
[52]*Haberith Haḥadašah* (Jerusalem, 1979) 151.

Samaria.[53] "A day's journey" for a slower-moving pilgrimage caravan would have been much less than a third of this.[54]

The expressions "relatives" and "acquaintances" also derive from pilgrimage terminology in general, and that of Elkanah and Hannah specifically. 1 Sam 1:21 states that Elkanah "and all his house" (וכל-ביתו) went up (to Shiloh) to offer to the Lord the yearly sacrifice and to pay his vow. This is expanded in Judaic tradition in a major way. *Eliyyahu Rabbah* (8)9 states, for example, in regard to 1 Sam 1:3 that Elkanah used to go up (to Shiloh) four times a year, three times as required for the pilgrimage festivals, and once in regard to his own requirement. In explanation of 1:21, the midrash continues by saying that Elkanah went up, "and his wife, and his sons, and his daughters, and his brothers and his sisters, and all 'his relatives' [קרוביו] with him, and all the members of his household – he led them all up with him." This was so that they would neither learn idolatry from the Canaanites and the transgressors, nor do anything which did not accord with the Torah.[55]

The midrash continues with a variation of this theme. Elkanah leads them all with him so that they will make the pilgrimage on the road and lodge in the broad part (plaza, marketplace) of a city. There the men gather by themselves, as do the women. The men get into a conversation, as do the women, grown-ups and little ones. This continues until the city is set in motion. Curious, the local people ask where the pilgrims are going. They reply, to the house of God in Shiloh, from which Torah and commandments proceed. Asked why they don't go up together with them, the local people immediately break into tears and agree to this. The following year there are five households, the next year ten; the next year the whole (city) is excited about making the pilgrimage. Finally, about sixty households go up from there. Elkanah takes a different route each year when he goes up (to Shiloh).[56] Because of him, many Israelites grow in virtue. As a reward for such behavior,

---

[53]Cf. *m. B. Meṣ.* 2:6 (Albeck 4.70; Danby 349); Josephus, *Vita* 269 (52); Str-B 2.149; and Safrai, *Die Wallfahrt* 135-140.

[54]Cf. the various lengths of "a day's journey," with the Hebrew and Aramaic terminology, given in Str-B 2.149, as well as *Ant.*, 15.293. The expression is already found in the MT. Jonah 3:4 states, for example, that the prophet went "a day's journey" into Nineveh, exaggeratedly called "three days' journey in breadth" in v 3.

[55]Cf. Friedmann 47, as well as Braude and Kapstein's somewhat paraphrastic translation on pp. 149-150.

[56]This may be influenced by the motif of Samuel's going on circuit year by year to three other Israelite cities and judging the people there before returning to his home town of Ramah (1 Sam 7:16-17). Cf. *Kallah Rabbati* 6,54a (Soncino 483), where the rabbis teach that "Samuel journeyed from city to city, and from province to province to teach us Torah...," as in 1 Sam 7:16-17.

God promises to grant him a son (Samuel), through whom many more will grow in virtue.[57]

In regard to Elkanah's behavior described above, and in reference to 1 Sam 1:3, R. Ze'ira, probably a first generation Babylonian Amora associated wit the Palestinian R. Yoḥanan (bar Nappaḥa),[58] also states in *y. Ber.* 9:5,14c: "If your motherland becomes weak, arise and fortify it, as Elkanah did when he led Israel on the pilgrimage festivals."[59] The German translator C. Horowitz interprets the first phrase here as in *Eliyyahu Rabbah*: "becomes old (and forgets its obligations [in the Torah])."[60]

In the medieval collection of all Judaic interpretations of Scripture then available, *Yalquṭ Shem'oni* 2.77 on 1 Sam 1:3 says in a variant of the *Eliyyahu Rabbah* narrative above: through Elkanah's activity there were five households in one year, in another ten, "until they all went up on pilgrimage." The "sixty households" of the whole city in *Eliyyahu Rabbah* is generalized here to "all." Elkanah is praised as gradually causing, by both positive example and persistent work, all the cities of Israel, i.e., all Israel, to go up to Shiloh for the pilgrimage festivals.

The same section of *Yalquṭ Shem'oni* on 1 Sam 1:3 cites an unknown midrash to the effect that Elkanah "was exalted in his household, he was exalted in his courtyard, he was exalted in his city, he was exalted in all Israel. And all his going up was nothing but a parable of himself." That is, through his efforts to get as many others as possible to join him in "going up" (עלה) to the Temple in Shiloh, Elkanah concomitantly caused himself to "go up" (נתעלה) or become elevated/exalted before God. This is one reason he is also considered to be one of the righteous.[61]

---

[57]Cf. Friedmann 47-48, Braude and Kapstein 150. See also *Yal.* 2.77. The motif of Elkanah's taking a different route to Shiloh each year in order to gather together more people and lead them up to Shiloh, is also found in *Midr. Sam.* 1/1,5,7 and 3/2 (Wünsche, *Aus Israels Lehrhallen* 5.7,11,12 and 22), as well as in *Eccl. Rab.* 5:19 §1 (Soncino 8.157, with n. 4). "God answers him in the joy of his heart" in the latter passage could be interpreted as in *Eliyyahu Rabbah*, i.e., that God grants Elkanah a reward for his behavior, a son, Samuel, by Hannah. In *Pesiq. R.* 43/3 (Friedmann 179b, Braude 757) mention is made of Hannah's going up to the Sanctuary on the festival pilgrimages, plural. Elkanah is certainly assumed to be with her, as in 1 Sam 1:24-25. In 43/1 (Friedmann 179a, Braude 755) Hannah "regularly" goes up and prays in the Sanctuary (of Shiloh). See also *Tg. Neb.* 1 Sam 1:3 cited above on Elkanah's going up to Shiloh "from the time of festival to festival."

[58]Strack and Stemberger, *Introduction* 93.

[59]Neusner/Zahavy 1.349.

[60]*Der Jerusalemer Talmud. Berakhoth* 246.

[61]Cf. the very beginning of *Yal.* 2.77. On this, see also *Ruth Rab.* 4/3 on Ruth 2:1 (Soncino 8.51), and a parallel in *Num. Rab.* Naso 10/5 on Num 6:2 (Soncino 5.361).

Josephus, a native of Jerusalem whose mother tongue was Aramaic, writes at the end of the first century C.E. in *Ant.* 5.342 in regard to 1 Sam 1:1 that Elkanah was a "citizen of the middle class," or "of moderate means."[62] This early Palestinian Judaic tradition, certainly not from the historian himself, probably implies that Elkanah's pilgrimage activity throughout the cities of Israel at all the annual festivals caused him many financial expenditures, which he was willing to take upon himself in spite of his lack of wealth.

The term "relatives" in Luke 2:44, used of the direct relations of Joseph and Mary, pilgrims to the Passover Festival in Jerusalem, thus derives from Palestinian Judaic tradition on Elkanah's "whole household" in 1 Sam 1:21, where the term "relatives" is specifically mentioned: קרובים. (For a different term for "relatives," which would provide assonance with "parents" and "caravan," see section III below.)

The term "acquaintances" in Luke 2:44 derives from Elkanah's taking those from his "courtyard" and his "city" (Ramah), whom he thus "knew," also on pilgrimage to the Temple in Shiloh. Commenting on someone's finding something lost by another at one of the three pilgrimage festivals in Jerusalem in *m. B. Meṣ.* 2:6, the Tosefta in 2:17 speaks of informing of this loss "relatives," "neighbors," "acquaintances" and "townsfolk."[63] The Hebrew here for "acquaintances" is מיודעים[64], which corresponds exactly to οἱ γνωστοί in Luke 2:44.

Finally, the Palestinian Jewish Christian hearers of Luke 2:41-51a may also have appreciated the narrator's artistic skill in creating assonance in the passage. The Hebrew could have been:

ידעו	:	"they did[n't] know," in v 43.
מיודעים	:	"acquaintances," in v 44.
מדוע	:	"Why?" in vv 48 and 49.
ידעתם	:	"Did[n't] you know?" in v 49.

The latter also maintains on the basis of *"one* [a] man" in 1 Sam 1:1 that he was the foremost man in his generation.

[62]For the latter translation, cf. Ginzberg, *The Legends* 6.215, n. 4. See, however, *b. Ber.* 10b (Soncino 58) and *Ned.* 38a (Soncino 120), regarding the "house" (1 Sam 7:17) of Elkanah's son Samuel as always accompanying him wherever he traveled. This is interpreted as a sign of wealth.

[63]Zuckermandel/Liebermann 374; Neusner 4.81. I have slightly changed the order. P. Billerbeck in Str-B 2.149 cites another phrase with "relatives, neighbors and acquaintances."

[64]On the term "acquaintance," cf. BDB 394, pu. ptc. of ידע, as well as Jastrow 565, ידע, pa. pass. ptc. See also the phrase "relatives and acquaintances" in Job 19:14, and A. Schlatter, *Das Evangelium des Lukas* (Stuttgart: Calwer, 1931) 205.

8.   The Temple in Jerusalem, and the Temple in Shiloh.

A.

After Jesus' parents made their Passover pilgrimage to Jerusalem, they set out on their return home to Nazareth. Discovering that Jesus was not in the caravan, they returned to Jerusalem, and after three days (of searching) they found him in the "Temple" (τὸ ἱερόν), sitting in the midst of the teachers, both listening to, and questioning them (Luke 2:46). In v 49, a favored interpretation of the phrase ἐν τοῖς τοῦ πατρός μου εἶναι is as in the RSV and NRSV: Jesus says he must "be in my Father's house" = the Temple.[65]

The emphasis here in 2:46, and possibly in v 49, on the boy Jesus' being in the Temple in Jerusalem also derives from the boy Samuel's being in the Temple in Shiloh.

B.

1 Sam 1:3 states regarding Elkanah that he went on an annual pilgrimage from his own city, Ramathaim/Ramah, to "Shiloh," spelled שִׁלֹה here, in 2:14 and 3:21, and שִׁלוֹ in 1:24 and 3:21. This city was located some 33 kilometers or 20 miles north-northeast of Jerusalem.[66] Here the "house of the Lord" (בֵּית יהוה) was found (1:7, 24; 3:15),[67] called the "Temple of the Lord" (הֵיכל יהוה; Septuagint ναός) in 1:9 and 3:3, and the "tent of meeting" (אֹהל מוֹעֵד) in 2:22. The ark, including two cherubim, upon which the Lord of hosts was thought to be enthroned (4:4), signified God's dwelling among men, and was found within the Temple (3:3).[68]

Samuel's parents brought him to the house of the Lord, the Temple, at Shiloh, and dedicated him there to the Lord (for service: 1 Sam 1:24-28a). There, too, (in Judaic tradition at the age of two) "he worshiped the Lord" (1:28b),[69] without his parents, just as Jesus was alone in the Jerusalem Temple without his parents in Luke 2:46. Here Samuel

---

[65]Cf. the similar expression of the temple of Zeus in Josephus, *Ant.* 8.145, and the parallel in *Cont. Ap.* 1.118. I favor another interpretation, based on an original Aramaic. See section III below.

[66]Cf. McCarter Jr., *I Samuel* 59, who notes that it is the modern (uninhabited) Khirbet Seilun. His map on p. 46 shows the relationship of Ramathaim/Ramah to Shiloh. See also the art. "Shiloh" by W. Reed in *IDB* 4.328-330; "Shiloh (City)" by S. Holm-Nielsen in *IDBSup* 822-823; and D. Schley, *Shiloh.* A Biblical City in Tradition and History (JSOTSup 63; Sheffield: JSOT, 1989), who notes that E. Hengstenberg of Berlin already argued in 1839 for interpreting the "festival" of 1 Samuel 1 as Passover (p. 22).

[67]Cf. the expression "house of the Sanctuary" in *Tg. Neb.* 1 Sam 1:7, 24; 2:1, 29, 32; 3:3 and 15.

[68]Cf. also 4:3-6, 11, 13, 17, 19, 21-22.

[69]Cf. BDB 1005 on שחה, hithpalel, third masc. sing., as in Isa 44:17.

ministered to the Lord (2:11, 18; 3:1). Here, too, he "grew in the presence of the Lord" (2:21), and "continued to grow both in stature and in favor with the Lord and with men" (2:26; cf. 3:19a), as Jesus did in Luke 2:40 and 52. In Judaic tradition, when Samuel was twelve (see section ten below), the Lord also appeared to him here and called him (chapter three) as his "Father," with Samuel as God's "son" (on this, see section fourteen below).

The Palestinian Jewish Christian author of Luke 2:41-51a borrowed terminology and motifs from the pilgrimage of Samuel's parents with him to the Temple in Shiloh partly because it was frequently compared to the Temple in Jerusalem in Judaic sources. According to *m. Zebaḥ.* 14:4-8, the tabernacle (משכן) was first set up (in the wilderness), then moved to Gilgal, Shiloh, Nob, Gibeon and Jerusalem.[70] Based on the "house" of 1 Sam 1:24, the Mishnah in 14:6 states that the building in Shiloh was a "house of stones," with hangings, called the "resting place" (מנוחה)[71]. According to *b. Zebaḥ.* 118b[72] and *y. Meg.* 1:12, 72d,[73] the ark was in the Tent of Meeting at the following places for the following lengths of time:

In the wilderness	39 years
Gilgal	14 years
Shiloh	369 years
Nob	13 years
Gibeon	44 years
The First Temple in Jerusalem	410 years
The Second Temple in Jerusalem	420 years

This table shows that in Judaic tradition, the only site anyhow comparable to Jerusalem's total of 830 years was Shiloh, with 369 years. This was a major reason why the two were often compared in Judaic sources, for example in *m. Meg.* 1:11.[74]

It should also be noted that in LXX Jer 48:5 (41:5), Shiloh is not transcribed into Greek as Σηλω(μ), but as Σαλημ[75]. This easily recalls

---

[70]Albeck 5.53-54; Danby 489-490.

[71]Albeck 5.53; Danby 490, with n. 2. See also *b. Zebaḥ.* 118a (Soncino 583).

[72]Soncino 585-589, with notes. See also *t. Zebaḥ.* 13:6 (Neusner 5.59).

[73]English in Neusner 19.91; German in Hüttenmeister 89, with n. 650.

[74]Danby 203. Cf. *Sipre Deut.* 68 on Deut 12:11 (Hammer 122); 74 on Deut 12:17 (Hammer 127); and 107 on Deut 14:25 (Hammer 154; see also pp. 174 and 289); *Gen. Rab.* Vayechi 95, MSV, on Gen 46:28 (Soncino 2.917); and *Num. Rab.* Naso 10/24 on Num 6:21 (Soncino 5.404).

[75]Cf. Holm-Nielsen, art. "Shiloh (City)" 822, cited in n. 66.

Jerusalem as Ἰερουσαλήμ, also called Σαλήμ in LXX Gen 14:18[76]. If there
was also a Hebrew background to Shiloh as Salem, this may help to
explain why a scribe copied *Eccl. Rab.* 5:19 §1 as: "Elkanah...used to lead
Israel and bring them up to *Jerusalem* every year by a different route."[77]
He knew that Elkanah led Israelites every year on pilgrimage up to
Shiloh, as in 1 Samuel 1. C. Horowitz may have had a similar wording in
his MS of *y. Ber.* 9:5, 14c, where he translates: "Elkanah led the Israelites
to go up to *Jerusalem* for the pilgrimage festivals."[78] If both of the latter
passages are simply scribal errors, this also shows how easy it was for a
Palestinian Jewish Christian to transfer imagery and motifs from a
pilgrimage to the Temple in Shiloh to a pilgrimage to the Temple in
Jerusalem, as in Luke 2:41-51a.

9. Shiloh and the Messiah.

Gen 49:10 states that "The scepter shall not depart from Judah, nor
the ruler's staff from between his feet, until Shiloh (שִׁילֹה)[79] comes [or,
until he comes to Shiloh], and to him shall be the obedience of the
peoples." This verse, from Jacob's deathbed blessing of his twelve sons,
was interpreted in Judaic sources at an early time, especially of the
Messiah.

This is shown, for example, in the Qumran fragment 4Q Patriarchal
Blessings (4QPBless or 4QpGen 49), where "until [Shiloh comes]" is
interpreted as "'Until' the Messiah of Righteousness comes, the Branch of
David...."[80] The Qumran writings date at the latest to 66 C.E., and some
are much earlier.[81]

In rabbinic sources, Gen 49:10 is definitely treated as referring to the
Messiah. In *b. Sanh.* 98b the school of R. Shila, in a pun on his name, say
in regard to the Messiah: "His name is Shiloh, for it is written, 'until
Shiloh come' (Gen 49:10)."[82] *Gen. Rab.* Vayechi 98/8 on Gen 49:10 also

---

[76]See also Salem as parallel to Zion in Ps 75(76):3, in Aquila, Symmachus and
Theodotion also spelled Σαλήμ.
[77]Soncino 8.157.
[78]*Der Jerusalemer Talmud. Berakhoth* 246. Horowitz based his translation on the
Gilead edition of New York, 1949. I do not find the term in the Krotoshin edition,
and Zahavy in Neusner 1.349 also omits it.
[79]For Hebrew variants of "Shiloh," cf. the apparatus of *BHK ad loc.*
[80]Cf. the Hebrew in Lohse, *Die Texte aus Qumran* 246. The English translation I
give is that of Dupont-Sommer, *The Essene Writings from Qumran* 314-315.
[81]Cf. Dupont-Sommer, *The Essene Writings* 8.
[82]Soncino 667, where puns are made on other names as well. For a parallel, see
Lam. Rab. 1:16 §51 (Soncino 7.137).

comments on "'Until Shiloh comes': this alludes to the royal Messiah."[83] Finally, *all* the targums on the biblical verse (Jerusalem or Jonathan, the Fragment Targum, Neofiti, and even the usually reticent Onqelos) interpret it messianically.[84]

In *Pseudo-Philo* 49:7, written in Hebrew in Palestine at about the time of Jesus, Gen 49:10 is also alluded to in regard to the son to be born from Elkanah, "who will rule among you and prophesy." D. Harrington's English translation italicizes the allusion to the biblical verse: "And *from this time on, a ruler will not be lacking* from you for many years."[85] This is Samuel, whose birth is described in chapter 51 in other messianic imagery.[86] Since the first chapter of First Samuel is quoted and alluded to numerous times in the narrative after 49:7, it is very probable that the author associated the Shiloh of 1 Sam 1:3 and 24 with the Shiloh of Gen 49:10. The messianic imagery applied by *Pseudo-Philo* to Samuel is very noteworthy.

The above passages from Qumran, rabbinic writings, and *Pseudo-Philo,* interpreting the Shiloh of Gen 49:10 as the Messiah, and applying this same verse to Samuel, who continues to be described in messianic imagery, makes it quite possible that the Palestinian Jewish Christian author of Luke 2:41-51a also knew of these associations. If so, this was one more reason for him to apply imagery and motifs from the pilgrimage of Samuel's parents with him to the Temple in Shiloh, to his description of the pilgrimage of Jesus' parents with him to the Temple in Jerusalem. He firmly believed that Jesus was the Messiah, already when he was twelve years old.

---

[83]Soncino 2.956; Theodor/Albeck 3.1259, with the passages cited by them in n. 1. See also *Tanḥuma* Genesis Vayeḥi 10 on Gen 49:10 in Singermann 295. In his art. "Shilo, 2" in *IDB* 4.330, N. Gottwald discusses various philological possibilities for the interpretation of the phrase "until Shiloh comes."

[84]Cf. Etheridge, *The Targums* 152, 331 and 336; Klein, *The Fragment-Targums* 1.66 and 158, and 2.31 and 119; Rieder, *Targum Jonathan ben Uziel on the Torah* 1.77; Díez Macho, *Neophyti 1.* Tomo I, Génesis 331 and 635; and Aberbach and Grossfeld, *Targum Onkelos to Genesis* 284-285, with the relevant notes. As remarked concerning *b.* Yoma 53b (Soncino 251), the first part of the verse as interpreted by this targum was "part of the High Priest's prayer in the Holy of Holies on the Day of Atonement" (Aberbach and Grossfeld 285, n. 19), showing the early liturgical employment of the verse.

[85]Cf. *OTP* 2.364. The Latin is found in Harrington, *Les Antiquités Bibliques* 1.326: Et *ex* hoc non *deficiet* ex vobis *princeps* plurimis annis.

[86]Cf. 51:3 and 6, where his horn will be exalted very high, an allusion to 1 Sam 2:10, with king = anointed one; and Samuel as "the light from which wisdom is to be born" (51:4) and "the light to the peoples" (Isa 51:4) in 51:6, also with "a light for this nation" (*OTP* 2.365-366). On "light" as a designation for the Messiah, see Str-B 2.139 and 726.

10. The Age of the Boy Jesus in the Temple of Jerusalem, and the Age of the Boy Samuel in the Temple of Shiloh.

A.

Luke 2:42 states that when Jesus was (or turned – ἐγένετο) twelve years old, his parents went up (to Jerusalem) according to the custom of the festival/feast. There are two main reasons for this specific age, and not eleven, thirteen, or another. One has to do with Jesus the "Nazarite," connected with the legal age at which a "Nazirite" may make his own vows (see section fifteen below). The second is the age of the boy Samuel in Judaic tradition when he is called by the Lord in 1 Samuel 3.

B.

According to 1 Sam 1:24-28 in Judaic tradition, as pointed out above, when Hannah weaned Samuel at the age of two, she and her husband took him up to the Temple in Shiloh and lent him to the Lord. There the boy (MT הנער; LXX τὸ παιδάριον) ministered to the Lord (2:11). This is repeated in 2:18, 21, 26 and 3:1. In the meantime Samuel had "grown," and he "continued to grow" in stature, i.e., in size and age (2:21, 26). No age is given in Scripture for the time of Samuel's encounter with God in the Temple of Shiloh. Yet in three major strands of Judaic tradition, he, like Jesus in the Temple of Jerusalem, is twelve years old at this point.

1) Josephus.

In *Ant.* 5.348 (10.4) the Jewish historian writes at the end of the first century C.E. that God called Samuel by name as he slept (in the Temple of Shiloh). By way of introduction, Josephus remarks just before this that Samuel had now completed his twelfth year (had turned twelve) when he began to prophesy.

This number is important to note since Judaic tradition unanimously cites Samuel's life span as fifty-two.[87] Samuel was a Levite,[88] and as such he could only do service until the age of fifty (Num 4:23 and 8:25). Since Hannah lent her child, weaned at two, to the Lord "as long as he lives" (1 Sam 1:28 and v 11), and he was to abide in the Temple of Shiloh "for ever" (v 22), Judaic tradition added the figures of fifty and two to produce fifty-two.[89] The other forty years, producing the age of twelve, are now accounted for in 2) and 3).

---

[87]Cf. the references in the latter part of n. 35, as well as *Seder 'Olam* 13 (Milikowsky 297-298 and 487), and Ginzberg, *The Legends* 6.234, n.70.
[88]Cf. 1 Chr 6:1-13 (Eng. 16-28).
[89]Cf. *Eliyyahu Rabbah* (6)7 in Braude and Kapstein 127, with n. 66, and Friedmann 37.

2) Seder 'Olam 13.

This official Judaic chronology notes regarding Samuel the seer that all his days were only fifty-two years. To explain this, it first cites 1 Sam 1:9, "Now Eli the priest was sitting," coupled with: "She [Hannah] was deeply distressed" (v 10). As in many rabbinic quotations, where only the beginning is cited, the hearer/reader is assumed to know the continuation. Here it is that Hannah promises to lend her son Samuel to the Lord "all the days of his life" (v 11). This is the basis for the further calculation of Samuel's life span. *Seder 'Olam* continues by stating that "he" was appointed judge. Then a phrase from 4:18 is quoted: "and he judged Is[rael] forty [years]." While the latter text originally referred to Eli, this chronology appears to apply the phrase to Samuel, for it continues the calculation of his life span by saying: "There remain thirteen years. Subtract one year for his being gestated; it turns out (that he lived) fifty-two years."[90]

Here it is assumed that Samuel judged Israel for forty years, i.e., as of the age of twelve, making his life span fifty-two. This is corroborated by MS Constantinople of 1516 C.E., which aside from the Mantua *editio princeps* of 1513 is the only MS which "has any text-critical value."[91] In the calculation of Samuel's life span, it adds after "for his being gestated" (Hannah's "carrying him" in her womb): "and twelve years for his childhood/youth" י׳ ב לנערותו.[92]

This independent MS tradition of *Seder 'Olam* thus agrees with Josephus in the number twelve for Samuel's "childhood/youth." At the end of this period, after the Temple experience in Shiloh, he began to prophesy (1 Sam 3:19–4:1a). The latter time span of prophesying, also described as his judging Israel "all the days of his life" (7:15), was thought to be for forty years.

3) Midrash Psalms 25/6.

In various MSS and in printed editions of this midrash, section 25/6 ends by citing Jer 15:1 ("Though Moses and Samuel stood before Me..."). It then compares these two figures in various ways, also stating that as the one ruled forty years, so did the other.[93] In other words, if Samuel died at fifty-two, he began to rule Israel (as judge) at the age of twelve.

---

[90]Translation by Milikowsky 487, Hebrew 297-298.

[91]Milikowsky 34, 82-83.

[92]Milikowsky 298, apparatus.

[93]Cf. Buber, *Midrasch Tehillim* 212, n. 24, for the MSS Florence 13, Rome 81, Merzbacher and Ginzburg, the printed edition of Venice, and afterwards all the printed editions. Braude in *The Midrash on Psalms* 351 does not draw attention to this important MS tradition, not even in his notes. See Ginzberg, *The Legends*

This comparison of Moses and Samuel in regard to the time they ruled Israel may be the original text of *Midrash Psalms* at this point, for in 1/3 on Jer 15:1 the two figures are compared in five ways, including their both ruling, and being summoned by a call from God (cf. Exod 3:4 and 1 Sam 3:4).[94] The fact that the ruling and calling are mentioned together may indicate that in 25/6 Samuel is also thought to have begun his forty year rule of Israel as judge from the time he was called in the Temple at Shiloh, at twelve.

* * *

Samuel's age as twelve for the time he was called in the Temple of Shiloh, when he began to prophesy and rule Israel in Judaic tradition, here in Josephus, *Seder 'Olam* and *Midrash Psalms*, is part of a very early Judaic topos of wisdom and understanding as already belonging to famous Israelites at exactly the age of twelve. This includes not only Samuel (to be analyzed in section twelve below), but also Solomon, Josiah and Daniel.

a)   Solomon.

The definitely pre-Christian Septuagint at 3 Kgdms (1 Kgs) 2:12 already states: "Solomon sat on (ascended) the throne of David his father when he was twelve." This is corroborated in Eupolemus 30:8,[95] *Seder 'Olam* 14, which elucidates the calculation,[96] and elsewhere.[97] Solomon's "wisdom and understanding beyond measure" are already praised in Scripture (1 Kgs 5:9, Eng. 29). Because of his uttering 3000 proverbs and 1005 songs (5:12, Eng. 32), the Book of Proverbs was attributed to him (1:1; 10:1; 25:1), as was the apocryphal Wisdom of Solomon.

b)   Josiah.

Josephus in *Ant.* 10.50 (4.1) states that Josiah was made king at the age of eight (48), and "when he was twelve years old" (cf. 2 Chr 34:3) he gave proof of his piety and righteousness...." "Reviewing the acts of his forefathers, he 'wisely' (συνετῶς) corrected the errors they had made...," employing "his natural wisdom (σοφία) and discernment (ἐπίνοια-51)" in

---

6.234, n. 69, who remarks that Julius Africanus agrees with the forty years reign. See the text in Migne, *PG* 10.75-76.

[94]Buber 4, Braude 6.

[95]Cf. *OTP* 2.867 and 863 on the date as "presumably" 158/157 B.C.E., probably in Palestine.

[96]Milikowsky 303-305 and 489-490.

[97]Cf. Ginzberg, *The Legends*, 4.125 and texts cited in 6.277, n. 1.

order to do so.[98] Like Solomon, Josiah already at the age of twelve precociously displays his wisdom and understanding/discernment.

c) Daniel.

Finally, the youth Daniel in LXX Susanna 45 is given a spirit of "understanding" (σύνησις). With this he rescues the falsely accused Susanna by sitting among the elders and wisely condemning them (50, 64). In the Syro-Hexapla at this point he is twelve years old.[99] In the longer Greek version of Ignatius to the Magnesians 3, this incident is described so: "For Daniel the wise, at twelve years of age, became possessed of the divine Spirit, and convicted the elders...."[100] Here, too, an Israelite hero is considered wise and understanding already at the age of twelve.

It is this topos of early Palestinian Judaism, as shown in Solomon, Josiah and Daniel, to which the twelve-year-old Samuel belongs, and not Hellenistic figures such as the twelve-year-old grandson of Ramses II, Si-Usire,[101] who like other pagan figures adumbrates his later wisdom already at an early age.[102] Nor is the number twelve for Jesus in Luke 2:42 a misunderstanding of thirteen in Aramaic.[103] It was rather based on the time Samuel began to prophesy in the Temple at Shiloh in well-attested, early Judaic tradition: twelve.

---

[98]Cf. the English translation by R. Marcus here.

[99]Cf. Brown, The Birth 482.

[100]English in The Ante-Nicene Fathers 1.60. The passage also mentions Samuel, Solomon and Josiah. See also the "Epistle of Maria the Proselyte to Ignatius" (120-121).

[101]Cf. E. Klostermann, Das Lukasevangelium (HNT 5; Tübingen: Mohr, 1929²) 45. See also W. Grundmann, Das Evangelium nach Lukas (THNT 3; Berlin: Evangelische Verlagsanstalt, 1984¹⁰) 94.

[102]Cf. Cyrus, Alexander the Great, Augustus and Apollonius of Tyana in R. Laurentin, Jésus au Temple. Mystère de Paques et Foi de Marie en Luc 2, 48-50 (EB; Paris: Librairie Lecoffre, 1966) 147-150, as well as Buddha on p. 156. I do not deny that the Hellenistic motif also influenced Palestinian Judaism, certainly via Hellenistic Judaism. Yet the Palestinian Jewish Christian author of Luke 2:41-51a based his narrative of the twelve-year-old Jesus in the Temple on the figure of the twelve-year-old Samuel in the Temple, as shown in the Palestinian Judaic sources of Josephus (a native of Jerusalem, whose native tongue was Aramaic), Seder 'Olam, and Midrash Psalms.

[103]Against P. van der Horst, "Notes on the Aramaic Background of Luke II 41-52" in JSNT 7 (1980) 62.

11. Mary and Joseph's Anxiety, and Hannah's Anxiety.

A.

In Luke 2:48 Mary says to Jesus in the Temple in Jerusalem, after she and Joseph have been searching for him for three days in the city: "My son, why did you act this way towards us? Behold, your father and I have been 'anxiously' searching for you."[104] The Greek for "anxiously," "in distress," "greatly worried," is the present participle of ὀδυνάομαι in the sense of "mental and spiritual pain."[105] The same form and sense are found in Acts 20:38, where the Ephesian elders are especially "sorrowful/pained" at what Paul tells them before his leaving. This is the only other such occurrence in the NT.[106] In Luke 2:48, this specific Greek term also derives from the story of Samuel's birth and youth.

B.

Parental anxiety at a son's being gone too long is found in the apocryphal book of Tobit, the present form of which is definitely pre-Christian and most likely from the diaspora. Qumran fragments, however, attest an Aramaic original and an early Hebrew translation.[107] Tobit says in 9:4, "my father is counting the days, and if I delay long, 'he will be greatly distressed' (ὀδυνηθήσεται λίαν)." Here the same verb is employed regarding a greatly worried father as in Luke 2:48.

Yet the term ὀδυνάομαι in the anecdote of the twelve-year-old Jesus derives from the story of Samuel's birth and youth. In the patriarchally-oriented Judaism of Jesus' time, it would have been usual for his father to address the remarks of Luke 2:48 to Jesus, especially since the boy was very close to the age of responsibility (see section fifteen below). The fact that Jesus' mother Mary does so instead is based on the Palestinian Jewish Christian narrator of 2:41-51a borrowing a specific term from 1 Samuel 1 regarding Hannah, the mother of Samuel, at the Temple of Shiloh.

Hannah was barren, while Elkanah's second wife Peninnah had children (1 Sam 1:2). Peninnah regularly provoked Hannah sorely, irritating her (vv 6-7). This caused Hannah to be "sorely troubled" (v 15) and to have "great anxiety and vexation" (v 16).

---

[104]The NRSV has here: "in great anxiety."

[105]BAGD 555.

[106]Luke 16:24 and 25 have the physical meaning of "to be in anguish" because of flames in Hades.

[107]Cf. G. Nickelsburg, *Jewish Literature Between the Bible and the Mishnah* 35 and 40, n. 45. According to J. Fitzmyer, *The Dead Sea Scrolls. Major Publications and Tools for Study* 35-36, 4QTob ar[b] contains parts of Tob 8:21–9:4, but has not yet been published.

The same motif occurs in 1 Sam 1:10, where Hannah at the Temple in Shiloh is "deeply distressed" (מָרַת נֶפֶשׁ). The Hebrew verb employed here is מרר.[108] The hiphil form is translated in LXX Zech 12:10 by ὀδυνάομαι. In 1 Sam 1:10, however, the Septuagint has κατώδυνος ψυχῇ, from the same root.[109] The verb κατοδυνάω also translates מרר at Exod 1:14. Without a known Semitic original, it is also found in Tob 8:20 S regarding "the anxious/distressed soul of my daughter."

I therefore suggest that the Palestinian Jewish Christian author of Luke 2:41-51a employed מרת נפש or its Aramaic equivalent of Joseph and Mary's being "anxious" in v 48. This expression is used of his "model" for Mary, Hannah, in the Temple both in the Hebrew of Sam 1:10, and in the Targum.[110] When the Semitic account was later translated into Greek in Hellenistic Jewish Christianity, ὀδυνάομαι was used, which as indicated above is attested elsewhere as a rendering of מרר.[111]

12. The Boy Jesus' Wisdom and Understanding, and The Boy Samuel's Wisdom and Understanding.

A.

In all four NT gospels Jesus is represented as regularly teaching the people. This includes the major motif of his also teaching in the Jerusalem Temple, where the multitude is "astonished" at the quality of his teaching.[112] Elsewhere people are also "astonished" at Jesus' teaching and ask about the "wisdom" (σοφία) given him (by God – Mark 6:2 par.). The adult deeds of Jesus are retrojected into his youth, however, only in the Palestinian Jewish Christian narrative of the twelve-year-old boy Jesus in the Temple at Jerusalem in Luke 2.

In the two verses later added to frame Luke 2:41-51a, Jesus is described as a child who grew and became strong, filled with "wisdom" (σοφία – v 40), and who increased in "wisdom" (σοφία – v 52) and in stature. Within the original narrative itself, his parents find their twelve-year-old son Jesus in the Jerusalem Temple, "sitting in the midst of the teachers [of the Torah], both listening to them and asking them

---

[108]BDB 600: to be bitter; with the soul, to be in bitter distress.

[109]LSJ 931 only cites 1 Kgdms 1:10 on this form: "in great pain or affliction." The verb κατοδυνάω on p. 928 is: "afflict grievously."

[110]Cf. Sperber, *The Bible in Aramaic* 2.94: מריא נפש For the Aramaic verb, see Jastrow 847.

[111]Cf. also *Pseudo-Philo* 50:6, which employs *anxiaretur sensu* of Hannah's soul being "anxious, disturbed" in 1 Samuel 1 (*OTP* 2.364; *Les Antiquités Bibliques* 1.330-331).

[112]Cf. Mark 11:17-18 par.; 12:14 and 17 par.; 12:35 par.; 14:49 par.; John 7:14-15, 28; 8:2, 20; and 18:20. On astonishment at Jesus' teaching, see also Mark 1:22 and 27 par.

questions. Now all those who heard him were 'astounded' at his 'understanding' and his answers to their questions" (vv 46-47). The Greek for "understanding" in v 47 is σύνεσις.[113] This scene also causes Jesus' parents to be "astonished" (v 48),[114] which the boy does not comprehend. He therefore asks them: "Did you not know that...?" (v 49). This saying, which Jesus spoke to them, the parents in turn "did not understand" (v 50). The latter Greek verb is the aorist of συνίημι,[115] from the same root as the above noun σύνεσις.

Here in the present context of Luke 2:40-52, amazing "wisdom" and "understanding" are attested for a mere "boy,"[116] not yet of legal age (thirteen) or fully responsible for his words and deeds in first century C.E. Palestinian Judaism[117]. As remarked in section ten above, Jesus as a wise and understanding twelve-year-old belongs to a very old Judaic tradition of wise and understanding twelve-year-olds: Solomon, Josiah and Daniel. The main influence exerted on Luke 2:41-51a, and later also on vv 40 and 52, however, derives from the wise and understanding twelve-year-old Samuel.

B.

Samuel's wise adult behavior in regard to the Torah, like that of Jesus, was also later retrojected in Judaic sources to his youth, early childhood, and even Hannah's pregnancy with him.

1) Adulthood.

The minor tractate of the Babylonian Talmud, *Kallah Rabbati* 6, 54a, states: "The Rabbis taught: When a Sage dies, all the people have the duty to mourn for him." An example of such a wise man is Samuel (1 Sam 28:3 and 25:1), who was mourned because he "journeyed from city to city and from province to province to teach us Torah, something which no other prophet had done." For this 1 Sam 7:16-17 is cited, where Samuel judged Israel annually when he went on circuit.[118]

---

[113]Cf. BAGD 788, as well as the article συνίημι by H. Conzelmann in *TDNT* 7.888-896.

[114]The antecedent of "they" in "And when they saw him" is Joseph and Mary, not "all who heard him" in v 47, for they are themselves astounded. The lapse is on the part of the narrator. It does not indicate that v 47 is a later addition (see section IV below).

[115]BAGD 790.

[116]In Luke 2:43 Jesus is characterized as a παῖς, and in v 48 as a τέκνον; v 40 employs παιδίον.

[117]Cf. *b. Ketub.* 50a (Soncino 287); *m. 'Abot* 5:21 (Danby 458); *Nid.* 5:6 (Danby 751), and other texts cited by Str-B 2.144-147. J. Wettstein in *Novum Testamentum Graecum* 1.667 had already called attention to a number of these in 1752.

[118]Soncino, *The Minor Tractates* 483.

Samuel taught the people the Torah in his function as a Levite.[119] Just as his father Elkanah went on an annual pilgrimage to the Temple in Shiloh, taking new people with him each time from various cities so as to "train them in the observance of the commandments," so his son Samuel later did the latter also, causing many people to grow in virtue because of himself.[120] Since he administered justice to Israel all his life in various places (1 Sam 7:15-17), Samuel's was one of the three most famous Israelite courts in Judaic tradition, where the Holy Spirit showed itself.[121] On account of his acumen in the Torah, Samuel was even labeled "head of the academy."[122]

2) *Youth.*

This exemplary acumen in the Torah on the part of the adult Samuel was then thought to have already prevailed in his youth. Dependent for the most part on *m. 'Abot* 1:1,[123] *'Abot R. Nat.* B 1 states that Moses received the Torah from Sinai and passed it on to Joshua, who passed it on to the elders, who passed it on to the judges, who passed it on to Eli, for which 1 Sam 1:9 is cited. Eli then passed it on to Samuel, as in 2:26 – "Now the boy Samuel continued to grow both in stature and in favor with the Lord and with men."[124] Here Eli is represented as Samuel's teacher in the Torah, before the calling of Samuel by God in chapter three, in Judaic tradition at the age of twelve. *Num. Rab.* Bemidbar 3/8 on Num 3:15 calls Eli Samuel's "master,"[125] as does *y. 'Erub.* 5:1, 22b in regard to Samuel's ministering to the Lord under Eli in the Temple in 1 Sam 3:1.[126] Elsewhere Eli is characterized as "the president of the

---

[119]Cf. 1 Chr 6:1 (Eng. 6:16) and 13 (Eng. 28). On the Levites as originally also teachers of the Torah, see Neh 8:7-9; 2 Chr 17:7-9 and 35:3; as well as the discussion in the art. "Priests and Levites" by R. Abba in *IDB* 3.879-880.

[120]Cf. *Eliyyahu Rabbah* (8)9 in Friedmann 48, Braude and Kapstein 150. See also *Pseudo-Philo* 51:3: "he will show to the [Israelite] nations the statutes...," in *OTP* 2.365, with n. "f" on 15:6.

[121]Cf. *t. Mak.* 11:14 (Neusner 3.197); *Midr. Ps.*17.A/16 and 72/2 (Braude 1.226, 559-560); *b. 'Erub.* 45a (Soncino 312); *Yebam.* 77a (Soncino 518-519); *B. Qam.* 61a (Soncino 353); *Mak.* 23b (Soncino 168); *y. Roš. Haš.* 2:9, 58b (Neusner/Goldman 16.73); *Gen. Rab.* Vayesheb 85/12 on Gen 38:26 (Soncino 2.797), with a parallel in *Eccl. Rab.* 10:17 §1 (Soncino 8.278); *Ruth Rab.* 4/6 on Ruth 2:5 (Soncino 8.56); and *Eccl. Rab.* 1:4 § 4 (Soncino 8.13).

[122]Cf. *Lev. Rab.* Vayyikra 2/3 (Soncino 4.21), with a parallel in *Ruth Rab.* 2/5 on Ruth 1:2 (Soncino 8.29).

[123]Danby 446.

[124]Saldarini 25-26, Schechter 2.

[125]Soncino 5.82; the time period includes Samuel's youth.

[126]Neusner 12.147, with רבו. On this expression, see also *b. Ber.* 31b below.

Sanhedrin,"[127] which especially qualified him to impart great Torah learning to his pupil Samuel. Finally, R. Eleazar (b. Pedat), a third generation Babylonian and Palestinian Amora who studied under R. Yoḥanan and took over his school in Tiberias,[128] interprets the "wise man" (חכם) who becomes wiser of Prov 9:9 as alluding to the boy Samuel's behavior at his calling in the Temple of Shiloh in 1 Sam 3:9-10.[129]

3) Early Childhood.

a)

The Temple is also the scene of a major incident displaying the child Samuel's great Torah learning, a narrative important in a number of respects for Luke 2:41-51a. R. Eleazar (b. Pedat), who above also called the boy Samuel a "wise man/sage" in the Temple, passed on[130] an Aramaic narrative related to the "child" of 1 Sam 1:27 in *b. Ber.* 31b.[131] As noted above, Samuel has just been weaned and is considered to be two years old here in Judaic tradition when he is deposited with Eli in the house of the Lord at Shiloh (1 Sam 1:24-28).

> At this time Samuel as a child "taught" (מורה) in the Temple a halakhah before his teacher (רבו) Eli, as the "ritual slaughtering" (שחט)[132] of a bull in 1 Sam 1:25 is interpreted. Eli, elsewhere also considered the high priest of the time,[133] had told Samuel's parents to call a priest to come and ritually slaughter the animal. When the child saw them searching for a priest to do so, he asked them why they were searching. He said: "Ritual slaughter is valid (כשר) [when done] by a lay person!" His parents then brought Samuel to Eli, who asked him: "From where do you know this?" He answered him, "Is it written, 'The priest shall slaughter'? It is written, 'The priests shall present' [the blood, Lev 1:5]. The priestly office begins as of the reception [of the blood]. This

---

[127]Cf. *Tanḥuma* B Shemini on Lev 9:1 (Bietenhard 2.39; Buber, Leviticus 23); *Tanḥuma* Shemini 2 on Lev 9:1 (Eshkol 516), both with אב בית דין; as well as other sources noted in Ginzberg, *The Legends* 6.220, n. 24.

[128]Strack and Stemberger, *Introduction* 98.

[129]See *b. Šabb.* 113b in Soncino 554.

[130]It is very improbable that Eleazar himself composed all the haggadoth he relates on Samuel. He appears to have had a special interest in collecting them. Cf., for example, the context of the incident in *b. Šabb.* 32b cited below. The haggadoth are definitely Palestinian, probably passed on to Eleazar through the school of R. Yoḥanan, his teacher (see n. 128).

[131]Soncino 194. Connected to this in *Midr. Sam.* 3/6 on 1 Sam 1:24 (Buber 53, Wünsche 24) is a similar incident on the child Samuel which illustrates Prov 20:1 ("Even a child [נער] makes himself known by his acts").

[132]Jastrow 1546-1547.

[133]Cf. Josephus, *Ant.* 5.338, 345, 348, as well as the *Tanḥuma* passages and other references in n. 127.

demonstrates the validity of ritual slaughter by a lay person."[134] Eli then tells the boy Samuel he has answered "very well."[135] Nevertheless, because he has taught a legal decision before his master, he must die. This is why Hannah comes and cries the contents of 1 Sam 1:26 before Eli. When Eli proposes that he punish Samuel, but pray to God to give Hannah a better (lit. "greater") one than the child, she replies that she had prayed "for *this* child" (1 Sam 1:27).

Here Samuel, thought to be only two years old, is presented as a child prodigy, instructing his own parents in the Temple in regard to ritual slaughtering. Since they are incredulous, they go to the authoritative figure, Eli the (high) priest. Himself astonished, Eli praises the child's answering "very well." In addition, however, Samuel teaches his own master a halakhah. Very early Judaic sources support Samuel's halakhic teaching, yet they, too, condemn a pupil's teaching before his master.[136]

This scene of the child Samuel in the Temple of Shiloh is the basic background for the boy Jesus in the Temple of Jerusalem, where, also at the Passover pilgrimage, he listens to the teachers and asks them questions. All who hear him are "amazed" at Jesus' understanding, and at the answers he gives to the teachers' questions. Like Elkanah and Hannah, Jesus' parents are also "astonished" (at his being in the Temple, but primarily at his [wisdom and] understanding there – Luke 2:46-48). The relevance of other motifs and expressions from the narrative of the boy Samuel in *b. Ber.* 31b to Luke 2:41-51a will be discussed below in sections thirteen and fourteen.

Two very early Judaic texts dealing with the wisdom and understanding of the child Samuel at the time he was weaned by

---

[134]For lay people allowed to slaughter especially at Passover, cf. *m. Pesaḥ.* 5:6 (Danby 142): "An Israelite slaughtered his [own] offering and the priest caught the blood"; Philo, *Mos.* 2.224; *Spec. Leg.* 2.145-146; and *Quaes. Exod.* I 10 on Exod 12:6b; as well as the rabbinic sources cited in Safrai, *Die Wallfahrt* 220-221.

[135]In his paraphrase of this expression (שפיר קא), Ginzberg in *The Legends* 4.60 speaks of Eli's "astonishment." Cf. Luke 2:47-48. On the phrase, see also Luke 20:39, "Teacher, you have spoken well," and the Matthean rendition in 22:33 as the people's being "astonished at his teaching."

[136]On the validity of a lay person's slaughtering in general, cf. for example *m. Ḥul.* 1:1 (Danby 513), and the Tosefta on this (Neusner 5.65); *m. Zebaḥ.* 3:1 (Danby 471); and *Sifra* Vayyikra on Lev 1:5 (Neusner 1.102; Winter 30). R. Eliezer (b. Hyrcanus), a second generation Tanna (Strack and Stemberger, *Introduction* 77), states in *Sifra* Shemini on Lev 10:1 (Neusner 2.135; Winter 264) that he had received as a tradition from his own teachers: "whoever teaches law in his master's presence is liable to death." A scriptural basis for this decision is given in *b. Yoma* 53a (Soncino 249), with Lev 16:1 and 1:7. In *b. Sanh.* 5b (Soncino 18), it is stated that a disciple must be three parasangs away from his teacher when giving a legal decision.

Hannah at the age of two (1 Sam 1:24-28) and left in the Temple to serve
the Lord (2:11) are the Septuagint version of Hannah's prayer in 1 Sam
2:1-10, and comment on it in *Pseudo-Philo.*

b)

1 Kgdms 2:10 greatly expands the Hebrew text. Among other things
Jer 9:22-23 (Eng. 23-24) are quoted in v 10c-j in a translation independent
of the Septuagint, pointing to the early date of this tradition.

The MT of Jer 9:22 states: "Let not the 'wise man' glory in his
'wisdom' (חכם בחכמתו)," for which the Septuagint has ὁ σόφος ἐν τῇ
σοφίᾳ αὐτοῦ, but First Kingdoms ὁ φρόνιμος ἐν τῇ φρονήσει αὐτοῦ.
Then the MT of Jer 9:23 says that he who glories should glory in this,
"that he 'understands' and 'knows' Me (השכיל וידע אותי)."[137] Both the
Septuagint and First Kingdoms have the verb συνίημι for "understand"
here, as well as γινώσκω for "know."

All three of these terms occur in Luke 2: "wisdom" in the later
framework verses 40 and 52; "to understand" in v 50, with
"understanding" in v 47; and "to know" in connection with God in v 49.

1 Kgdms 2:10 1, at the conclusion of the verse, also speaks of the
Lord's exalting the horn of His anointed one (χριστός). This may have
been a major impetus for the Hellenistic Jewish Christian translator of
the narrative of the twelve-year-old Jesus in the Temple to employ the
same Greek terms noted above when he rendered the original Semitic
into Greek. He recognized its background in 1 Kingdoms 1-3.

c)

Pseudo-Philo, as remarked above Palestinian, from about the time of
Jesus, and originally in Hebrew, paraphrases Hannah's prayer in 1 Sam
2:1-10 in 51:3-6. Here she predicts that her son Samuel "will show to the
nations the statutes" (3).[138] He is "the light from which 'wisdom'
(sapientia) is to be born" (4).[139] Hannah has born "the light to the
peoples" of Isa 51:4, whereby the Gentiles are probably meant. Yet
Samuel is also he who is to stay in the Temple and serve "until he be
made a light for this nation," Israel (6).[140] Directly before the latter
phrase, God's "anointed one" and "king" from 1 Sam 2:10 are
mentioned. They are certainly meant here of Samuel, for in 51:7 the
people now festively present him to Eli in the Temple and "anoint" him,

---

[137]On שכל as a verb and noun with the meaning "to understand,"
"understanding," cf. BDB 968.
[138]*OTP* 2.365, with n. "f," referring to 15:6.
[139]*Les Antiquités Bibliques* 1.334 and 2.365.
[140]*OTP* 2.366.

praying that the prophet "may be a light to this nation for a long time."[141]

That Samuel is the anointed king of 1 Sam 2:10, who in fact is anointed at this point, is peculiar to *Pseudo-Philo*. Again, as in the ancient traditions behind the Septuagint of Hannah's prayer, it shows how a Palestinian Jewish Christian describing the twelve-year-old Jesus in the Jerusalem Temple could also employ Judaic traditions on the two-year-old Samuel here for the future Christian Messiah. Samuel is not only thought to be in the elite group of Israelite wise and understanding twelve-year-olds, like Solomon, Josiah and Daniel. Already at the age of two he is recognized in *Pseudo-Philo* as the light of Israel and the nations, from which "wisdom" is to be born. He is the "anointed one."

4) Samuel in Hannah's Womb.

Predictions of Samuel's later wisdom and understanding were even retrojected in Judaic tradition to the time in which Hannah was pregnant with him.

Midr. Sam. 2/12 comments on the phrase "and the God of Israel grant your 'petition'" in 1 Sam 1:17. Here Eli says to still barren Hannah: "The son whom you will have will capture much booty (שלל)[142] in the Torah."[143] That is, Eli predicts that Hannah's future child Samuel will become a great Torah scholar.

This motif is also found in Judaic comment on 1 Sam 1:11. Here Hannah vows in the Temple that if the Lord gives her "seed of men" (זרע אנשים; RSV "a son," NRSV "a male child"), she will give it to the Lord "all the days of his life, and no razor shall touch his head." *Midr. Sam.* 2/7 on this expression "seed of men" interprets it as meaning "understanding men," as in Deut 1:13, "wise and understanding (חכמים ונבנים)." This is repeated two more times.[144] Here Hannah's future sons (1 Sam 2:21), primarily Samuel, are to be wise and understanding.

The Hebrew for "razor" in 1 Sam 1:1 is מוֹרָה[145]. Literally the sentence in which it is found reads: "And a razor shall not come upon his head." If "razor" is vocalized as מוֹרֶה, however, it means "teacher."[146] Then the clause can be interpreted: "And no teacher shall surpass him," i.e., his Torah learning will be so great that no other scholar will come up to him.

---

[141] *Ibid.*
[142] Jastrow 1585: "booty, gain."
[143] Buber 52, Wünsche 5.21.
[144] Buber 49, Wünsche 5.18.
[145] BDB 559.
[146] BDB 435, from the same root as "Torah," which is "direction, instruction, law." The hiphil of ירה (BDB 435,5) can also mean "direct, teach, instruct."

This is the way the Targum also interpreted the expression. It reads: "And the dominion (מרוּת) of man will not be upon him."[147]

In these Palestinian traditions, now found in *Midrash Samuel* and the Targum, Samuel's wisdom and understanding are even carried back to the time before his birth in the form of predictions.[148]

* * *

I have documented the "wisdom and understanding" of the boy/child Samuel in Judaic tradition so extensively above because they provide the immediate background for the twelve-year-old Jesus' display of great understanding in the Jerusalem Temple (and wisdom in Luke 2:40 and 52). There is thus no reason whatsoever to exclude v 47 from the narrative because it emphasizes Jesus' understanding (on this, see also section IV below). Nor is there any reason to look for the origins of this motif, as found in the Lucan narrative of the boy Jesus, in Hellenistic, pagan sources. Hellenistic biography enjoyed describing its great heroes as child prodigies, "Wunderkinder," and these descriptions certainly exerted some influence on Judaic biographies. Cross-fertilization occurred. Yet the *direct* source for the great understanding (and wisdom) of Jesus in the Luke 2 Temple incident was the Palestinian account of the wisdom and understanding of the child/boy Samuel at the time of a Passover pilgrimage to the Temple in Shiloh.[149] The characteristics which were applied in Judaic tradition to the anointed one, Samuel, were later applied by a Palestinian Jewish Christian to his own Anointed One/Messiah, Jesus.

13. Searching, Finding, and a Question of One's Parents.

A.

Jesus' parents thought he was in their caravan returning from the Passover festival to Nazareth. Not knowing he had remained in Jerusalem, they "sought" (ἀναζητέω) him among their relatives and

---

[147]Sperber 2.94; Harrington and Saldarini 103. On the noun, see Jastrow 840: "authority, dominion," with a reference to Targ. 1 Sam 1:11. Cf. also *m. Nazir* 9:5, where R. Yose believes the Hebrew means this (n. 1 in Danby 293). R. Nehorai makes another word play with מוֹרָה: מוֹרָא, "fear" (BDB 432). On the relevance of מרות to Jesus' being "obedient" to his parents in Luke 2:51, see section III below.

[148]Cf. also *Eliyyahu Rabbah* (8)9, Friedmann 47, cited above on the prediction regarding Elkanah: he is to have a son who will also train the people in the observance of the commandments.

[149]Another example of this as a *Palestinian* motif is Josephus, who describes himself at about the age of fourteen in Jerusalem: "the chief priests and the leading men of the city used constantly to come to me for precise information on some particular in our ordinances." This showed his great "understanding" (σύνεσις): *Vita* 8-9.

acquaintances (Luke 2:44). When they didn't "find" (εὑρίσκω) him, they returned to Jerusalem, "seeking" (ἀναζητέω) him there (v 45). Then after three days (of searching), they "found" (εὑρίσκω) him sitting in the Temple (v 46). He was engaged in scholarly discussion with the teachers/Sages, characterized by the disputation-like method of the time: listening, asking questions, and answering them. When Joseph and Mary saw him in this context, fully unexpected by them, they were astonished. Jesus' mother then informed him that they had been "seeking" (ζητέω) him anxiously (v 48). Replying not to his mother, but to both parents, Jesus asks: Why were you "seeking" (ζητέω) me? Did you not know that...? (v 49).

The four-fold mention of "seeking/looking for/searching for" shows its importance in this relatively short narrative of eleven verses. The number is increased to five times if one supplements "after three days" with "of searching" in v 46. The verb ἀναζητέω is only found in the NT in vv 44-45 and in Acts 11:25. This means that the Evangelist Luke, for stylistic reasons, probably added ἀνα- to the simple verb form ζητέω he found in the Greek text available to him. He wanted to vary and thus improve the style.

Again, the emphasis on "seeking" and "finding," coupled with a question posed by a son to his parents at a Passover pilgrimage, derives from Judaic tradition on the child/boy Samuel in the Temple.

B.

The *b. Ber.* 31b account of the two-year-old Samuel in the Temple of Shiloh at the pilgrimage of Passover was cited above in section twelve in regard to his great acumen in the Torah. In the same narrative it is stated that Eli tells Samuel's parents to call a priest to come and ritually slaughter the bull they wanted to offer (1 Sam 1:25). Before they found one, Samuel saw them (his parents) "searching for" (Aramaic הדר בתר[150]) a priest to ritually slaughter it. Therefore "he [Samuel] said to them, 'Why do you go *searching for* a priest to ritually slaughter it?'" He then informed Elkanah and Hannah that a lay person is allowed to do this.[151]

The Aramaic for: "He said to them, 'Why do you go searching for...'" is the following: אמר להו: למה לכו לאהדורי בתר.... I suggest that the Aramaic-speaking Palestinian Jewish Christian author of Luke 2:41-51a borrowed the motif and even phraseology of this incident, perhaps in an earlier form available to him, and applied it to the twelve-year-old Jesus in the Temple. Verse 49 has in regard to Joseph and Mary: "And he said to them, 'Why have you been searching for....'" If the original Semitic

---

[150]Jastrow 334.
[151]Soncino 194.

narrative of Luke 2:41-51a was Hebrew, however, the term for "searching" was probably בקש.[152]

This haggadic narrative is now also found in *Midr. Sam.* 3/6 in Hebrew, which comments on the boy/child of 1 Sam 1:24 that he was two years old. Here Samuel, in the Temple of Shiloh, came and "found" (מצא) them (pilgrims) standing next to their offerings. After he asks them why they do not ritually slaughter, they answer that they are waiting for a priest to come, as in Lev 1:5. To this he answers that they themselves should arise and ritually slaughter. He asks: "Is it not an early tradition that ritual slaughter, including that of most holy things, is valid [even] when done by lay people, women and servants/slaves?" When Eli came and "found" (מצא) them slaughtering, he asked them: "Who permitted you this ritual slaughtering?" They answered him: "A child/boy" (נער אחד). Eli then tells them to bring him to him, as in 1 Sam 1:25. He "sought/wanted" (בקש) to punish Samuel, even by death, but Samuel's mother Hannah then intervened for him, as in *b. Ber.* 31b above.[153]

Here in this variant, Temple pilgrims play the role of Samuel's parents in the *b. Ber.* 31b account. He himself "finds" them in the Temple, wanting to ritually slaughter, and Eli then "finds" them doing so at the instigation of the two-year-old boy. Then he "seeks" to punish Samuel. The motif of "finding," although only explicitly stated in this late midrashic collection of Judaic traditions on Samuel, thus may also belong to an earlier form of the original narrative, where Samuel's parents do not "find" the priest they are "searching for" to ritually slaughter their offering of a bull. From there the "finding" may also have entered Luke 2:45-46.

* * *

Finally, it may also be noteworthy that "searching for" an article lost at a festival pilgrimage to Jerusalem was apparently a common occurrence. Jesus' parents are pictured in Luke 2:46 as searching for him in Jerusalem for three days before finding him, which adds to the dramatic tension. This is because the population of the city at Passover swelled from some 25-30,000 to possibly 180,000.[154] Searching for a twelve-year-old boy at all the caravan meeting sites and festival lodging

---

[152]Jastrow 188.

[153]Buber 53, Wünsche 5.24.

[154]Cf. J. Jeremias, *Jerusalem in the Time of Jesus* (London: SCM, 1969) 77-84. Jeremias later considered the latter figure possibly "a little too high" (p. 84). S. Safrai in *Die Wallfahrt* 97 speaks of "10,000's"; one cannot be more exact. A. Edersheim in *The Life and Times of Jesus the Messiah* (Grand Rapids, Michigan: Eerdmans, 1942) 1.243 estimates that the Temple alone held ca. 210,000 persons.

opportunities in the greater Jerusalem area would have been a formidable task, easily thought to last three days.

In *m. B. Meṣ.* 2:6 early Sages discuss the procedure of a man's proclaiming what he has found at a festival pilgrimage. R. Judah (b. Ilai), a third generation Tanna,[155] says the finder of a lost object should proclaim it at the three pilgrimage festivals (in Jerusalem) and for seven days after the last one in order to allow the loser to spend three days going home, three days returning, and one day to proclaim his loss.[156] It is possible that precisely this figure of "three days" may have influenced the author of Luke 2:41-51a when he states in v 46 that Jesus' parents had searched for him for "three days" before finding him at the feast of Passover in the Jerusalem Temple.

There was even a special blessing pronounced upon a person who "lost" something at a pilgrimage festival. *Sem.* 7:11, 46a states: "To one who 'lost' some object they say, 'May He who dwells in this House [the Jerusalem Temple] put it into the heart of the 'finder' to return it to you at once.'" An incident is then related of a rabbi who "lost" his copy of the Torah in Jerusalem, (probably wanting to have it corrected according to the master copy in the Temple Courtyard at a pilgrimage). He soon discovered that it had been "found."[157]

The motifs of "searching for" and "finding" in Luke 2:41-51a derive from Judaic haggadah on the child/boy Samuel in the Temple at Shiloh. Nevertheless, "losing" and "finding" an object lost at a festival pilgrimage to Jerusalem seems, because of the very large number of pilgrims to the city, to have been a common occurrence. The imagery is therefore very appropriate to a Passover pilgrimage to the Jerusalem Temple, as in Luke 2:41-51a.

Excursus on Jesus' Sitting with the Teachers in the Temple

Luke 2:46 states that after returning to Jerusalem, Jesus' parents sought their son and found him "sitting" (καθέζομαι) in the Temple, in the midst of the teachers/Sages, listening to them and responding to their questions. Two issues are involved here: 1) the location of scholarly discussions in the Temple precincts at the Passover festival, and 2) the custom of sitting while engaged in scholarly debate or teaching.

---

[155]Strack and Stemberger, *Introduction* 84-85.

[156]Albeck 4.7, Danby 349. See also Safrai, *Die Wallfahrt* 54, n.68.

[157]English in Socino, *The Minor Tractates* 354. On this incident as probably related to a pilgrimage festival, cf. Safrai, *Die Wallfahrt* 262-263.

1)

The Tosefta, a Tannaitic document, states in *Sanh.* 7:1 regarding the court of seventy or seventy-one, the Sanhedrin: "On Sabbaths and on festivals they came only to the study house which was on the Temple mount. [If] a question was brought before them, if they had heard the answer, they told them. If not, they stand for a vote." It adds: "From there did the law go forth and circulate in Israel."[158]

The Temple Mount (הר הבית) was the entire Temple area, enclosed by the four Porticos. Where the study house or academy (בית המדרש) was exactly located is not known. It may, more probably, simply have been a specific, sheltered section of the magnificent open-air Royal Portico or Stoa along the southern wall.[159] The Tosefta's mention of "festivals" includes Passover, when the twelve-year-old Jesus is represented as engaging in scholarly debate with the "teachers" or Sages.[160] Since his mother Mary may also approach Jesus and the Temple teachers (Luke 2:46-49), one of the outer areas, where women were also allowed, is meant. Mary would not have been permitted, for example, to enter the Men's Court with Joseph and Jesus.

The Tosefta also speaks of a "question" (שאילה) being put to the Sages in the highest court. The term "answer" in Neusner's English translation is not found in the Hebrew, but is implied. This questioning and answering method of learning and arriving at a decision or conclusion

---

[158]Zuckermandel/Liebermann 425; Neusner 4.217. A variant tradition is found in *b. Sanh.* 88b (Soncino 586).

[159]Cf. the art. "Temple of Herod" by M. Ben-Dov in *IDBSup* (1976) 871, with the drawing on p.870. See also Edersheim, *The Life and Times of Jesus the Messiah* 2.742, who mentions the possibility that "the term 'Beth ha-Midrash' must be taken in the wider and more general sense of the 'place of Rabbinic exposition,' and not as indicating any permanent Academy." See also p. 247. In John 10:23 Jesus is mentioned as walking in the winter in the Portico of Solomon, the section on the eastern wall. If Luke 2:46-49 presumes this eastern Portico, there may be an intentional contrast between the great wisdom of the twelve-year-old boy Jesus and the wisest Israelite king, Solomon (cf. 11:31), who according to very early Judaic tradition ascended the throne at twelve. For Josephus' description of these Porticos, see Str-B 2.625-626 on Acts 3:11. According to Judaic tradition, R. Yoḥanan b. Zakkai fled Jerusalem at the time of the Jewish-Roman War of 66-70 C.E. and founded an (open-air) study house in the shade of vineyard trees at Yabne. See the literature cited in Strack and Stemberger, *Introduction* 75. This may thus be how the study house on the Temple Mount is meant: in the shade and shelter of a Portico.

[160]For the festival pilgrims as also concerned with study of the Torah, encouraged by their viewing the Sages of the Sanhedrin and their disciples doing this, cf. Safrai, *Die Wallfahrt* 260. See also Edersheim, *The Life and Times* 1.248, above.

was typical of the time.[161]   It is reflected in the "questions" and "answers" of Luke 2:46-47.

When the Palestinian Jewish Christian author of Luke 2:41-51a describes Jesus as sitting in the Temple, among the teachers, listening to them, asking his own questions, and answering theirs, he most probably implies that the twelve-year-old's wisdom and understanding are even greater than those of the country's best scholars, the members of the Sanhedrin who issued authoritative opinions on the Torah, which then circulated in all of Israel.   By answering their open questions (successfully), the boy Jesus is pictured here as already now being superior to the Sages of the supreme court of the land.[162]   He is so because he debates with them the concerns of "my Father" (v 49); that is, he is the Son of God and knows His will best.[163]

2)

The author of Luke 2:41-51a certainly knew of Jesus' teaching in the Jerusalem Temple, which he retroverted to his boyhood.   After "cleansing" the Temple at Passover, Jesus "taught" there, causing the multitude to be "astonished" (Mark 11:17-18).   M. Ben-Dov considers the Royal Portico on the south side to be the site of the affected merchants, and perhaps of the Sanhedrin.[164]   If so, Jesus' "teaching" here may have taken place at the authoritative source of the nation's teaching during the Passover festival.   A greater contrast cannot be imagined.   It would have greatly contributed in a negative way to his almost immediate arrest and to the outcome of Jesus' "hearing" before the Sanhedrin (Mark 14:43, 53; 15:1).

Mark 12:35 also mentions Jesus' teaching in the Temple.   When later arrested in the Garden of Gethsemane, the Galilean prophet states: "Day after day I was with you in the Temple teaching, but you did not seize

---

[161]Cf. the sources cited in Str-B 2.150-151, section 3.   Billerbeck thinks Jesus debated with scholars in the teaching room of a synagogue on the Temple Mount (p. 150).   See also Safrai, *Die Wallfahrt* 2.   There is no evidence for such a synagogue.   See the literature cited by H. de Jonge, "Sonship, Wisdom, Infancy: Luke II.41-51a" in *NTS* 24 (1978) 328-329.

[162]K. Bornhäuser in *Die Geburts- und Kindheitsgeschichte Jesu* (Gütersloh: Bertelsmann, 1930) 130-131 sees here Pharisaic theology versus Jesus' divinely bestowed wisdom.   He speaks of the teachers' viewing Jesus with animosity because of the latter's "decisive contradictions" of their positions.   However, there is nothing of a negative nature in the narrative, in which the Palestinian Jewish Christian author, who himself probably still attended the Temple, respectfully speaks of "teachers."

[163]Cf. the Evangelist John, who in 8:28 has Jesus, teaching in the Temple (v 20), say: "I speak thus as the Father taught me."   The motif is the same as in Luke 2.

[164]Art. "Temple of Herod" 871.

me" (14:49). This indicates a longer period of time than that now recorded in the Synoptics. The Evangelist John expands the same motif of Jesus' teaching in the Temple.[165]

The customary position for teaching and for learning from a teacher was that of sitting. A good example of this is the baraitha found in *b. Pesaḥ.* 26a regarding R. Yoḥanan b. Zakkai, a first generation Tanna.[166] He "was sitting in the shadow of the Temple and teaching all day."[167] H. Freedman notes here that Yoḥanan was explaining the regulations of Passover to the crowds shortly before the festival, as was usual.[168] "As his own school-house was too small for the large number who wished to hear him, he taught in the open, choosing this site on account of the shade afforded by the high walls of the Temple."[169] The inner southern side of the Temple Mount afforded most shade from the sun. Yoḥanan's great following would then not have to move from the eastern, and then to the southern and western sides, to avoid the sun. This also speaks for his sitting and teaching in the shadow of the southern or Royal Portico, where Jesus also may have taught in order to address as many local inhabitants and pilgrims to Jerusalem as possible.

Other passages in the NT mention Jesus' sitting while teaching,[170] and additional rabbinic sources also attest the practice.[171] When the Palestinian Jewish Christian author of Luke 2:41-51a represents Jesus as sitting among the teachers in the Temple and debating with them (vv 46-47), they are thus all pictured as sitting. He reflects the standard Judaic practice of the time. This also means that modern presentations of the twelve-year-old Jesus in the Temple (for example, Liebermann's) which have him, or both him and the teachers, standing demonstrate artistic license. Luke 2:46 correctly has Jesus (and the teachers) sitting.

14. Jesus as God's Son, and Samuel as God's Son.

A.

As a narrative, Luke 2:41-51a has two main emphases. One is the understanding (and wisdom) of Jesus already as a twelve-year-old boy, in the same Judaic chain of tradition as Solomon, Josiah, Daniel, and above all Samuel. The other, the more important, is Jesus as the Son of

---

[165]Cf. 7:14, 28; 8:2, 20; and 18:20.
[166]Cf. Strack and Stemberger, *Introduction* 74-75.
[167]Soncino 117.
[168]He compares 6a-b (Soncino 23-24).
[169]Soncino 117, n. 1.
[170]Cf. Mark 4:1; 9:35; 12:41, 43-44; 13:3; Matt 26:55; Luke 5:17; and John 8:2.
[171]Cf. the traditions noted in Str-B 1.997 on a teacher's sitting, and 2.763-765 on a pupil's sitting. See also 2.33-37.

God. Here in Luke 2 a highly christological statement is made of Jesus' Sonship about eighteen years (cf. 3:23) before a voice comes from heaven at his baptism, saying: "You are My beloved *Son;* I am well pleased with you" (3:22).[172]

Luke 2:41 and 43 speak of Jesus' "parents." Verse 48 mentions his "mother," as does v 51. In v 48 Mary addresses Jesus as τέκνον, which the RSV correctly translates as "son." This is shown, for example, in 1 Kgdms 3:16, where Eli's calling Samuel "my son" (בני) in the MT is also simply τέκνον in Greek. The Hebrew New Testaments of both Delitzsch and the United Bible Societies also have בני, "my son," for the τέκνον of v 48. In the same verse Mary says, "Your father [Joseph] and I have been searching for you anxiously." To this Jesus replies in v 49: "Did you (pl.) not know that it was necessary for me to discuss [as a scholar, in the Temple] the concerns of my Father?"[173] Regardless of how one interprets the difficult phrase ἐν τοῖς...εἶναι, a very strong contrast is presented here by the author between Jesus' earthly "father" (Joseph), and his "Father" in the Jerusalem Temple, the heavenly Father, God.[174] The attention of the listener, later the reader, of this narrative is emphatically directed to Jesus at the age of twelve as already being the Son of God, for the latter is his true Father.

Again, this son/father-Father imagery derives from Judaic tradition on the child/boy Samuel in the Temple at Shiloh.

B.

The Hebrew text of 1 Samuel 3 already has Eli say "my son" (בני) to Samuel twice at the scene of the boy's being called by God in the Temple (3:6 and 16). Eli knew very well that Elkanah was Samuel's real father (1:19-20). Yet because the boy ministered to the Lord in the Temple in the presence of the priest (2:11, 18), Eli considered him his adopted son. Judaic tradition, as noted above, has Samuel's parents lend him to the Lord in the Temple, under the care of his master or teacher Eli, at the age of two. Since the early haggadic tradition still found in Josephus has Samuel begin to prophesy at the age of twelve, Eli will have had ten

---

[172]Cf. the variant in MS "D" from Ps 2:7, "You are My *Son;* today I have begotten you."

[173]For this interpretation of ἐν τοῖς...εῖναι, cf. section III below.

[174]The Jerusalem Temple was considered to be the site of God's "indwelling" presence. In addition to n. 68 in section II, see, for example, 2 Sam 6:2 for His sitting enthroned on the cherubim of the ark, removed by David to a tent in Jerusalem (v 17). 2 Macc 2:4-8 describes the hiding of the ark by the prophet Jeremiah at Nebuchadnezzar's destruction of Jerusalem in 587 B.C.E. Nevertheless, the heavenly Father was still thought to "dwell" in the Second Temple, including Herod's rebuilt version of it. See section 13.B above on the blessing, "May He who dwells in this House...."

years in which to educate him in the Temple, as his father Elkanah would otherwise have done at home. In addition, just as Elisha could call his teacher Elijah "my father" in 2 Kgs 2:12, so rabbinic scholars were thought of as if they had "begotten" their pupils.[175] That is, they were their spiritual "fathers," who imparted wisdom to them.

In 1 Samuel 3, Samuel is pictured as "lying down within the Temple of the Lord, where the ark of God was" (v 3). Since God was thought to be enthroned above the cherubim of the ark and to speak from there (Num 7:89),[176] the heavenly Father was directly next to Samuel when He called him four times. The first three times the boy thinks Eli has called him. Only after receiving Eli's advice does he recognize that it is the Lord who is speaking to him (3:10).

The issue of whose son Samuel really is (Elkanah's, Eli's or the heavenly Father's), is discussed extensively in Judaic texts. In *Pseudo-Philo*, Palestinian and from about the time of Jesus, chapter 53 deals with the call of Samuel in the Temple in 1 Samuel 3. As in rabbinic sources (see below), God's calling Samuel is associated here with His calling Moses from the burning bush in Exodus 3. Moses, an adult, was afraid of that fire, so God decides here in *Pseudo-Philo* first to speak to the eight-year-old Samuel, "beloved" *(dilectus)* before Him[177], in a voice like that of a man. Then, when the boy has understood this, God will speak to him like God (53:2).[178] When He calls Samuel the first time, Samuel recognizes the voice as that of Eli, whom he addresses as "father," and Eli addresses him as "my son." Eli then repeats "my son" (none of these are in 1 Sam 3:4-5). When a voice from heaven calls Samuel a second time, the boy also goes to Eli. He now asks him, however, why his "father" Elkanah has called him, for he has heard Elkanah's voice. Eli instructs him: "With the two voices by which God has already called to you, he has become like a 'father' [Elkanah] and a master [Eli]; now with the third he will be like God" (53:3-6). Eli then instructs Samuel how to recognize whether it is God who is really calling him. When this indeed

---

[175]Cf. for example *b. Sanh.* 19b (Soncino 102), and *B. Meṣ.* 33a (Soncino 204; Danby 350 on m. 2:11). See also the words of Joshua to Moses in *Midr. Prov.* 14 (Visotzky 74): "My father who has raised me from my youth, my master who has taught me wisdom!" This is already found in *Sifre Deut.* Niṣṣabim 305 on Deut 31:14 (Hammer 297; Neusner 2.294).

[176]Cf. *Num. Rab.* Naso 14/21 on Num 7:89 (Soncino 6.640) with 1 Sam 3:10. See also Exod 25:22 and Isa 6:1, as well as n. 174.

[177]Cf. God's statement to Jesus at his baptism in Luke 3:22. Here God speaks to Jesus "from heaven," as does God to Samuel in *Pseudo-Philo* 53:3.

[178]Cf. God's speaking to Moses in the voice of his father in *Exod. Rab.* Shemoth 3/2 on Exod 3:6 (Soncino 3.58) and Ki Thissa 45/5 on Exod 33:18 (Soncino 3.522), noted in *Les Antiquités Bibliques* 2.222.

occurs, Samuel "knew that the word of his 'Father' had come down" (53:7). God then tells him negative things which will happen to Eli. Samuel asks how he can prophesy the destruction of "him who nourished me." He also asks: "And who has brought me up?" (53:11; cf. 12). Eli then again calls Samuel "my son," as in 1 Sam 3:16. He informs the boy that when his mother Hannah came to the Temple to pray (1 Sam 1:9-18), he had told her: "Go forth, for what will be born from you will be a 'son' for me" (53:12, based on 1 Sam 1:18). Humble before God, who has revealed Himself to the boy, Samuel in conclusion states: "I am under His power" (53:13).[179]

Here, in a Palestinian writing roughly contemporary with Jesus, the question of who Samuel's real father is, already latent in the biblical text, is greatly expanded in a dramatic scene. Three fathers are possible: Elkanah, Eli, and the heavenly Father, God. In the Temple, however, it is the heavenly Father who speaks with Samuel. This same question is borrowed from Judaic tradition on the boy Samuel in the Temple by the Palestinian Jewish Christian author of Luke 2:41-51a and transferred to the boy Jesus in the Jerusalem Temple. Jesus asks his parents, including his "father" Joseph (v 48):[180] "Did you not know that it was necessary for me to discuss [as a scholar, in the Temple] the concerns of my Father?" (v 49).

Jesus' statement, based on Judaic haggadah on the twelve-year-old Samuel in the Temple, is highly christological.[181] As stated above, about eighteen years before God publicly calls Jesus His Son at his baptism, the hearer, later the reader of this narrative is clearly made aware here of Jesus as the Son of God, the heavenly Father.

Rabbinic traditions also deal with Samuel's call in 1 Samuel 3, one of them clearly corroborating the motifs in *Pseudo-Philo*.[182] *Midr. Ps.* 1/3 comments on Moses and Samuel in Jer 15:1 by stating that what is said of the one is also said of the other. One example is their calls in Exod 3:4

---

[179]Cf. *OTP* 2.367-368, and *Les Antiquités Bibliques* 1.340-346.

[180]On the Palestinian Jewish Christian origin of Mary's "virginity" at her bearing Jesus, based on Judaic traditions concerning the virginity of the mother of Israel's first redeemer, Moses, at his birth, see my *Weihnachtsgeschichte* 38-44.

[181]Against P. Winter, who maintains that Luke 2:49 has no "connotation of christology," in his art. "Lc 2:49 and Targum Yerushalmi" in *ZNW* 45 (1954) 145-179. *Fg. Tg.* Exod 15:2 with "*He* is our Father!" has no relevance to Luke 2:49 except that little children call God their Father. It is rather the twelve-year-old Samuel in Judaic tradition who is the author's model.

[182]It should also be noted that the fragmentary 4QVis Sam is "The Vision of Samuel," 4Q160 in *Qumran Cave 4*, ed. J. Allegro, 9-11. The first piece on p. 9 has sections of 1 Sam 3:14-17. This is definitely pre-70 C.E. and shows another segment of early Palestinian Judaism as interested in Samuel's calling.

and 1 Sam 3:4.[183] In *b. Šabb.* 113b, R. Eleazar refers the "wise man" who becomes wiser in Prov 9:9 to Samuel at his call in 1 Sam 3:9-10.[184] *Exod. Rab.* Bo 16/4 on Exod 12:21 designates Moses and Samuel as of equal value, as in Ps 99:6. Yet they differ in that while Moses went to God, God Himself went to Samuel to speak with him (1 Sam 3:10).[185]

Finally, *Midr. Sam.* 3/6 on Samuel as a two-year-old teaching a halakhah in the Temple has Eli as his master desire to punish him by death. However, Eli says to the mother Hannah he will pray so that another (child) come (be born) in his place. Hannah defends Samuel by saying that "for *this* child I prayed" (1 Sam 1:27). She continues: Whether this or that is the case, "he is not mine and he is not yours" (לא דידי ולא דידך הוא). Then 1:28a is quoted: "I have lent him to the Lord."[186] Here it is clearly stated, as in *Pseudo-Philo*, that Samuel belongs neither to his parent(-s) nor to Eli, but to God, the heavenly Father. The midrash continues in 3/7 on 1:28b ("And he [the two-year-old Samuel] worshiped the Lord there"): R. Isaac[187] said, Everything takes place because of worship. The first example he cites is Gen 22:5, where Abraham returned from Mt. Moriah (for the rabbis, Jerusalem) safely because he worshiped God there.[188] The real parallel to the rescue of the boy Samuel from Eli's threatening him with death, however, is not explicitly stated, but assumed. It is the rescue by God of Abraham's only or beloved son, the boy Isaac, from being killed at the *'Aqedah* or binding on the altar. A ram was offered in his place (22:13).[189]

The above rabbinic tradition is not cited as Tannaitic. Nevertheless, it corroborates the definitely early Judaic statements in *Pseudo-Philo* 53 about whose son the child Samuel at his calling in the Temple in 1 Samuel 3 really was: not Elkanah's, not Eli's, but his heavenly Father's. The same is true of the boy Jesus in Luke 2:49.

---

[183]Braude 1.6. Cf. also *Midr. Sam.* 9/5 (Wünsche 5.62).

[184]Soncino 554. He is the same rabbi cited above in *b. Ber.* 31b.

[185]Soncino 3.209-210.

[186]Buber 53, Wünsche 5.24-25.

[187]Probably R. Isaac II the Smith, a third generation Palestinian Amora and pupil of R. Yohanan in Tiberias (Strack and Stemberger, *Introduction* 98), as was R. Eleazar b. Pedat.

[188]Buber 53, Wünsche 5.25. Cf. the parallel in *Gen. Rab.* Vayera 56/2 on Gen 22:5 (Soncino 1.492-493), where 1 Sam 1:19 is also cited to mean God caused Hannah to become pregnant with Samuel because of Elkanah's and her worshiping in the Temple.

[189]Cf. the statement by God to the people regarding Samuel in *Pseudo-Philo* 49:8, "And I will love him as I have loved Isaac, and his name will be before Me always" (*OTP* 2.364; *Les Antiquités Bibliques* 1.326).

15. Jesus the Nazarite/Nazirite, and Samuel the Nazirite.

A.

Luke 2:51 states that after the incident in the Jerusalem Temple, Jesus went down with his parents and came to "Nazareth" (Ναζαρέθ), where he was obedient to them. In the present Lucan context this recalls the earlier return from Jerusalem to "their own city," Nazareth, in v 39. The same Greek spelling of Nazareth as in 2:51 is found in the best texts of 1:26 and 2:4. Only 4:16 has Nazara (Ναζαρά), a reading also found in Matt 4:13.[190] Jesus the "Nazarene" is expressed in the gospels both by Ναζαρηνός (for example Luke 4:34 and 24:19) and Ναζωραῖος (for example Luke 18:37).

The variant spellings of "Nazareth" and "Nazarene" show different traditions already in the Semitic. A word play with the messianic "branch" (נֵצֶר) of Jesse from Isa 11:1 (cf. also Jer 23:5; 33:15; Zech 3:8 and 6:12) stands behind the Greek of Matt 2:23, "Nazareth" and "Nazarene."[191] Since the Greek language could not reproduce the Semitic *ṣadē*, *zeta* was employed for it.

As P. Billerbeck points out, one of the most common hermeneutical methods of the rabbis was to say: "Do not read..., but read...." In haggadic contexts, the validity of slightly changing a vowel or consonant for purposes of exegesis was never questioned by them.[192] I suggest therefore that the Palestinian Jewish Christian author of Luke 2:41-51a also compared the twelve-year-old Jesus in the Temple with the twelve-year-old Samuel in the Temple in Judaic tradition because Jesus was a "Nazarite" (Hebrew נֹצְרִי), and Samuel a "Nazirite" (נָזִיר)[193]. He reasoned: "Do not read נָזִיר, but read נֹצְרִי." This was a bridge he created to also apply Judaic motifs and vocabulary regarding Samuel the "Nazirite" to Jesus the "Nazarite." If the author was also bilingual, his knowledge of

---

[190]Nazareth with τ instead of θ is a variant found in Matt 2:23; Mark 1:9; and John 1:45-46.

[191]On this, cf. Str-B 1.92-96.

[192]Cf. Str-B 1.93-94, and the special study by Rosenzweig cited in n. 1 of p. 94.

[193]In Rabbinic Hebrew, for example, ס and שׂ can, here by mutation, be used for the same word, as is true for ס and צ. Cf. M. Segal, *A Grammar of Mishnaic Hebrew* (Oxford: Clarendon, 1958), with examples on p. 33. See also Aramaic examples cited by G. Dalman, *Grammatik des jüdisch-palästinischen Aramäisch* (Leipzig: Hinrichs, 1927²) 104, and on Nazareth/Nazarite 152, n. 2 of the preceding page, and 178, n. 2. It may also be noted that the biblical city Zoar, צֹעַר in Deut 34:3, is זְעֵיר in the Fragment Targums and Neofiti 1. For a fuller discussion, which should also include Gen 19:20 and 22, see my *Weihnachtsgeschichte* 64. For mutilation of נָזִיר into נָזִיק, נִזְחַ and פּוֹזִחַ, see *m. Nazir* 1:1 (Albeck 3.195; Danby 280). This shows that intentional changes were sometimes made for the purpose of vows. An intentional change could also have been made with נָזִיר : נֹצְרִי. See also G. Dalman, *Orte und Wege Jesu* (Gütersloh: Bertelsmann, 1924) 62-63.

the Greek letter *zeta* in Ναζαρέθ and Ναζωραῖος/Ναζαρηνός may have recalled for him a Nazirite, spelled Ναζ[ε]ιραῖος and Ναζ[ε]ίρ in the Septuagint.

Another reason for applying Nazirite imagery from Samuel to Jesus was the fact that Palestinian Jewish Christian tradition had also described the adult Jesus at the very end of his life as a "Nazirite." On the evening before his death in Jerusalem, he ate the Passover meal with his twelve disciples and stated after one of the prescribed four cups of wine: "Truly, I say to you, I shall not drink again of the fruit of the vine [= wine] until that day when I drink it new in the kingdom of God" (Mark 14:25; cf. Matt 26:29 and Luke 22:18).[194]

Jesus' words allude to the eschatological or messianic banquet, when the righteous in Paradise will be invited by God to drink of the wine preserved for them since the six days of creation.[195]

The "Nazirite" (נזיר) vows to "separate himself" from wine (Num 6:2-4). Jesus the Nazirite's foregoing wine as a Nazirite recalls a statement by R. Levi, a third generation Palestinian Amora,[196] regarding Joseph the "Nazirite" of Gen 49:26. From the time his brothers sold him until their reunion banquet in Egypt (Gen 43:34), Joseph was "separated" from them. R. Levi says Joseph here was literally a Nazirite. "During the whole of the twenty-two years that he did not see them, he tasted no wine...."[197]

Early Palestinian Jewish Christians applied this motif from Judaic tradition on Joseph to Jesus at the "Lord's Supper." From now until his future reunion with his disciples, the Nazirite was also to be a "Nazirite," drinking no wine. This Nazirite imagery, a firm part of the earliest gospel tradition, thus also may have aided the Palestinian Jewish

---

[194]On the benediction over the Passover wine, cf. *m. Pesaḥ.* 10:2 (Danby 150; see also *Ber.* 8:1-Danby 8). It is given as "[Blessed be He who] creates 'the fruit of the vine'" in *m. Ber.* 6:1 (Danby 6) and *t. Ber.* 4:3 (Neusner 1.20). See also J. Jeremias, *Die Abendmahlsworte Jesu* (Göttingen: Vandenhoeck & Ruprecht, 1967⁴) 176.

[195]Cf. Isa 25:6; Luke 14:15-24; *b. Sanh.* 99a (Soncino 671); and other sources cited by Ginzberg, *The Legends* 5.29, n. 79, 294, n. 93; *b. Pesaḥ.* 119b (Soncino 616); *Exod. Rab.* Beshallaḥ on Exod 16:4 (Soncino 3.309-310); other older sources noted in *The Legends* 6.272-273, n. 129; and J. Behm, art. δεῖπνον etc. in *TDNT* 2.34-35.

[196]Strack and Stemberger, *Introduction* 98.

[197]Cf. *Gen. Rab.* Vayechi 98/20 on Gen 49:26 (Soncino 2.970-971; Theodor and Albeck 3.1271, and the footnotes on lines 4-7). See also the parallel in Mikketz 92/5 on Gen 43:34 (Soncino 2.852), as well as *b. Šabb.* 139a (Soncino 702), *Midr. Prov.* 1 (Visotzky 25), and Deut 33:16.

Christian author of Luke 2:41-51a in applying Nazirite imagery from Samuel to the Nazirite Jesus.[198]

B.

Hannah in the Temple vows a vow that if God will give her a son, she will set him before the Lord "as a Nazirite" (NRSV) all his life, "and no razor (מוֹרָה) shall touch his head" (1 Sam 1:11). The latter phrase regarding her future son is found only here in the MT, as well as of Samson the Nazirite (נָזִיר) in Judg 13:5 and 16:17. Not shaving one's hair is one of the major stipulations of Naziriteship (Num 6:5). The Septuagint at 1 Kgdms 1:11 adds that "he shall drink neither wine nor intoxicating drink," referring to Num 6:3.[199] In *m. Nazir* 9:5 R. Nehorai, a third generation Tanna,[200] maintains on the basis of the same phrase involving a razor in 1 Sam 1:11 and Judg 13:5 that Samuel was a Nazirite.[201]

The 4QSam[a] text at 1 Sam 1:22, probably from the first half of the first century B.C.E., also reads regarding Hannah's promise to dedicate Samuel in the Temple: "[And I will gi-]ve him as a Nazirite [נזיר] for ever."[202] This reading is adopted by the NRSV.

Finally, the Hebrew of Sir 46:13 speaks of Samuel as "a נזיר of the Lord in prophecy."[203] The writing stems from the first quarter of the first century B.C.E.[204]

All these very early sources attest that the boy/child Samuel was considered a Nazirite already before his birth and at the time of his calling in the Temple.

Although there was a Judaic tradition placing Samuel's age here as twelve, like that of the wise and understanding Solomon, Josiah and Daniel, another factor most probably played a role in regard to the specific age of twelve. The vows made by a Jewish boy already thirteen years old were considered by the rabbis to be valid. The vowing of a boy

---

[198]In Judaic tradition, only four figures are mentioned as Nazirites: Joseph, Samson, Samuel and Absalom. Cf. Ginzberg, *The Legends* 7.339. This encouraged their being compared with one another.

[199]Cf. Philo, *Ebr.* 143 on 1 Sam 1:11. Josephus, *Ant.* 5.344, states regarding this verse: "his manner of life should be unlike that of ordinary men," very probably referring to the same motif. See also 5.347: "his locks were left to grow and his drink was water."

[200]Strack and Stemberger, *Introduction* 86.

[201]Albeck 3.222, Danby 292-293.

[202]Cf. the text in E. Ulrich, Jr., *The Qumran Text of Samuel and Josephus* 165; for the dating, see p. 10. See also P. McCarter, Jr., *I Samuel* 56.

[203]Cf. I. Lévi, *The Hebrew Text of the Book of Ecclesiasticus* 64. It is based on MS "B" from the Cairo Genizah.

[204]Cf. Nickelsburg, *Jewish Literature* 64.

only twelve years old, however, still was questionable. He first had to be examined to determine if he was sexually mature.[205] This is illustrated by the precocious answer given by the boy Ḥananya b. Ḥananya, a Tanna from ca. 120 C.E.,[206] whose father applied the Naziriteship to him as a minor in *t. Nid.* 5:15. Rabban Gamaliel was about to examine the boy to determine whether or not he was sexually mature and capable of vowing independently. The (twelve-year-old) then asked his examiner: "Why are you so troubled? If I am subject to the authority of father, lo, the authority of father is upon me, and lo, I am a Nazir. And if I am subject to my own authority, lo, I am a Nazir from this point forward."[207] The Tosefta concludes the incident by stating that he became a (great) teacher (מורה) of instruction in Israel.

The Judaic view of a sexually immature twelve-year-old boy as still dependent on his father in regard to making the vow of a "Nazir" may also be in the background of the twelve-year-old Jesus in the Jerusalem Temple. Displaying great understanding (and wisdom), he stood under the authority of his own Father. Nevertheless, as a twelve-year-old, he went home to "Nazareth" with his parents, being obedient to them, or accepting their authority.

* * *

The above fifteen biblical and Judaic traditions regarding Elkanah and Hannah, who take their child Samuel on their annual Passover pilgrimage to the Temple in Shiloh, lie behind the narrative in Luke 2:41-51a of Joseph and Mary's taking Jesus along on their annual Passover to the Temple in Jerusalem. While one may disagree with part of one or even with several of the individual comparisons, cumulatively the large number argues very strongly for the Palestinian Jewish Christian author of the Lucan narrative as basing it almost exclusively on motifs and phraseology from the 1 Samuel 1-3 account, especially as developed in Judaic tradition.

III
The Original Language

The commentators agree that Luke's style can be seen throughout 2:41-51a.[208] J. Fitzmyer even maintains that there "are fewer Semitisms

---

[205]Cf. *m. Nid.* 5:6 (Albeck 6.391, Danby 751).
[206]Cf. Str-B 5/6.135.
[207]Zuckermandel/Liebermann 646; Neusner 6.220. See also the notes in *b. Nazir* 29b (Soncino 104-105). Billerbeck called attention to this text in Str-B 2.151.
[208]Cf., for example, R. Brown, *The Birth of the Messiah* 480-481, and the special study by J. Jeremias cited in section IV, n. 237.

in it than in the rest of the infancy narrative.[209] Nevertheless, in contrast to many other major expositors of the pericope up to now, I would maintain that the Third Evangelist only later improved stylistically an anecdote he already found in Greek.[210] It had become available to him via Greek-speaking Jewish Christians, who in turn had translated it from the original Semitic, probably already in Palestine, perhaps in Syria, where there were also many bilingual communities. In various parts of section II above, I suggested that the original language was definitely Semitic, more probably Aramaic, perhaps Hebrew. Here I would briefly like to review those arguments and to supplement them with others.

1)

The major emphasis on the "festival/feast," also still found in the Targum of 1 Samuel 1-2, caused the author of Luke 2:41-51a to specifically mention the "festival/feast" in vv 41 and 43. (Cf. II.3 above.)

2)

The Targum of 1 Sam 1:20, "and it happened at the time of the completion of the days," still contains the closest parallel to the phrase "And having completed the days" of Luke 2:43. The "return" of the same verse in Luke may also derive from the "return" of 1 Sam 1:19. (Cf. II.5 above.)

3)

The Targum of 1 Sam 1:11 regarding Samuel changes the "razor" (מוֹרָה) of the MT into מְרוּת, "authority": "And the authority of man will not be upon him."[211] For a Palestinian Jewish Christian acquainted with this text or an earlier form of it, this could mean that no human authority would supersede that of the boy Samuel, then that of the boy Jesus.

In section II.12, I suggested that the above Hebrew term מורה could also be vocalized מוֹרֶה, "teacher."[212] That is, no teacher of the Torah would supersede Samuel, as shown in Judaic tradition on his wisdom and understanding. This may also have provided the Palestinian Jewish Christian author of Luke 2:41-51a with his term "teachers" in v 46, מוֹרִים. If he borrowed the term "anxiously" in v 48 from the Hebrew מָרַת נֶפֶשׁ of the nearby verse 1 Sam 1:10, even more assonance was present. The same holds true for the Targum's "bitter of soul," מרירא נפש.[213]

---

[209]*The Gospel According to Luke* I-IX 435.

[210]There are no indications that Luke himself knew Hebrew or Aramaic.

[211]Sperber 2.94; cf. Harrington and Saldarini, *Targum Jonathan of the Former Prophets* 103, with "dominion." For the noun, see Jastrow 840.

[212]Jastrow 596 on ירה, ירי and its Aramaic equivalent, as well as 749 on מוֹרָה II.

[213]See the sources cited in n. 211.

In Luke 2:51 the author also states that Jesus went down with his parents, came to Nazareth, "and was obedient to them": καὶ ἦν ὑποτασσόμενος αὐτοῖς.   This can be expressed in Hebrew by והיה נכנע למרותם, "and he submitted/humbled himself to their authority."[214] This is based on biblical and later Hebrew expressions.[215] The same is also possible, however, in Aramaic.[216] The Semitic original of v 51 may thus also have added to the narrative's assonance: מורים, מרת, נפש and מרות, or the Aramaic equivalents of these.

4)

Luke 2:41 and 43 speak of Jesus' "parents," which I suggested above in section II.1 to be the Aramaic שיירא or Hebrew שיירה. This would be an intentional word play with "caravan" in v 44, Aramaic שיירא or Hebrew שיירה (see section II.5 above). The "relatives" of v 44 in Hebrew could be קרובים, based on Judaic interpretation of the "whole household" of 1 Sam 1:21 (cf. section II.6 above). Yet they also could be expressed in Hebrew by שְׁאָר, שְׁאִיר.[217] If so, this would provide even more assonance with "parents" and "caravan" in the Semitic, even though the same root is not involved.

Here I would like to strengthen the latter proposal by suggesting that Jesus' "remaining" (behind) in Jerusalem in Luke 2:43 (ὑπομένω) may also derive from the root שאר. The Aramaic ithpa. and ithpe. of the verb mean to be left over, remain, be left behind, and the Hebrew nithpa. to be left over.[218] There may thus be a total of four similar sounding words in the short pericope of 2:41-51a. This was certainly appreciated by the original hearers, who considered it to be a mark of the author's narrative ability.[219]

5)

The latter was also true of word plays with שוב and ישב in the narrative. The Hebrew of "they returned" in vv 43 and 45 can be ישובו, that for "remained" in v 43 ישב,[220] that for "answers" in v 47 תשובות, that for "and 'he said/replied' to them" in v 49 השיב (not אמר or ענה), which

---

[214]So the United Bible Societies' Hebrew New Testament of 1979 *ad loc.*

[215]For the niphal of כנע, see BDB 488; on מרות, see Jastrow 840.

[216]Cf. Jastrow 650 on the ithpa. or ithpe. of כנע, and 840 on מרותא.

[217]Cf. Jastrow 1509.

[218]Cf. Jastrow 1509, Levy 4.492 and 548.

[219]Contrast A. Loisy, *L'Évangile selon Luc* (Paris, 1924; reprint Frankfurt/Main: Minerva, 1971) 131, who speaks of Luke 2:41-51 as "a mediocre fiction."

[220]This is an alternative to the term שאר suggested above. On the motif of Jesus' "remaining" in the Temple, cf. also Hannah's statement to Elkanah in 1 Sam 1:22 regarding the child Samuel: he will "remain" (ישב) in the Temple forever. The next verse also has "remain" twice.

may mean he "refuted" them.[221] Also the same sound is found in Jesus' "sitting" (ישׁב) in the Temple in v 46. Here, therefore, a total of five very similar sounding words are found, one more than above in 4). In combination, they attest the narrator's great love of assonance and his linguistic skill.

6)

The same is true of the root ידע, perhaps also employed five times. The Hebrew for "to know" in Luke 2:43 and 49 could be ידע, that for "acquaintances" in v 44 מְיוּדָּעִים, and that for "why" in vv 48 and 49 מַדּוּעַ.

7)

The most difficult phrase in Luke 2:41-51a is found in v 49, where Jesus asks his parents: "Did you not know that I must be ἐν τοῖς of my Father?" The favorite interpretation of this is "being in the house of my Father," or "being concerned with the affairs of my Father."[222]

P. van der Horst has, however, convincingly shown that ἐν...εἶναι derives from the Aramaic הוי ב or הוה ב, literally "to be in/among," here, however, meaning "to discuss, to dwell upon, to argue, to investigate by questioning, to raise questions," etc.[223] It is only found in this meaning in Aramaic, and not in Hebrew.[224] Here the phrase could be translated: "Did you not know that I must discuss [with the Temple scholars] the matters of my Father's [Torah]?" It fits the context very well, where Jesus in the Jerusalem Temple is pictured as sitting among the teachers, listening to them, asking them questions, and giving them answers (to their questions: 2:46-47). This is probably the strongest argument for Aramaic as the original language of 2:41-51a.

---

[221]Cf. Jastrow 1528 on שׁוב as go back; BDB 442-443 on ישׁב 2) as remain, stay, tarry, which is translated in Num 22:19 by ὑπομένω; Jastrow 1703 on תשובה as reply, answer; and 1528 on the hif. of שׁוב as to reply, refute.

[222]Cf. R. Brown, *The Birth of the Messiah* 475-477, who weighs the many arguments, favors the first, and mentions a minor third opinion. D. Sylva in "The Cryptic Clause en tois tou patros mou dei einai me in Lk 2,49b" in *ZNW* 78 (1987) 132-140 considers the phrase to be a double entendre in Luke's usage: "I must be concerned with my father's words in the temple" (p. 134). He does not deal with its origin.

[223]Cf. his "Notes on the Aramaic Background of Luke II 41-52" in *JSNT* 7 (1980) 61-66, quotation p. 63. He also considers the story to have been "originally Palestinian" (p. 64). See also M. Mielziner, *Introduction to the Talmud* (New York: Bloch, 1968⁴) 237-238: "to investigate a subject by questioning," noted by van der Horst. One example from the Palestinian Talmud is *Beṣa* 4:2, 62c (Neusner 18.96). In his *A Dictionary of Jewish Palestinian Aramaic of the Byzantine Period* (Ramat-Gan: Bar Ilan University, 1990) 161, 4., M. Sokoloff does not note this. He only has: "to treat/deal with." I thank Dr. N. Oswald of Berlin for the latter reference.

[224]Cf. Jastrow 338.

8)

As noted in section II.8 above, the expression τὸ ῥῆμα ὃ ἐλάλησεν in Luke 2:50 could be a word play in Hebrew: הדבר שדיבר.

9)

The use of καί to introduce nine of the eleven verses in Luke 2:41-51a is also Semitic.[225] The two exceptions are vv 44 and 47 with δέ, which most probably show the stylist Luke at work. This is even reduced to only one incident if what is now v 44 did not originally begin as it now does, but already at: "*And* his parents did not know it, but thought him...." Originally, of course, there was no verse numbering at all in the NT manuscripts.

10)

The episode of the two-year-old Samuel in the Temple teaching a legal point to his parents, the priests and Eli, in rabbinic tradition president of the Sanhedrin, is found in Aramaic in *b. Ber.* 31b. A Hebrew version is found in *Midr. Sam.* 3/6. The great relevance of this narrative to various points in Luke 2:41-51a was pointed out above.

11)

Josephus in his retelling of the episode of Samuel's birth and childhood up until the age of twelve in the Temple in *Ant.* 5.341-351, appears to be dependent on an Aramaic source here.[226]

* * *

The above eleven points cumulatively speak very strongly for a Semitic original for Luke 2:41-51a. Unfortunately, our knowledge of first century Palestinian Aramaic is still quite limited. It is also known that writings such as *Pseudo-Philo,* much of the Qumran literature from the period before 70 C.E., the early midrashim, and prayers were still composed in Hebrew, although the masses spoke Aramaic. Because of point seven, however, I think the scale tips slightly in favor of Aramaic. Hebrew, however, should not be excluded. The assertion of a Semitic original in either of the two languages is the main point I wish to make here in regard to the interpretation of the narrative of the twelve-year-old Jesus in the Temple.

---

[225]Cf. BDF § 442 (p. 227).
[226]Cf. the notes of H. Thackeray and R. Marcus in the LCL edition, especially 153, n. "h," 154, n. "a," and 156, n. "b."

Table of Semitic Word Plays in Luke 2:41-51a

The following table provides a better overview of possible Semitic word plays in the narrative of the twelve-year-old Jesus in the Temple. I here give the Hebrew form, for which an Aramaic one is also usually available.

I.

a)		שְׁיָרָה	:	γονεῖς, "parents," in 2:41 and 43.
b)		שְׁיָרָה	:	συνοδία, "caravan," in 2:44.
c)	nithpael,	שאר	:	ὑπομένω, "to remain behind," in 2:43.
d)		שְׁאִיר/שְׁאָר	:	συγγενεῖς, "relatives," in 2:44.

II.

a)		שׁוּב	:	ὑποστρέφω, "to return," in 2:43 and 45.
b)		שׁוּב	:	ὑπομένω, "to remain," in 2:43.[227]
c)	hiphil,	שׁוּב	:	εἶπον (λέγω), "he replied," in 2:49.
d)		תשובות	:	ἀποκρίσεις, "answers," in 2:47.
e)		יָשַׁב	:	καθέζομαι, "to sit," in 2:46.

III.

a)	מוֹרִים	:	διδάσκαλοι, "teachers," in 2:46.
b)	מָרַת נָפֶשׁ	:	ὀδυνώμενοι, "anxiously," in 2:48.
c)	(נכנע ל) מָרוּתָם	:	ἦν ὑποτασσόμενος αὐτοῖς, "he submitted to 'their authority,'" in 2:51.

IV.

a)	ידע	:	γινώσκω, "to know," in 2:43 and 49.
b)	מְיוּדָעִים	:	γνωστοί, "acquaintances," in 2:44.
c)	מַדּוּעַ	:	τί, "why?", in 2:48 and 49.

V.

הַדָּבָר שֶׁדִּיבֶּר: τὸ ῥῆμα ὃ ἐλάλησεν, "the saying/matter which he told," in 2:50.

IV
The Extent, Content, and Age of the Original Narrative

A. The Extent and Content.

Luke 2:39 could easily have concluded the Lucan infancy narrative. It corresponds to Matt 2:23, which is followed by an introduction of John the Baptist at the Jordan. Both Luke 2:39 and Matt 2:23 get the infant Jesus back to the city of Nazareth, in Galilee, from which he later comes

---

[227]This is an alternative to שאר above.

as an adult to be baptized by John in the Jordan River (Luke 3:21; cf. 4:14-16; Matt 3:13; cf. 4:12-13).

Luke 2:40 would be unnecessary if vv 41-52 did not follow it. It is a transitional verse, speaking of Jesus' growth physically and spiritually until the time when, at the age of twelve, he accompanied his parents on a pilgrimage to Jerusalem. It is modeled on v 52 and was probably inserted by a Palestinian Jewish Christian collector of the birth narratives when he added the originally independent narrative of 2:41-51a to them (see below).

Modern English translations such as the RSV, NRSV, Phillips, the New English Bible, and Good News for Modern Man all begin the incident of the twelve-year-old Jesus in the Temple with Luke 2:41.[228] Yet only the first two end it at v 51, making v 52 a separate sentence. Good News for Modern Man makes a new sense unit out of both verses, 51-52.

Where did the incident originally end? It is easiest to begin an answer to this question by excising 2:51b, "and his [Jesus'] mother kept all these things in her heart." It clearly derives from the pen of Luke, who stated basically the same thing of Mary in 2:19.

J. Fitzmyer considers 2:51-52 to be "clearly of Lucan composition," and thus not to belong to the original narrative.[229] Yet v 51a in speaking of Jesus' "going down" (from Jerusalem) and going (back) with his parents to Nazareth corresponds symmetrically to the opening two verses, where in 41-42 they "went up" to Jerusalem (from Nazareth). Verse 51a thus belongs to the original author's narrative artistry.

The phrase "and he [Jesus] was obedient to them [his parents]" in v 51a, involving the assonance of מרות ("authority") with other similar terms in the Semitic original, as shown above, also displays the author's linguistic artistry. The phrase is suspect to some commentators because it contrasts with Jesus' independent spirit in deciding to stay in Jerusalem alone, to dispute with the Temple scholars, and to speak in what at first appears to be a disrespectful manner to his parents. Yet Jesus was not yet thirteen, when a Jewish boy of the time was held completely responsible for his words and deeds. His obedience to his parents, exemplifying the Fourth Commandment,[230] also included his father Joseph. The original hearer of the incident thus not only received

---

[228]The originally independent narrative most probably had "Jesus' parents" here for "his parents."

[229]*The Gospel According to Luke I-IX* 435.

[230]K. Rengstorf in his *Das Evangelium nach Lukas* (NTD 3; Göttingen: Vandenhoeck & Ruprecht, 1958[8]) 51 correctly asks: Can there be a Messiah in the people of the Torah who for himself nullifies the Fourth Commandment?

a positive impression of Jesus' filial piety, but was once again confronted with the second and major issue of the entire narrative: Who was/is Jesus' true father/Father?

As I pointed out in section I, almost all the commentators agree that Luke 2:52 is based on 1 Sam 2:26 (cf. 2:21b and 3:19) regarding the boy Samuel, with the exception of the term "wisdom." This means that the verse also reflects the section 1 Samuel 1-3, just as many other motifs and terms in Luke 2:41-51a do. To this extent it may have been added as a kind of addendum or afterthought by the original author. There are, however, two other possibilities.

One is that the Palestinian Jewish Christian community in which the narrative of 2:41-51a was produced, already added it to other similar materials regarding the birth and infancy of Jesus.[231] Since, for example, Mary's Magnificat in 1:46-55 is based to a great extent on Hannah's song in 1 Sam 2:1-10, and the description of the prophetess Anna in Luke 2:36-38 is based in part on 1 Sam 2:22 in Judaic tradition, an early collector of these Jesus birth traditions may have himself added Luke 2:52 to verses 41-51a. He correctly based v 52 upon a verse from the childhood of Samuel, which he knew to be the background of the narrative. He then added the term "wisdom" in v 52 to underline Jesus' great "understanding" shown in the Jerusalem Temple. Since this collector knew of no other episode in Jesus' early life between his infancy and baptism, v 52 rounded off the entire collection and enabled it to be used in the Christian community as material related to the events preliminary to Jesus' baptism. There, in contrast to 2:41-51a, God openly speaks of Jesus as His beloved "Son" (3:22).[232]

Another possibility, much less probable, is that Luke somehow recognized the background of 2:41-51a in 1 Samuel 1-3, and himself modeled v 52 on 1 Sam 2:26 to provide a transition between the story of the twelve-year-old Jesus and John's baptizing in the Jordan River. If this is correct, he also added v 40 in a somewhat varied style, basing it on his own creation in v 52. For the later Greek-speaking reader acquainted with the Septuagint's version of Samuel's birth and childhood, this framework was a tip in regard to the origin of the story. In addition, the reader could draw his own comparisons between the famous Israelite and Jesus.

Of these three possibilities for the origin of Luke 2:52, I consider the second the most probable: it was appropriately added by a collector of

---

[231]Cf. also H. Schürmann, *Das Lukasevangelium, Erster Teil* (Herder 3; Freiburg: Herder, 1981) 139.
[232]This would mean that Luke himself probably added 2:40, basing it on what he found in 2:52. As a good stylist, he varied it somewhat.

the birth narratives in the original Palestinian Jewish Christian community in which they were composed.[233]

The only other two elements in 2:41-51a which have been called into question in a major way are vv 44 and 47. B. van Iersel considers v 44 to be from Luke because for him it contains "novelistic elaborations" typical of the Third Evangelist.[234] While Luke certainly sometimes expands the traditions he takes over, here this is definitely not the case. The verse logically explains the latter part of v 43, and it shows good acquaintance with Palestinian pilgrimage customs, which one would not expect from the "Hellenist" Luke. Thirdly, the Semitic terms for "caravan" and "relatives" are word plays with the term "parents" at the end of v 43. They are not visible in the Greek, showing it to be a translation, not a gloss from the redactor Luke.

Van Iersel also considers 2:47 to be of "profane character," with novelistic details. For him, the original story did not stress the twelve-year-old's intelligence, but only God as Jesus' Father in v 49.[235]

This is a wrong alternative. The original author clearly compared the twelve-year-old Jesus in the Temple with the twelve-year-old Samuel in the Temple. Both the motif of Samuel's great understanding there, and the question of who his real father/Father was, are strongly emphasized in Judaic tradition. The Palestinian author applied *both* of these to the twelve-year-old Jesus. In emphasizing his understanding and the astonishingly good answers he gave to the scholars' questions (2:47), the author indicated to his hearers that the boy Jesus was at least equal to the precocious child/boy Samuel, if not superior to him.

Finally, it has been maintained that Luke has a propensity for hendiadys, as ostensibly shown in the expressions "their relatives and acquaintances" in 2:44, and "his understanding and his answers" in v 47.[236] While Luke may have introduced double expressions elsewhere, as in 2:34 ("fall and rising") and 37 ("night and day"), this is improbable in these two instances.

Jesus' parents would have sought him not only among their own relatives, but also among the acquaintances and neighbors who were

---

[233]For an analysis of Luke 2:1-20 as also belonging to this same Palestinian Jewish Christian community, see my *Weihnachtsgeschichte* 11-58.

[234]Cf. his "The Finding of Jesus in the Temple. Some Observations on the Original Form of Luke 2, 41-51a" in *NovT* 4 (1960) 171.

[235]*Ibid.*, 165-166 and 169. He posits an original story of vv 41-43, 45-46, and 48-51a (p.172). See also H. de Jonge, "Sonship..." 345.

[236]On v 44, see Bovon, *Das Evangelium nach Lukas (Lk 1, 1-9, 50)* 156, on v 47 p. 157; Fitzmyer, *The Gospel According to Luke I-IX* 441 on v 44, and 442 on v 47, referring to his discussion on 2:37; and Brown, *The Birth of the Messiah* 474 on v 44, and 475 on v 47.

members of the caravan from Nazareth or that region of Galilee. As in Elkanah's gaining more and more people to join him on his pilgrimages to the Temple, not only his own relatives, so here the large number of participants was described by the author of 2:41-51a. The motif of searching becomes even more intense in Jerusalem, where it is for three days. The term "acquaintances" in 2:44 was intentionally mentioned by the original author in addition to "relatives." It does not derive from Luke.

The same is true for "his understanding and his answers" in v 47. Jesus is represented not only as listening to and asking questions of the Temple scholars in v 46, which shows his grasp of the issues and precocious understanding. He is also pictured as successfully answering the difficult questions put to him by the elite members of Israel's supreme religious authority. Already at the age of twelve he is not only their match, but their superior. This prefigures the high quality of his later adult teaching, for example when no one could refute him (6:9; 13:17; 14:6; 20:7, 26, 40). "His answers" in 2:47 was intentionally mentioned by the author of 2:41-51a; it also does not derive from the Third Evangelist.

If there are Lucan changes other than those described above, they are relatively insignificant. The original narrative thus extended from 2:41-51a almost as it is now found, except for Luke's minor stylistic improvements, such as the καὶ ἐγένετο at the beginning of v 46.[237]

B. The Age.

Luke 2:41-51a betrays no knowledge of the angel Gabriel's annunciation to Mary in Nazareth that she will bear "the Son of the Most High" (1:32), "the Son of God" (1:35). Nor does it show an acquaintance with Elisabeth's addressing Mary as "the mother of my Lord" in 1:43, nor with Joseph and Mary's hearing Simeon in the Jerusalem Temple speak of his now having seen God's "salvation" (2:30; cf. v 38 with Anna, and v 11). Finally, the mention of Jesus' "parents" in 2:41 and 43, as well as Mary's speaking to Jesus regarding Joseph as "your father" in v 48, can hardly be reconciled with the motif of the virgin birth in 1:34-35.

This shows that the anecdote of 2:41-51a is older than the birth narratives to which it was later appended. The earliest gospel, that of Mark, was probably written shortly before or, more probably, very

---

[237]Contrast the opinion of H. de Jonge in "Sonship..." 347: "The localization of the episode in Jerusalem, the feast of the Passover, the pilgrimage, the traveling party and the journeys of Jesus' parents to and from Galilee, may all be due to Luke's invention." For elements of Lucan style in the incident, cf. J. Jeremias, *Die Sprache des Lukasevangeliums* (Meyer, Sonderband 3; Göttingen: Vandenhoeck & Ruprecht, 1980) 99-103.

shortly after the catastrophe of the Roman victory over Palestinian Jews and the destruction of Jerusalem in 70 C.E.[238] It has no birth narrative. Yet two later gospels, Matthew and Luke, both in part dependent on Mark, do. This indicates that the birth narratives derive from a later period, when enough time had passed for interest to develop in this type of biographical legend. What was later true of Jesus, his great understanding of the Torah and his being the Son of God, were now thought to be already present in his childhood.

The story of the twelve-year-old Jesus in the Temple shows not only good acquaintance with Palestinian pilgrimage customs and of scholarly debate within the Jerusalem Temple precincts. It also has a respectful attitude toward the Temple cultus (the Passover offerings made by Jesus' parents are not explicitly mentioned, but are simply assumed), and toward the Jewish nation's leading teachers of the Torah.[239] This probably indicates that the Palestinian author himself still attended the Temple services, i.e., before 70 C.E. He may have been a member of one of the churches of Judea, of which Paul speaks in Gal 1:22, or even of the Jerusalem Christian community. In section III I argued for one of the Semitic languages, Aramaic, or possibly Hebrew, as the language of the original narrative. This also speaks for a Palestinian origin. It then took a certain amount of time for the narrative to reach the Hellenist Luke after it was translated into Greek within a Greek-speaking Jewish Christian community.

All of the above factors argue for Luke 2:41-51a as having originally been composed in Palestine within the period somewhat before the fall of Jerusalem in 70 C.E. (50-66?). More, unfortunately, cannot be said.

V
The Purposes and Genre of the Original Narrative

Before the genre of Luke 2:41-51a is ascertained, its purpose must be described. Here scholarly opinion varies, in part greatly.

A. The Purposes

The most recent major commentator on Luke, F. Bovon, believes that the "anecdote had the function of apologetically removing the aggravation of Jesus' modest origin by [emphasizing] his relationship to

---

[238]Cf. for example J. Marcus, "The Jewish War and the Sitz im Leben of Mark" in *JBL* 3 (1992) 460; D. Lührmann, *Das Markus-Evangelium* (HNT 3; Tübingen: Mohr, 1987) 6; and J. Gnilka, *Das Evangelium nach Markus (Mk 1–8, 26)* (EKKNT II/1; Zurich, Benziger; Neukirchen-Vluyn, Neukirchener, 1989³) 34.
[239]On this, cf. also J. Ernst, *Das Evangelium nach Lukas* (RNT 3; Regensburg: Pustet, 1977) 122.

the heavenly Father." Its life setting was an inner-Jewish discussion, especially the Christian answer to Jewish reproaches regarding Jesus' very modest beginnings. Jewish intellectuals had ridiculed the deficiencies in the education of Jesus and of those in the early church.[240]

Although I also view the pericope as deriving from Jewish (Palestinian) Christianity, there are no indications that it functions as an apology. If that were the case, the mention of the "teachers" in 2:46 would be much harsher, more aggressive. Only here does the term "teacher" occur of Jewish scholars in Luke's Gospel. In his editing the narrative, he could easily have changed the original term, for example, to "scribe," adumbrating Jesus' later hostile encounters with these experts in the Torah.[241] The retention of the neutral, even honorific term "teachers" refutes Bovon's thesis. In addition, the mention of Nazareth in 2:51a has here no negative connotation, as in Nathanael's question in John 1:46.

S. Gilmour maintains that "the stress in Jesus' story is on Jesus' early interest in matters of religion. 'Jesus Learning in the Temple' would be a better title."[242] He is joined here by K. Rengstorf, who states: "The presentation betrays no interest whatsoever in a child prodigy."[243] R. Brown agrees that the "center of the story is not the boy's intelligence...."[244] J. Fitzmyer also maintains that the wisdom motif "is only mentioned in the Lucan secondary conclusion (v. 52)...."[245]

The latter three commentators belong to the great majority of scholars who see the main message of the pericope in the christological affirmation of 2:49. Jesus is described here as the Son of God, and his place as such is in his Father's house, the Temple.[246] A variant of this view is that of G. Schneider, who sees the story as a confession of Jesus as the Son of God, expressed in language as an answer to the kerygma of Christ. Yet for Schneider there is more emphasis in the narrative on Jesus' obedience than on his being the "Son of God."[247] While the latter may be true if considered in regard to Jesus' later obeying his heavenly

---

[240]Cf. his *Das Evangelium nach Lukas (Lk 1,1-9,50)* 154 (quotation), 155 and 157.

[241]R. Brown, *The Birth of the Messiah* 488, views the "teachers" here similarly.

[242]Cf. his "The Gospel According to St. Luke" in *IB* 8.67.

[243]See his *Das Evangelium nach Lukas* 51.

[244]Cf. *The Birth of the Messiah* 483.

[245]See his *The Gospel According to Luke I-IX* 437.

[246]J. Ernst, *Das Evangelium nach Lukas* 123, wrongly sees the whole weight of the narrative as lying on Jesus' "remaining" in Jerusalem: the Messiah Jesus was not at home in Bethlehem or Nazareth, but only in the holy city of Jerusalem . Nevertheless, Ernst's discussion of Jesus' "sonship" on pp. 125-126 is helpful.

[247]Cf. *Das Evangelium nach Lukas, Kapitel 1-10* (ÖTKNT 3/1; Gütersloh: Mohn, 1977) 75.

Father by going to Jerusalem and accepting God's will for him on the Cross, at the end of the Gospel, this plays no major role in the original narrative of the twelve-year-old Jesus, which first circulated by itself.

There are actually two points made in the original anecdote of 2:41-51a. The first is to place Jesus in the series of Jewish child prodigies already at the age of twelve: Solomon, Josiah, Daniel, but primarily Samuel. Jesus is meant to continue this tradition; in fact, he is depicted as the epitome of it. Through the demonstration of his equality with, and even superiority to the nation's leading scholars of the Torah in the Temple at Jerusalem, his later great "understanding" is also adumbrated. A motif from Jesus' adult ministry is here retrojected to his childhood. This does not mean, however, that Jesus is here perceived as divine wisdom, which reveals itself.[248]

The second, and main point of Luke 2:41-51a is that espoused by the majority of scholars, described above: Jesus, even before the words of his Father to him at the baptism (in Luke at 3:22), reveals that he is the Son of God and belongs in the Temple, the house of his heavenly Father. Here he is engaged with others in determining what is the proper interpretation of the Torah, the will of God for mankind.

As I have extensively pointed out in section II, these two points were already present in Judaic tradition on the child prodigy Samuel, who also as a small child displayed his great understanding in the Torah in the Temple, and at the age of twelve his special relationship to his real Father there. The Palestinian Jewish Christian author of 2:41-51a preserved these two points from his model, which caused his own narrative to be "zweigipfelig."[249] Although unaware of the background of the narrative in Judaic tradition on the child/boy Samuel, R. Bultmann had already correctly recognized that the story's two points were closely related from the outset.[250]

Finally, another broader purpose of the narrative was to fill in the long chronological gap between Jesus' birth ca. 4 B.C.E. and the outset of his public ministry at the baptism. The Third Evangelist maintains that Jesus was about thirty years old at that point (3:23). Palestinian Jewish Christians felt that this gap somehow had to be filled. Their "pious curiosity" then went to work. This is what I. Heinemann means when he states regarding one direction of the *haggadah:* it is the "creative [re-]

---

[248]Against Laurentin, *Jésus* 138-141, who emphasizes Sir 24:1-12.

[249]Cf. this term as employed by W. Wiefel, *Das Evangelium nach Lukas* (THKNT 3; Berlin: Evangelische Verlagsanstalt, 1988) 83. He follows two other authors here (his n. 10).

[250]Cf. his *The History of the Synoptic Tradition* (New York: Harper & Row, 1963) 300.

writing of history" which embellishes biblical narratives, supplementing them with details, etc.[251] Just as Chronicles rewrote Samuel and Kings, changing passages and adding many details, so the Septuagint, *Pseudo-Philo* and Josephus, for example, retold 1 Samuel 1-3, changing the Hebrew text in decisive ways to create a new narrative regarding the child/boy Samuel.

The Palestinian Jewish Christian author of Luke 2:41-51a did the very same thing, retelling biblical and Judaic traditions on the child/boy Samuel to fit his own hero, Jesus. This he could do all the more easily because in Judaic tradition Samuel was also considered to be twelve years old in the Temple. Decades later, the same type of "gap filling" occurred in the Apocryphal Gospels. There events from the earlier childhood of Jesus are described, for instance in the "Infancy Gospel of Thomas" when he was eight (12:1-2), six (11:1-2), and five (2:1-5).[252] The "gap filling," typical of Judaic haggadah, continued.

B.   The Genre

After ascertaining the original double purpose of Luke 2:41-51a, as well as that it was typical of Judaic, haggadic "gap filling" to satisfy pious curiosity, it is easier to describe its genre. M. Dibelius considered this narrative to be that "story of Jesus whose quality shows most clearly the marks of Legend...."[253] He speaks of "legendary biography" in this regard.[254] The same is true for R. Bultmann.[255]

R. Brown labels the narrative a "biographical apophthegm: the illustration of a saying (in this case, a christological saying [2:49]) shaped out of a life setting."[256] J. Fitzmyer prefers to borrow a term from V. Taylor and call 2:41-51a "the Gospel's first pronouncement story."[257]

The latter two terms are too precise because they see the entire narrative as a biographical expansion only of the saying in v 49.   As

---

[251]Cf. the summary by G. Stemberger in Strack and Stemberger, *Introduction* 260. See also the statement regarding haggadah by B. Grossfeld in *The First Targum to Esther* (New York: Sepher-Hermon, 1983) iv: "legendary recountings of incidents to supply gaps in the canonical history."

[252]Cf. Hennecke and Schneemelcher, *New Testament Apocrypha* 1.396 and 392-393.

[253]See his *From Tradition to Gospel* (New York: Scribner's, no date; first German edition 1919) 106.

[254]*Ibid.*, 108.

[255]Cf. *The History* 300, and the term "biographical legend" of a religious hero on p. 245. He concedes that it is not "always easy to draw" the line between legends and biographical apophthegms *(ibid.)*.

[256]Cf. *The Birth of the Messiah* 483.   He can also call it "an apophthegm or paradigm, i.e., a short story centered around a saying." See also his n. 17.

[257]See his *The Gospel According to Luke I-IX* 436.

shown in section *A.* above, this is wrong because in both the Judaic "model" of the child Samuel in the Temple, and here, there is also a second point: the child's great understanding. The anecdote of 2:41-51a therefore not only centers on v 49, although this question of the twelve-year-old Jesus dominates the pericope. It actually has two points. For this reason, although one could speak of 2:41-51a as a "biographical apophthegm based on two points," I prefer Bultmann and Dibelius' more general term of "legendary biography" or "biographical legend." It also fits, for example, the incident of the two-year-old Samuel in the Temple, explaining a point of the Torah to his parents, the priests, and others in *b. Ber.* 31b, and *Pseudo-Philo* 53, which deals with the child Samuel's call in the Temple by his three different "fathers." As noted above, the same type of "biographical legend" continued in regard to the child Jesus in the Apocryphal Gospels.[258]

<h1 style="text-align:center">VI</h1>
<h2 style="text-align:center">The Question of Historicity</h2>

Up to the time of the Enlightenment, Luke 2:41-51a, like the rest of the Bible, was considered by Christians to be divinely inspired Holy Scripture and therefore automatically historical. Since then, however, especially after Protestants began to employ the historical-critical method (in this century also appropriated more and more by Roman Catholic scholars), doubts as to the historicity of the narrative of the twelve-year-old Jesus in the Temple have grown. Today, there are very few exegetes who maintain that the incident took place just as it is described in Scripture.

One example of the latter is R. Laurentin, who considers Mary to be an eye-witness in Luke 2:51; therefore for him the account is historical.[259]

---

[258]In "The Infancy Story of Thomas" in Hennecke and Schneemelcher, *New Testament Apocrypha* 1.393-401, for example, Jesus' teacher Zacchaeus is modeled on Samuel's teacher Eli. In the Syriac variant, Jesus is represented as saying to Zacchaeus: "But thou thinkest that thou art my father" (p. 399). In the "Protevangelium of James" (1.374-388), much material from 1 Samuel 1-3 has been incorporated, as noted by O. Cullmann (p.373). It has been applied here to the birth of Mary and her being raised in the Temple until the age of twelve, when Joseph receives her by lot (8.1-3, pp. 378-379). Someone well acquainted with Judaic traditions on the birth and childhood of Samuel should relate them to this narrative. Cullmann does not recognize these developments whatsoever.

[259]Cf. his *Jésus* 111. He also sees Jesus' Resurrection alluded to in the phrase "after three days" in 2:46, which is very farfetched (pp. 101-102). K. Bornhäuser in *Die Geburts-und Kindheitsgeschichte Jesu* 134-135 (cf. p. 143) also sees Mary as the person who handed on the content of Luke 2:41-51. F. Hauck in *Das Evangelium des Lukas* (THKNT 3; Leipzig: Deichert, 1934) 46 says there is no reason to believe Jesus did not utter the key saying in 2:49b. It may not be completely historical,

Unfortunately, such an attitude completely misses the points of the narrative. Early Palestinian Jewish Christians believed that he who showed great understanding in the Torah and taught accordingly during his adult min istry, also in the Temple, was the Son of God on the basis of his Resurrection from the dead. One such an early Christian therefore retrojected these two motifs to Jesus at the age of twelve. As a Jew, he was accustomed to this type of haggadic embellishment of the life of Israelite heroes, such as Moses.[260] His main model, however, was the childhood of the wise and understanding Samuel, who at the age of twelve was called by God in the Temple, where the question arose of who his real father/Father was. These two motifs he wove into a new narrative, a "biographical legend" of Jesus, with great artistic skill.[261] He himself knew that his new story was not "historical" in the modern sense. He wanted his hearers to consider it edifying, yet also gently provocative in the positive sense of the word. They should ask: What was the source of Jesus' great understanding at such a tender age? To what extent was he already then the Son of God? Was Joseph and Mary's inability to understand their son in the Temple part of the hearers' own experience, culminating in the difficult question of the meaning of Jesus' suffering on the Cross? Finally, the earliest Palestinian Jewish Christian hearers would have noted and appreciated the application of motifs and terminology from Judaic traditions on the infancy and childhood of Samuel to the twelve-year-old Jesus. They would have asked: How was Jesus similar to, yet in major ways different from, the OT hero?

Today, thanks to NT scholars' greater acquaintance with Judaic, including rabbinic, sources, the influence of Palestinian haggadah on the Gospels has been recognized and appreciated more and more. This is a great enrichment in regard to better understanding many gospel texts,

---

yet it approximately corresponds to Jesus' growing self-consciousness (p. 47). A. Plummer in *The Gospel According to S. Luke* (ICC 33; Edinburgh: Clark, 1956[5]) 80 also considers the whole incident to be historical.

[260]I trace, for example, the Judaic Moses birth traditions as applied to the birth of Jesus in Luke 2:1-20 in my volume *Weihnachtsgeschichte* 11-58.

[261]It is ironic that OT scholars today have recognized that in the MT of 1 Samuel 1, motifs and terminology from an earlier birth story regarding Saul have been applied to that of Samuel. One major sign of this is the double word play in the Hebrew of 1:28, where Samuel is "dedicated/lent" (שָׁאוּל) to the Lord. See, for example, P. McCarter, Jr., *I Samuel* 62 on 1:20, 63 on 1:27-28, and 65; as well as G. Caird, "The First and Second Books of Samuel" 2.881, citing A. Lods. Thus a Saul birth story was applied to the birth and childhood of Samuel, which was then applied to the childhood of Jesus. In turn, the Apocryphal Gospels borrowed from the latter and applied the material to the child Jesus at an even earlier age, and to the child Mary. See n. 258.

which, although not literally historical, conveyed *religious truths* first to Palestinian Jewish Christians, and later in Greek translation to Hellenistic Jewish Christians, and finally to non-Jewish Christians, even today.

* * *

The lack of understanding on the part of Jesus' parents in regard to who he really was, displayed in Luke 2:50, continued on the part of his family and other inhabitants of Nazareth when Jesus became an adult and began his public ministry. As the figure of Samuel provided the major Judaic background for 2:41-51a, so the same prophet and the first king or anointed one of Israel, Saul, play major roles in the Judaic background of the rejection in his home town of Jesus, the Anointed One. To this I now turn.

2

Jesus' Rejection at Nazareth (Mark 6:1-6a par.), and Samuel's Anointing Saul as King (1 Samuel 10)

Introduction

Between the raising of Jairus' daughter from the dead (5:21-43) and the commissioning of the twelve disciples (6:7-13), the Evangelist Mark relates the narrative of Jesus' rejection in Nazareth, his home town (6:1-6a). This vivid, brief story at first seems to be well rounded out, of one cast, and to bear the signs of authenticity. Closer examination, however, reveals what E. Grässer calls "rents and seams" in the incident.[1] After the inhabitants' positive astonishment at Jesus' teaching in their synagogue, they marvel at the mighty works he has done. Yet they themselves have not experienced any now. Then, without any apparent reason, they take offense at Jesus. They call him "the carpenter," name his mother and brothers, and mention his sisters. Yet, strangely, no reference is made to his father Joseph. Jesus reacts by stating that a prophet is not without honor except in his home town. This is made extensively long by the addition: "and among his relatives, and in his

---

[1]Cf. his "Jesus in Nazareth (Mc 6, 1-6a). Bemerkungen zur Redaktion und Theologie des Markus" in *Jesus in Nazareth*, ed. W. Eltester (BZNW 40; Berlin: de Gruyter, 1972) 11. The essay also appeared as "Jesus in Nazareth (Mark VI. 1-6a). Notes on the Redaction and Theology of St. Mark," in *NTS* 16 (1969/70) 1-23. I cite from the German. For secondary literature on this pericope, see J. Gnilka, *Das Evangelium nach Markus (Mk 1-8,26)* 226-27, as well as U. Luz, *Das Evangelium nach Matthäus*, 2. Teilband, Mt. 8-17 (EKK 1/2; Zurich: Benziger; Neukirchen-Vluyn: Neukirchener, 1990) 383. Cf. also H.M. Humphrey, *A Bibliography for the Gospel of Mark. 1954-1980* (New York: Mellon, 1981) 67-68; and *The Gospel of Mark. A Cumulative Bibliography 1950-1990*, ed. F. Neirynck et al. (BETL 102; Leuven: University Press, 1992) 583.

house/family." After the narrator categorically relates that Jesus could not do a single mighty work in the town, an exception is nevertheless mentioned. Finally, the term πατρίς is found in the four gospels only in this narrative (Mark 6:1, 4; Matt 13:54, 57; Luke 4:23-24; John 4:44). The expression σοφία is employed by Mark only in 6:2, as is true for τέκτων in 6:3 (in the NT elsewhere only in Matt 13:55). The adjective ἄτιμος occurs in the gospels only in 6:4 and the parallel Matt 13:57. The term συγγενής in 6:4 is also singular in Mark.

The above inconcinnities and philological observations point to the narrative of Jesus' rejection in Nazareth as an entity appropriated by Mark from elsewhere.[2] In another study on the beheading of John the Baptist in the same chapter (6:14-29), I have proposed that Judaic traditions on the beginning of the book of Esther inform that narrative.[3] Here I would like to suggest that many elements from the biblical story of Samuel's anointing Saul king in 1 Samuel 10, including its development in Judaic tradition, provided an early Palestinian Jewish Christian with the raw materials he needed to present Jesus[4] as not only rejected by the leaders of his people in Jerusalem at the end of his life, and earlier by his family, but also by his own townspeople in Nazareth.[5]

After a brief sketch of the Saul narrative (I), I shall point out twelve verbal expressions, motifs, and a question structure found in Mark 6:1-6a as deriving from that narrative in the MT and in Judaic tradition (II). Included in section II 10) is a special treatment of the Messiah as the eschatological "carpenter" who is to (re-)build the Temple. Then the original narrative and Mark's redactional work are outlined (III). This is followed by the questions of the narrative's original language (IV) and its historicity (V). Finally, section VI sharpens the contours of the original narrative by describing what it is not.

---

[2]On Mark's redactional activity, cf. the article by Grässer in n. 1. It must be substantially revised, however, in light of the conclusions of this essay. See section III below on the pre-Marcan form of the narrative.

[3]See *Water into Wine and the Beheading of John the Baptist. Early Jewish-Christian Interpretation of Esther 1 in John 2:1-11 and Mark 6:17-29*, pp. 39-74.

[4]The author of *Midr. Ps.* 18/7 (English in Braude, *The Midrash on Psalms* 1.236) has David cite the words of Samuel to Saul in 1 Sam 10:1 as spoken to him, David. The transfer of motifs and terms regarding Saul from the Samuel chapter to Jesus by the author of Mark 6:1-6a was nothing unusual in Palestinian Judaism.

[5]The two books of Samuel in Judaic tradition also provided the background for other NT narratives. In addition to essays one and three in this volume, John 11:45-54 relies, for example, on 2 Samuel 20, as I point out in the essay "The Death of One for All in John 11:45-54 in Light of Judaic Traditions" in my *Barabbas and Esther and Other Studies in the Judaic Illumination of Earliest Christianity* 29-63.

I
Samuel's Anointing Saul as King

In 1 Samuel 8 Israel "rejects" the Lord from being their King and requests the prophet Samuel to appoint them a king to govern them like all the nations. After warning them of the king's future misuse of them, Samuel receives an order from the Lord to make them a king anyway.

This begins the "rather quaint tale"[6] of Saul's search for the lost asses of his father in chapters 9-10, leading to his being anointed as king of Israel. Not finding the animals after traversing various areas, Saul is informed by his servant of the prophet Samuel "in this city" (Ramah, Samuel's home town – 8:4), a man "held in honor" (9:6). The day before, the Lord had told Samuel to anoint the Benjaminite prince of His people Israel. Saul is to "save" His people from the Philistines (9:16).

Samuel then anoints Saul prince (10:1), and at Gibeah a band of prophets meets Saul. The spirit of God comes mightily upon him, and he prophesies. In Gibeah those who know him from before ask what has come upon the son of Kish: "Is Saul also among the prophets?" Someone from there (the city) also asks: "And who is their father?" This becomes a proverb (מָשָׁל): "Is Saul also among the prophets?" (vv 11-12). Returning home after prophesying, Saul does not speak with his father but with his relative about the lost and found asses, yet not about his receiving the kingship.

At this point a different (the so-called "Late") source relates how Saul is chosen king by lot (10:17-27). Modest, he hides among the baggage, but is found and acclaimed king. Some who approve of him accompany him home to Gibeah, but others ask derogatively: How can "this one" save us? They despise him and refuse to give him a present, which would be appropriate to a king. Saul reacts by remaining silent in regard to their disapproval (v 27).

Later, Saul's behavior causes Samuel to inform him that his kingdom will not continue; the Lord will seek out a successor (13:14). Among other things, Saul's refusal to kill Agag the Amalekite causes God to "reject" him as king (15:23, 26).

* * *

In his commentary on the anointing of Saul as king, Artur Weiser speaks of the "popular peculiarity belonging to this saga, interwoven with fairy-tale motifs." He maintains that here the laws of the "development of legends" must be considered. The narrative possesses a

---

[6]P. McCarter, Jr., *I Samuel* 184.

"colorful vividness" and dramatic tension. A "popular saga" dated the anointing of Saul back to his younger years.[7]

In the following I shall point out the relevance of numerous verbal expressions, motifs, and a question structure from this "vivid, legendary" narrative of Samuel's anointing Saul king in the MT, and its development in Judaic sources, to the rejection of the messianic (or anointed) king, Jesus, by the people of his home town, Nazareth.

II
Verbal Expressions, Motifs, and a Question Structure from the Samuel-Saul Narrative in Mark 6:1-6a

1. The Anointed King.

A. Mark.

Mark, our earliest known evangelist, wrote his gospel backwards, so-to-speak. Only because Jesus, the Christ or Anointed One (הַמָּשִׁיחַ; ὁ χριστός), was crucified and raised by God from the dead, was it worthwhile to preface these events with an "extended introduction," forming the gospel. In Mark the terms "the Christ/Anointed One" and "king" play very important roles, as they do in the Saul narrative.

At his "trial" Jesus is asked by the high priest: "Are you the Christ, the Son of the Blessed?" (14:61). In addition, the chief priests and scribes revile Jesus on the Cross in 15:32 with the words: "Let the Christ, the King of Israel, come down now from the cross, that we may see and believe." Long before Peter, on the way to villages of Caesarea Philippi, confesses Jesus to be the Christ in 8:29, the reader also knows of Jesus' being the Anointed One. Already in 1:1 Mark has informed the reader that his gospel concerns Jesus "Christ," the Son of God. Although "Christ" here has become a proper name, its original meaning of "the Anointed One" still could be heard in the term.

Except for its application to Herod Antipas in Mark 6:14, 22, 25-27 and in a general sense in 13:9, the expression "king" in Mark occurs only at Jesus' trial. Jesus as "the king of the Jews" occurs here five times, showing its major importance to the Evangelist (15:2, 9, 12, 18, 26 – the inscription of the charge against Jesus on the Cross). As noted above, 15:32 combines the two terms: "the Christ, the King of Israel."

This association and combination of "Messiah/Anointed One" and "king" was very natural in the first century C.E., as is shown by the

---

[7]See his *Samuel. Seine geschichtliche Aufgabe und religiöse Bedeutung. Traditionsgeschichtliche Untersuchungen zu 1. Samuel 7-12* (FRLANT 81; Göttingen: Vandenhoeck & Ruprecht, 1962), 48, 49 and 53, respectively.

extremely frequent rabbinic expression מלך המשיח, "the King, the Messiah," "the messianic King."[8]

In Mark 6:1-6a Jesus is neither designated the Anointed One[9] nor king. Instead, he indirectly designates himself a prophet by stating in v 4: "A prophet is not without honor, except in his home town, and among his relatives, and in his house/family." Yet the Palestinian Jewish Christian author of the narrative behind 6:1-6a himself firmly believed that Jesus was the messianic King. For this reason an OT narrative, 1 Samuel 10, appealed to him as the major source of his materials with which to describe Jesus' rejection in Nazareth. There both "to anoint" and "king" occur as major motifs.

B. Saul.

In the narrative of Saul's anointing, the elders of Israel ask for a "king" to govern them like all the nations. While Samuel first rejects this request, the Lord persuades him nevertheless to grant it, and Saul then becomes king (8:5, 6, 7, 9, 10, 11, 18,19, 20; 10:19, 24).[10]

In 9:16 the Lord reveals to Samuel that he should "anoint" (מָשַׁח, LXX χρίω) Saul to be prince over His people Israel and to "save" (עָשַׁע; LXX σῴζω)[11] them. In 10:1 Samuel takes a vial of oil, pours it on Saul's head, kisses him and asks: "Has not the Lord 'anointed' (מְשָׁחֲ; LXX χρίω) you to be prince over His heritage?" The Septuagint at this point retains what most probably has fallen out of the Hebrew:[12] Saul will "save" (σῴξω) the Lord's people. He has "anointed" (χρίω) him to be a ruler. Targum Jonathan on 10:1 labels the oil Samuel employs here משחא (MT שֶׁמֶן), and it also employs משח for the anointing. In addition, it emphasizes Saul as "king" by substituting מלכא for the נגיד, "prince," of the MT.[13]

The above association of "king," "anointing" and "saving" appealed to the author of Mark 6:1-6a as his source of materials for a description of Jesus' rejection in Nazareth because, as stated above, he firmly believed

---

[8]Cf. Str-B 1.6-7.

[9]See below, however, for the term "carpenter" as a messianic designation.

[10]These verses are found in the so-called "Late Source." Cf. also 9:17 and 10:16, 25, as well as 1 Kgdms 10:1.

[11]Cf. Matt 1:21 for the Hebrew word play behind "Jesus," עָשַׁע, who will "save" (עָשַׁע) his people from their sins.

[12]Cf. the apparatus of *Biblica Hebraica*, ed. R. Kittel et al. 418, and McCarter, *I Samuel* 171.

[13]Cf. Sperber, *The Bible in Aramaic*. II. *The Former Prophets According to Targum Jonathan* 111. An English translation is offered by D. Harrington and A. Saldarini in *Targum Jonathan of the Former Prophets* 118.

that Jesus, the "Savior," was the "Christ/Anointed One," the messianic "King."[14]

2. Jesus' Home Town.

A. *Mark.*

In 6:1 the author writes: "He [Jesus] went away from there[15] to his home town (πατρίς)." As remarked above, this Greek term occurs in the gospels only here, in v 4, and in Matt 13:54, 57; Luke 4:23-24; and John 4:44, all connected with Jesus' "prophet" saying. While the RSV[16] translates "his own country" in Mark 6:1, this is wrong here because of two reasons. First, Jesus in v 2 begins to teach in the synagogue, which cannot be *the* synagogue of Galilee, but that of a definite place, a city/town. (The reader knows as of 1:9 that Jesus comes from Nazareth of Galilee. See also 1:24, and later 14:67 and 16:6.) In addition, 6:3 mentions Jesus' mother and brothers and then notes that Jesus' sisters are "with us," i.e., not somewhere in the region of Galilee but in the town of Nazareth. Secondly, the Greek term πατρίς can mean "home town" as well as "fatherland, homeland."[17] The meaning "native city/town/place" is found in Philo, *Leg. ad Gai.* 278, which names the city Jerusalem, and in other passages of the Alexandrian author.[18] Josephus has a large number of such passages, for example *Ant.* 10.114, where the prophet Jeremiah returns to his *patris*, Anathoth.[19] (On *Ant.* 6.67, see

---

[14]The *Stichwort* "anointing" also caused the author of Luke 4:16-30, which differs in major ways from Mark 6:1-6a, to cite Isa 61:1 in v 18. "The Spirit of the Lord is upon me" was also suitable for his narrative because the Spirit of the Lord came upon Saul in 1 Sam 10:6 and 10.

[15]Most probably Capernaum on Lake Tiberias. Cf. 5:21.

[16]The New Revised Standard Version now has "home town" in Mark 6:1 and 4.

[17]For both meanings close together, cf. Josephus, *Vita* 417-18. On the term, see BAGD 636-37.

[18]Cf. *Fug.* 107; *Som.* 2.124; *Leg. Gai.* 158, 277, 279, 281, 283 and 290. The term *patris* as native country is associated with "relatives" and "house," as in Mark 6:4, in *Conf.* 76; *Her.* 26; *Abr.* 31 and 62; *Spec. Leg.* 1.52; and *Praem.* 17.

[19]The Jewish historian has *patris* at least fifty times in this sense. At least twenty-two sites are named or clear from the context:
1)   Abel Beth-Maacah: *Ant.* 7.289.
2)   Alexandria : *Ap.* 2.34.
3)   Alurus: *Bell.* 4.523.
4)   Anathoth: *Ant.* 8. 10; 10.114-15.
5)   Antioch: *Bell.* 7.49.
6)   Armatha: *Ant.* 6.67 and 293; Ramah in *Ant.* 5.346.
7)   Auaris: *Ap.* 1.242.
8)   Beersheba: *Ant.* 9.157.
9)   Bethlehem: *Ant.* 6.227, 236; 5.271; 7.312.

below regarding Saul.) Next to Matthew, the earliest commentator on Mark 6:1 is the Evangelist Luke, who in his retelling of Jesus' rejection explicitly states in 4:16: "And he came to Nazareth, where he had been brought up."[20] If in the Semitic original of this Marcan narrative (on this, see below, section IV) the Palestinian Jewish Christian author employed either מדינתא or מדינה, the same double meaning prevailed in the Semitic as in the Greek *patris*.[21]

Nazareth in Jesus' time was an insignificant small town. This is shown by the fact that it lay on no major road, and by its being mentioned nowhere in the OT, the Apocrypha, the two talmuds, the midrashim, Philo and Josephus.[22] Its insignificance is also attested by John 1:45-46, where Philip informs Nathanael of Jesus of Nazareth, the son of Joseph. To this Nathanael replies: "Can anything good come out of Nazareth?"[23]

Jesus was rejected according to Mark 6:1-6a in his home town, Nazareth, by those who had excellent knowledge of him, his direct family and his relatives.

B. Saul.

The expression "home town" is also very important in the narrative of Saul's anointing. In 9:6 Saul's servant informs him concerning Samuel, whose home is Ramah (7:17): "Behold, there is a man of God in this city,

---

10) Ephra: *Ant.* 5.229, 232.
11) Gelmon: *Ant.* 7.228.
12) Gischala: *Bell.* 2.590, 621; *Vita* 71, 189, 235, 372.
13) Jerusalem: *Bell.* 1.199, 201; 4.380; 5.456, 458; 6.230; *Ant.* 10.230; 11.165; *Vita* 418.
14) Jotapata: *Bell.* 3.112, 260.
15) Modeei: *Ant.* 13.210.
16) Nob: *Ant.* 6.262, 268.
17) Rome: *Bell.* 7.9.
18) Saba: *Bell.* 3.229.
19) Sarasa: *Ant.* 5.317.
20) Sebee: *Ant.* 5.270.
21) Sepphoris: *Vita* 30.
22) Tiberias: *Vita* 338, 340, 344, 346, 349, 391.

[20]The translation "his own country" in John 4:44, however, is appropriate because of the mention of the region Galilee in vv 43 and 45.

[21]See S. Lachs, *A Rabbinic Commentary on the New Testament. The Gospels of Matthew, Mark and Luke* (Hoboken: KTAV, 1987) 55, 180 and 182, n. 33. Cf. also Jastrow, *A Dictionary* 734, with an example of a city.

[22]Cf. Str-B 1.92, as well as the article "Nazareth" by D. Pellett in *IDB* 3.524-26, with literature. R. Batey in "Is Not This the Carpenter?" in *NTS* 30 (1984) 250, however, posits a Roman road which "went through the outskirts of Nazareth" and led to Sepphoris.

[23]Cf. 7:52: "Search and you will see that no prophet is to rise from Galilee."

and he is a man that is held in honor." For "man of God" the targum has "a prophet of the Lord."[24] Writing at the end of the first century C.E., Josephus, a native of Jerusalem, whose mother tongue was Aramaic,[25] in *Ant.* 6.47 (4.1) mentions "the city of Armatha, in which a true prophet is." As I shall point out below, this forms part of the background for Jesus' "prophet" saying in Mark 6:4, also concerned with his home town.

Saul's home town is called "Gibeah of Saul" in 1 Sam 11:4. Samuel tells him that when he comes to the city of "Gibeah of God," he will prophesy (10:5-6). This town is simply called Gabatha at this point by Josephus in *Ant.* 6.56, and Gibeah in 1 Sam 10:10. The sites are identical. Here Saul indeed prophesies, with those who knew him from before asking how this could happen to him.

Most importantly, at 1 Sam 10:25, after Saul is chosen king – here by lot –, and Samuel instructs the Israelites in what the kingship will be like, according to Josephus in *Ant.* 6.67 (cf. also 293) Samuel departs to Armatha (Ramah), his "home town" *(patris).* This is an addition to Scripture. Saul then also departs to Gabatha, "where he grew up" (ἐξ ἧς ὑπῆρχε).[26] For this the MT has: "Saul also went to his home at Gibeah..." (10:26). This is one of only two instances, as noted above, of *patris* as "home town" in Josephus. It is very significant that Saul's departure for the town in which he grew up is made parallel to Samuel's return to his own "home town."

The latter context of *patris,* in the narrative of Saul's anointing as king, coupled with 1 Sam 9:6, provided the Jewish Christian author of Mark 6:1-6a with the motif and exact term of Jesus as a prophet with (-out) honor in his "home town" of Nazareth.

Finally, 1 Sam 10:10 says of Saul and his servant before the latter begins to prophesy: "When they came to Gibeah...." The LXX at this point renders Gibeah by "hill," yet more importantly changes the plural to the singular: "And he (Saul) comes from there to..." (καὶ ἔρχεται ἐκεῖθεν εἰς...). I would suggest that this formulation, certainly deriving from an early variant of the MT or a Judaic development of it, stands behind most of Mark 6:1a: "He went away *from there and came to* his home town" (καὶ ἐξῆλθεν ἐκεῖθεν, καὶ ἔρχεται εἰς τὴν πατρίδα αὐτοῦ). "Home town" was substituted here for Gibeah, Saul's home town. If this

---

[24]Sperber, *The Bible in Aramaic* II.109; Harrington and Saldarini, *Targum Jonathan of the Former Prophets* 117.
[25]See 93-94 C.E. for the completion of the Antiquities in *Ant.* 20.267; *Vita* 7; *Bell.* 1.3; *Ant.* 20.263; and *Cont. Ap.* 1.50.
[26]Literally, "from which he began/was": ὑπάρχω. H. St. J. Thackery and R. Marcus in the LCL edition translate: "whence he was sprung." Cf. Luke 4:16, "Nazareth, where he had been brought up."

is correct, 6:1a should not be viewed as a typical introduction due to the redactor Mark.[27] It, too, basically derives from Judaic development of the account of Saul's being anointed king by Samuel.

3. Teaching.

A. Mark.

The Jewish Christian author of 6:1-6a needed an appropriate setting for his narrative of Jesus' rejection in Nazareth. Palestinian himself, he may have known of a tradition that Jesus did not do a single mighty work, i.e., a healing or miracle, in his home town (v 5a). That could have taken place outdoors, for example at the only water supply of the site, a spring now called "Mary's Well," a favorite gathering place.[28] Yet for the reason I cite below in *B. Saul*, he appropriately selected the synagogue for Jesus' public appearance. Since the town was too small to have an academy (בית המדרש),[29] where Jesus could demonstrate his wisdom, the author selects the town's synagogue. To ensure maximum effect, he has Jesus teach there on the Sabbath, when all the males would be assembled to pray and hear a lecture or *derashah*/sermon,[30] if one was given.

Elsewhere in Mark, Jesus is very frequently addressed as "Teacher" (διδάσκαλος) by Pharisees, "Herodians," Sadducees, a scribe and his own disciples.[31] Again and again the prophet from Nazareth is described as "teaching," from Galilee to Jerusalem and Judea, to Trans-Jordan, "as his custom was" (10:1).[32]

The fact that Mark 6:1b has Jesus' disciples follow him to Nazareth from "there," most probably Capernaum, is not an editorial addition by Mark, as usually maintained.[33] Rather, the Jewish Christian author knew

---

[27]Against Grässer, *Jesus in Nazareth* 14, and most commentaries *ad loc.*

[28]See Z. Vilnay, *The Guide to Israel* (Jerusalem: Daf-Chen, 1979[21]) 463, and the well's location at number 12 on the map of p. 462. Vilnay notes on p. 464 that it is 47 km or 29 miles by present roads from Nazareth to Capernaum on Lake Tiberias, from which Jesus ostensibly came to Mark 6:1. The distance was shorter in Jesus' day. The straight distance is 34 km or 20.4 miles. Cf. Pellett, "Nazareth" 525.

[29]See Schürer, *The history of the Jewish people in the age of Jesus Christ*, 2.333-34, as well as the whole section on "Torah Scholarship," 322-38.

[30]See Mark 4:2 for Jesus' "teaching" many things in parables. There was seldom a fine line between legal and popular materials, halakhah and haggadah.

[31]See 4:38; 5:35; 9:17, 38; 10:17, 35; 12:14, 19, 32; 13:1; and 14:14 (Jesus labels himself "Teacher" here).

[32]The concordance lists fourteen occurrences of διδάσκω, as well as three of Jesus' teaching (διδαχή).

[33]See Grässer, *Jesus in Nazareth* 16, and the commentaries.

that disciples (תלמידים)[34] constantly seek the "wisdom" (see v 2b) of their master, on every possible occasion. If their teacher gave a lecture or sermon, they sought to be present if at all possible.[35] The author, not Mark, thus has them accompany Jesus to Nazareth and the synagogue, although they play no further role.[36]

B. Saul.

In the OT narrative of Saul's anointing as king, Samuel informs him in 1 Sam 10:5 that he will meet a band of prophets in Gibeah of God. This is fulfilled in v 10, when the spirit of God comes mightily upon Saul in Gibeah, his home town, and he prophesies. In v 11 Saul prophesies with the prophets, and the people then ask if he is among the prophets. In v 12 this becomes a proverb, "Is Saul also among the prophets?"

For all five occurrences Targum Jonathan has "teachers" (ספריא) instead of "prophets".[37] One of the major tasks of the *sofer* or scribe in the first century C.E. was to teach the Torah or law. For this reason he was called in Greek not only γραμματεύς, but also νομοδιδάσκαλος, "teacher of the law," as in Luke 5:17 and Acts 5:34.[38]

I suggest that the Palestinian Jewish Christian author of Mark 6:1-6a knew of this "teacher" tradition, still found in the present form of the targum.[39] Intimately related to the proverb associated with Saul in his home town, "Is Saul also among the teachers?", it provided him with the impetus to have Jesus "teach" in the synagogue of his home town, Nazareth, where a proverb concerning him also plays a major role (6:4).

---

[34]This recalls the same root employed for Jesus' beginning to "teach" (למד) in v 2a.

[35]Cf. the statement by M.-J. Lagrange in his *Évangile selon Saint Marc* (Ebib; Paris: Gabalda, reprint 1966) 147: "Les disciples sont du voyage, parce que Jésus ne va pas pour voir ses siens, mais pour prêcher."

[36]In Mark 1:21 the newly called disciples go to Capernaum with Jesus, where he enters the synagogue (with them) on the Sabbath and teaches, which leads to astonishment (v 22). The formulation here leads me to suspect that it is Mark's, based on his knowledge of 6:1-2. It should be noted that in 3:14, Jesus appoints the twelve "to be with him." This is meant literally, for disciples learn by example and discussion with their master. It was thus natural for the Jewish Christian author of Mark 6:1-6a to have Jesus' disciples enter the synagogue with him to learn more wisdom/Torah.

[37]Sperber, *The Bible in Aramaic* II.112; English in Harrington and Saldarini, *Targum Jonathan of the Former Prophets* 119, with n. 8.

[38]For the scribe as a teacher, see "Schürer, *The history* 2.332-34.

[39]Much of this targum appears to have assumed basically its present form by the first half of the second century C.E. Each particular tradition, however, must be considered on its own merits. Cf. Harrington and Saldarini, *Targum Jonathan of the Former Prophets* 13-14.

4. Astonishment.

A. Mark.

After Jesus finished teaching in the Nazareth synagogue, many who heard him "were astonished" (6:2 – ἐκπλήσσομαι). This verb means in the passive: to be amazed, astounded, astonished. It literally is to be "driven out of one's senses by a sudden shock."[40]

The Nazarites are struck with admiration[41] at Jesus' "wisdom" (σοφία), asking where he got "these things" (ταῦτα – v 2). Isn't he the artisan ("carpenter" – τέκτων), whose family members are well-known to the residents of the small town (v 3)? They are amazed, asking where Jesus could derive the contents of his teaching.

The Evangelist Mark employs seven different Greek expressions for being amazed, astonished, astounded.[42] While the typical reaction to a healing is so described, those who elsewhere experience Jesus' teaching are also amazed in three instances. In 1:22 the inhabitants of Capernaum are astonished (ἐκπλήσσομαι) at Jesus' teaching in their synagogue on the Sabbath, "for he taught them as one who had authority, and not as the scribes." Here the reason for their astonishment is explained, which is not, at least explicitly, the case in 6:2. After the "cleansing" of the Temple, Jesus teaches there (11:17). The chief priests and scribes fear him "because all the multitude was astonished (ἐκπλήσσομαι) at his teaching." Finally, some of the Pharisees and Herodians seek to entrap Jesus in his talk. They ask the teacher who "truly teaches the way of God" (12:14) whether they should pay taxes to Caesar or not. His clever answer results in the fact that "they were amazed (ἐκθαυμάζω) at him."[43]

In spite of the Evangelist Mark's clear presentation elsewhere of the people's "astonishment" at Jesus' teaching, leading one to think the expression in 6:2 could be redactional,[44] I propose that in this particular

---

[40]LSJ 517, BAGD 244.

[41]Cf. the example from Herodotus, fifth century B.C.E., cited by LSJ 517, II.2, end.

[42]
1) ἐκθαυμάζω – 12:17.
2) ἐκθαμβέομαι – 9:15; 14:33; 16:5, 6.
3) ἐκπλήσσομαι – 1:22; 6:2; 7:37; 10:26; 11:18.
4) ἐξίστημι – 2:12; 5:42; 6:51. See also ἔκστασις in 16:8.
5) θαμβέομαι – 1:27; 10:24, 32.
6) θαυμάζω – 5:20; 6:6; 15:5, 44 (the latter two of Pilate's "wondering").
7) φοβέομαι – 2:12.

[43]Mark 1:27 is a mixed form. After Jesus heals a man with an unclean spirit in the Capernaum synagogue, all are "amazed" (θαμβέομαι), saying it is a new "teaching."

[44]See above, n. 36, for my suggestion that 1:21-22 is redactional, based on 6:1-2.

instance the Jewish Christian author of the Nazareth episode derived it from Judaic accounts of Saul's being anointed king in his home town.

B. *Saul.*

In his retelling of Saul's being anointed king, Josephus has Samuel tell Saul that when he comes to Gibeah, he will meet an assembly of prophets. Divinely inspired, he will prophesy with them so that whoever sees him will "be astonished and marvel" (ἐκπλήττεσθαί τε καὶ θαυμάζειν) and say: "How (πόθεν) has the son of Kish come to this state of good fortune?" This then happens as Samuel foretells it (*Ant.* 6.56).

This "being astonished," here in the Attic Greek form, is found neither in the MT, LXX or targum at 1 Sam 10:11, the source of the narrative. Josephus is clearly dependent on early Palestinian Judaic tradition here. This argument is supported by the term "marvel," also employed in Mark 6:6, and by the expression πόθεν, associated in Josephus with the people's astonishment, just as in Mark 6:2.

The Gospel of Mark is generally thought to have been composed just before or after 70 C.E.[45] Mark therefore cannot have borrowed from Josephus, who finished the Antiquities at the beginning of the nineties (see above). The opposite is also the case. Josephus would certainly not have borrowed material from the Gospel of Mark regarding Jesus' rejection at Nazareth in order to describe the anointing of Saul as king. This is true even if Josephus, writing in Rome, had access to the Gospel, thought by some scholars to have been written in the same city.[46] There is no evidence whatsoever for Josephus' ever referring to a gospel. The Jewish Christian author of the account of Jesus' rejection at Nazareth is in part dependent on the same Palestinian Judaic traditions regarding Saul's anointing as the Jerusalem Jew Josephus was. These were most probably in Aramaic. (See section IV below.)

5. Relatives and Home/Family.

A. *Mark.*

The proverb quoted by Jesus in 6:4 says that a prophet is not without honor except in his home town. To this is added: "and among his relatives (συγγενεῖς), and among his family (οἰκία, lit. 'house')."[47] Matt 13:57 omits only the relatives at this point, while Luke 4:24 and John 4:44 omit both.

---

[45]See Gnilka, *Das Evangelium nach Markus (Mk 1-8,26)* 34-35 (perhaps in the first three years after 70 C.E.), as well as W. Kümmel, *Einleitung in das Neue Testament* (Heidelberg: Quelle & Meyer, 1983[21]) 70. See also here, p. 58, n. 238.

[46]See Kümmel, *op. cit.* 69-70.

[47]See BAGD 772 and 557, respectively, on these.

Jesus' "family" is explicitly enumerated in Mark 6:3, which has Mary, his brothers James, Joses, Judas and Simon, and his sisters, who are said to be "here among us," that is, in Nazareth. The latter appears to indicate that they, at the typical age of ca. fourteen,[48] married local men,[49] while Mary and the male children now resided in nearby Capernaum on the Lake of Tiberias.[50]

E. Lohmeyer believed that the mention of Jesus' relatives and family in Mark 6:4 was a later addition, modifying the general statement of the proverb to fit the special situation here.[51] This is incorrect because all these terms, home town, relatives and family, are found in Judaic tradition on the anointing of Saul, from which a Palestinian Jewish Christian borrowed them to portray Jesus' rejection at Nazareth.

B. Saul.

The lineage of Israel's first king is related at the beginning of the story of Saul's anointing in 9:1. In 14:49 the names of his three sons, two daughters, wife, father and uncle are given. Strangely, although 10:1 speaks of Kish's concern for his son, after Saul prophesies directly outside his home town of Gibeah, and his neighbors ask what has come over him, he goes home (10:13)[52] and is queried by his uncle (vv 14-16). Kish, like Joseph, is now missing.

The LXX at 10:14-16 has ὁ οἰκεῖος αὐτοῦ, "his family member," lit. "of the house,"[53] for Saul's "uncle." Again, however, it is Josephus in his retelling of the Saul incident who shows that the terms "relatives" and "family/house" belonged to this episode in Palestinian Judaic tradition.

In 1 Sam 10:7 Samuel tells Saul that after he has prophesied, "do whatever your hand finds to do." This is interpreted in *Ant.* 6.57, after the people of Saul's home town are "astounded" and "marvel" at him, to mean: "go to greet your father and 'relatives' (συγγενεῖς)." Yet only one relative is visited when Saul enters the house (οἰκία). In contrast to the MT of 10:14-17, where Saul's uncle (Ner; 14:50-51) is mentioned, Josephus makes the person Saul visits his son Abner, his "relative" (συγγενής). Of all the family members (οἰκεῖοι), Saul felt most affection

---

[48]Str-B 2.374.

[49]Cf. already J. Wellhausen, *Das Evangelium Matthaei* (Berlin: Reimer, 1914²) 71.

[50]Cf. Mark 2:1; 3:19b, 21, 31-35; 9:33, as well as Matt 4:13 and John 2:12a. Joseph is presumed to be dead. Contrast, however, John 6:42.

[51]*Das Evangelium des Markus* (Meyer I 2; Göttingen: Vandenhoeck & Ruprecht, 1963¹⁶) 110.

[52]This is preferable to the MT, which has "to the high place." Cf. the apparatus of *Biblia Hebraica ad loc.*; Josephus, *Ant.* 6.58, "But when he entered the house..."; and P. McCarter, Jr., *I Samuel* 172.

[53]See LSJ 1202 on οἰκεῖος: II. of the same household, family or kin, related.

for him; he "loved him more affectionately than all those of his blood."[54] Even though he was his "relative" (συγγενής), however, Saul did not reveal to him the secret of his kingdom (6.58-59).

Here the terms "house" (οἰκία) and "family members" (οἰκεῖοι), as well as "relatives" (συγγενεῖς), are strongly emphasized directly after the home town people's astonishment at Saul. The Jewish Christian author of Mark 6:1-6a appropriated them from Judaic tradition on Saul's anointing and included them in the proverb he himself composed: "A prophet is not without honor except in his home town." He then logically listed beforehand the members of Jesus' house or family.

6. A Proverb of a Prophet Without Honor.

A. Mark.

Jesus' reply to the Nazarites' taking offense at him is to quote what is clearly meant to be a proverb: "A prophet is not without honor except in his home town, and among his relatives, and among his family" (6:4). This is also the only time in Mark that Jesus applies the term "prophet" (προφήτης) to himself.[55] In addition, the motif of "lack of honor" (ἄτιμος) occurs only here in Mark.[56] Again, these usages are dependent on the episode of Saul's being anointed king of Israel by Samuel.

B. Saul.

When Saul prophesies among the prophets in his home town of Gibeah, it results in the inhabitants' coining a proverb about him (מָשָׁל; targum מתלא; LXX παραβολή): "Is Saul also among the prophets (נְבִיא; LXX προφήτης)?"

While its exact meaning is not clear, the proverb definitely implies astonishment on the part of the user. If the form of Saul's prophecy was ritual dancing, with "convulsive and ecstatic frenzy," it could have been viewed as madness.[57] To this Mark 3:21 may be related, where at Jesus' (later) home in Capernaum his family goes out to seize him because people were saying: "he is beside himself (ἐξέστη)." It is significant that Josephus in *Ant.* 10.114 has Judean leaders and impious men ridicule

---

[54]Translation by H. St. J. Thackeray and R. Marcus in the LCL edition.
[55]Against G. Friedrich in the art. προφήτης in *TDNT* 6.841; see, however, n. 379. Cf. also Mark 8:28 and 14:65.
[56]See the parallel in Matt 13:57, also singular in the gospel. The verb ἀτιμάζω occurs in Mark 12:4.
[57]See G. Caird, "The First and Second Books of Samuel" in *IB* 2.932, referring to 1 Sam 19:18-24 (the second occurrence of the proverb is here); 2 Kgs 9:11; Jer 29:26 ("every madman who prophesies"). See also 1 Sam 18:10 for Saul's "raving" within his house.

Jeremiah's prophesying, "as though he were out of his mind" (ὡς ἐξεστηκότα τῶν φρενῶν). Jesus' ostensible "madness" may have been connected to his prophesying, incomprehensible to those who knew him well and did not expect it of him.[58]

The proverb concerning Saul's prophesying may also imply astonishment at how someone of the fine lineage of Saul[59] could become involved with such people as ecstatic prophets, perhaps of a much lower social class.[60]

For the above reasons it is understandable that Josephus spoke of "astonishment" at this point (see above), as did the Jewish Christian author of Mark 6:1-6a, basing his account on the Saul episode, involving a proverb.

The expression "honor," "lack of honor" in the proverb of Mark 6:4 also derives from the Saul episode. As noted above, the framework of the saying is found in a positive formulation in 1 Sam 9:6. There Saul's servant informs him regarding the prophet Samuel, whose home was in Ramah (7:17): "Behold, there is a man of God in this city, and he is a man that is 'held in honor' (נִכְבָּד; LXX ἔνδοξος)." That is, the prophet Samuel is held in honor in his home town of Ramah. It is significant that in rabbinic tradition, two of the five terms of praise attributed to Samuel are "prophet" (1 Sam 9:9) and "honored" (9:6).[61]

The opposite of being held in honor is true of Saul after his prophesying, according to Judaic tradition mirrored in Josephus. The Jewish historian relates that after Saul was chosen king, Samuel returned to his home town (*patris*) of Ramah. Then Saul departed for Gibeah, where he grew up. He was accompanied there by "many" (πολλοί) good people, who paid him the "honor" (τιμή) appropriate to a king. Nevertheless, "more" (πλείονες) malicious people held him in contempt and derided the others present (*Ant.* 6.67, based on 1 Sam 10:27). The LXX at 10:27 states that they "held him in dishonor" (ἀτιμάζω).

Josephus states that Saul's military victory over Nahash the Ammonite (1 Samuel 11) was an "illustrious" (λαμπρός) deed, spreading

---

[58]It is not due to demonic powers as implied from what follows in 3:22.

[59]1 Sam 9:1 says Saul's father was a man of wealth; in v 3 he has servants. On Saul's immaculate pedigree in Judaic sources, see *b. Yoma* 22b (Soncino English 103), and L. Ginzberg, *The Legends of the Jews* 4.66 and 68, with the relevant notes.

[60]See H. Stoebe, *Das erste Buch Samuelis* 211; F. Stolz, *Das erste und zweite Buch Samuel* (Züricher Bibelkommentare, AT 9; Zurich: Theologischer Verlag, 1981) 70 (the prophets have no possessions); and H. Hertzberg, *I & II Samuel* (OTL; Philadelphia: Westminster, 1964) 86: "'How does a reasonable man, well placed in civic life, come to be in this eccentric company?' Among people who, as a contemptuous aside puts it, 'have no father,' i.e., come from anywhere!"

[61]Cf. *Mishnat R. Eliezer* 8 in Enelow, *The Mishnah of Rabbi Eliezer* 151.

his praise among the Hebrews, including a "marvelous fame" (θαυμαστῆς... δόξης) for courage. Some who had earlier despised him now "honored" (ἐπὶ τὸ τιμᾶν) him as the "noblest" (ἄριστος) of all men. Saul returned in "glory" (λαμπρός) to his home (*Ant.* 6.80). This is based on 1 Sam 11:11, which is followed in vv 12-13 by a reference backwards to the worthless fellows of 10:27, who had doubted how Saul could "save" (ישׁע; LXX σῴζω) the Israelites.

Josephus here draws on Palestinian Judaic traditions concerning the episode of Saul's becoming king of Israel. They are very early, as indicated in the ἀτιμάζω of the Septuagint at 1 Kgdms 10:27. They provided the Jewish Christian author of Mark 6:1-6a with the term "many" (πολλοί) in v 2; the motif of the Nazarites' "taking offense" (σκανδαλίζω) at Jesus in v 3; and the term "without honor" (ἄτιμος) in v 4. The latter, mentioned in connection with the prophet Samuel's returning to his "home town" (*patris*) of Ramah, caused the Jewish Christian author to think of the nearby 1 Sam 9:6. This, in turn, provided him with the framework for the proverb of Mark 6:4.

7. Unbelief.

A. *Mark.*

With the exception of 9:24, the term ἀπιστία, "unbelief," occurs in the gospels only at Mark 6:6 and its parallel, Matt 13:58.[62] Jesus marvels at the Nazarites' lack of belief in him. This motif also derives from the narrative of Saul's being anointed by Samuel.

B. *Saul.*

Josephus relates, as noted above, that more people than those who were for Saul's being king "despise" him (*Ant.* 6.67, based on 1 Sam 10:27). In the MT they do not believe that Saul can "save" them. Only after his military victory over the enemy do they "honor" him (*Ant.* 6.80).

The motif of lack of faith also occurs in *Ant.* 6.59 on 1 Sam 10:14-16. Saul relates to his "relative" Abner, the "family member" he loved most, everything about his search for his father's asses. Yet he does not mention his receiving the "kingdom" (βασιλεία) because this might cause envy and "lack of belief," "distrust" (ἀπιστία). Josephus then expatiates on this motif extensively, arguing that when God bestows "brilliant distinctions" on someone, even "relatives" immediately "regard these eminences with malice and envy."[63]

---

[62]The adjective ἄπιστός, "unbelieving," occurs only at Mark 9:19 (parallels in Matt 17:17 and Luke 9:41), Luke 12:46, and John 20:27.
[63]Translation by Thackeray and Marcus in the LCL edition.

I suggest that this "lack of belief" or "distrust" on the part of two groups, those associated with Saul's going to his home town of Gibeah after having been made king, and his relatives and family members, was borrowed by the Jewish Christian author of Mark 6:1-6a to describe the lack of belief in Jesus on the part of the inhabitants of his own home town, Nazareth, who mention Jesus' family members.

8. Three Questions.

A. Mark.

In 6:2-3 the inhabitants of Jesus' home town, Nazareth, ask three different questions. 1) "From where (πόθεν) did this man get these things?" 2) "And what is the wisdom granted to this man?"[64] 3a) "Is this man not the carpenter, the son of Mary and brother of James and Joses and Judah and Simon, b) and are his sisters not here with us?" The latter question is composed of two halves, both having to do with Jesus' identification via his immediate family.

The structure of three different questions, followed by the prophet proverb, also derives from the narrative of Saul's becoming king.

B. Saul.

In 1 Sam 10:11-12 three questions are also asked by the inhabitants of Saul's home town, Gibeah, after he unexpectedly prophesies. Those who know him from "before" (lit., "from yesterday and the day before yesterday" = "hitherto, from aforetime, previously"[65]) say to one another: 1) "What has come over the son of Kish?" 2) "Is Saul also among the prophets?" A man from there (Gibeah) then asks: 3) "And who is their father?" This leads to the coining of the Saul proverb.

The similarity of three questions asked regarding Jesus and Saul is striking. The Jewish Christian author of Mark 6:1-6a is here certainly dependent on the structure of the Saul narrative. As noted above, Josephus in *Ant.* 6.57 paraphrases the first question, beginning with πόθεν, as in Mark 6:2. This is hardly accidental.

9. Father.

A. Mark.

The only explicit mention in Mark of Mary, Jesus' mother, is found in 6:3; Jesus is the carpenter, the son of Mary. Matthew in the parallel passage at 13:55 speaks in contrast of Jesus as the carpenter's "son,"

---

[64]As indicated below, 6:2c is a later addition.
[65]BDB 1026 on שִׁלְשׁוֹם.

whose mother is Mary. At Luke 4:22 Mary and Jesus' siblings are omitted completely, the Evangelist asking: "Is this not Joseph's son?"

In Mark, our earliest gospel, Jesus' father is nowhere mentioned. In the related passage of 3:21, 31-35, the Evangelist defines Jesus' "family" as his mother, brothers and sister(s). If Joseph had still been alive at the time of Jesus' public ministry, the Jewish Christians responsible for handing on 3:21, 31-35 and 6:3 would certainly have mentioned him.[66]

There is no subtle reference to the virgin birth in the expression "the son of Mary."[67] Rather, it has a pejorative connotation. This is confirmed by the fact that only an illegitimate son was normally named after his mother.[68] Another argument for the negative connotation is that Jesus is referred to only indirectly three times in Mark 6:2-3 (τούτῳ twice, οὗτος): "this man." Like the phrase ὁ υἱός σου οὗτος in Luke 15:30, where the brother of the prodigal son refuses to say "my brother" or to use his name, the Nazarites here refuse to employ Jesus' name.[69]

The reader of Mark's gospel knows as of 1:1 (the Son of God) and v 11 (at the baptism the words "You are My beloved Son, with whom I am well pleased") that Jesus' true father is not Joseph, but the heavenly Father, God. The Nazarites fail to perceive this, therefore Jesus can do no mighty work there. He marvels at their unbelief (in the Father's power in him).

---

[66]Cf. Acts 1:14. The mention of Joseph in Luke 4:22 seeks to remove the negative association of Mark 6:3. It is later than Mark and unhistorical, as is John 6:42. The formulation "Jesus, son of Joseph" in Luke 4:22 and John 1:45 does not mean that Joseph was still alive. To differentiate Jesus from many others of the same name, the patronym was added. In the English index of the LCL edition of Josephus, for example, there are twenty-one different Jesuses. The addition of a patronym was almost always the case with the rabbis, for example, R. Yoḥanan ben (son of) Zakkai.

[67]Against Gnilka, *Das Evangelium nach Markus (Mk 1-8, 26)* 232. Cf. his discussion of the textual variants on p. 231, where he correctly prefers "the carpenter [Bauhandwerker], the son of Mary" because it is the most offensive.

[68]Cf. Judg 11:1-2; 1 Sam 26:6 and 2 Sam 23:18; R. Yose, the son of the woman of Damascus; perhaps Abba Saul, the son of the woman of Batnit; and *b. Sanh.* 106a (Soncino English 725): "She [Mary] who was the descendant of princes and governors played the harlot with a carpenter" (the Munich marginal reading, not "carpenters"); *Pesiq. R.* 21/6 (English in W. Braude, *Pesikta Rabbati* 1.422 – "If the son of a whore should say to you, 'There are two different gods'...."); and a Jew cited in Origen, *Contra Celsum* 1.28 (Str-B 1.678). See also John 9:29 ("but as for this man, we do not know where he comes from").

[69]Cf. W. Grundmann, *Das Evangelium nach Markus* (THNT, II; Berlin: Evangelische Verlagsanstalt, 1977[7]) 156: "Die erste Frage [v 2] redet von Jesus verächtlich als 'von dem da'...."

B. Saul.

Saul is the son of Kish, who sends his son to find lost family donkeys. When they are found, the father is concerned about his son (1 Sam 10:2). After Saul prophesies, people from his home town of Gibeah ask what has come over the son of Kish (v 11). A man of the town also asks: "And who is their father?" (v 12).[70] For the latter the LXX, Syriac and Old Latin have "his father."[71] In Judaic tradition, this question is interpreted as being contemptuous.[72] Strangely, after becoming king of Israel Saul does not return home to his father, but to his uncle (Ner, vv 14-16).

This major concern with Saul's father, who at the climax of the narrative of Saul's being anointed king is strangely absent, like Joseph,[73] appears to lie behind the formulation of Mark 6:3. The main reason the Jewish Christian author of 6:1-6a does not mention Joseph is that he wants the hearer of his anecdote to ask: "Who is Jesus of Nazareth? Who is his real Father?" The earthly father of Jesus, Joseph, may now be dead, but his heavenly Father grants new life through the teaching and mighty works of His son, if people, including the Nazarites, are willing to believe in him.

Finally, the above pejorative sense of "this man" three times in Mark 6:2-3 probably derives from 1 Sam 10:27. Worthless fellows ask after Saul has become king: "How can 'this man' (זֶה) save us?" They therefore despise him and offer him no presents appropriate to a king. Other examples of this contemptuous usage of זֶה are 16:8-9; 21:16; and 25:21.[74] This negative connotation of Saul as "this man" corroborates the negative connotation of Jesus as "this man," not the son of his father, but of Mary.

---

[70]Stoebe, *Das erste Buch Samuelis* 211 cites three commentators who relate the popular etymology of "prophet" here. A נָבִיא is equivalent to אֵין אָבִי, "I have no father." If this view prevailed in first century C.E. Palestine, it may have influenced the fact that the father of Jesus the prophet is not mentioned in Mark 6:3.

[71]Cf. H. Smith, *The Books of Samuel* (ICC 9/10; Edinburgh: Clark, 1899) 71, and McCarter, *1 Samuel* 172.

[72]Cf. *t.B. Meṣ.* 3:25 (English in J. Neusner, *The Tosefta* 4.92; Hebrew in M. Zuckermandel and S. Liebermann, *Tosephta* 378) regarding a proselyte who comes to study the Torah. He is now dead to his previous life as an idolator and should not be contemptuously reminded of it.

[73]On Joseph's absence, see above.

[74]BDB 260, 1.a

10. A Carpenter and Wisdom.

A. Mark.

The Nazarites are astonished at the "wisdom" (σοφία) displayed by Jesus when he teaches in his home town synagogue (6:2).[75] Only here does the term occur in Mark. The next verse has them ask whether Jesus is not the "carpenter" (τέκτων),[76] whose family members they personally know (v 3). In the NT the latter expression is only found here and in the parallel, Matt 13:55. The First Evangelist, however, intentionally changes Jesus from being "the carpenter" to "the son of the carpenter."[77]

In Mark, there is an implied contrast between one who displays "wisdom" in the synagogue and an artisan or craftsman. As I will show below, this is also true in Judaic sources.

Again, the source of the term "carpenter" by the Jewish Christian author of 6:1-6a is the OT narrative of Saul's being anointed king of Israel by Samuel.

B. Saul.

As it now stands, the MT at 1 Sam 10:27 has some worthless fellows ask derogatively how "this man," Saul, can save the Israelites. They despise him, for which the LXX has "bring him no honor," "dishonor." The relevance of these expressions to Mark 6:1-6a was pointed out above. Saul's reaction to these people's negative behavior is to be "silent." The Hebrew is וַיְהִי כְּמַחֲרִישׁ, "But he was like one who is silent." This is the hiphil participle of חָרֵשׁ, "to be silent, dumb, speechless," in the sense of exhibiting silence.[78] Saul is represented as "magnanimously overlooking these contentious people, as is appropriate for a ruler."[79] The rabbis

---

[75]For the "wisdom" (MT חָכְמָה, LXX σοφία) to come upon the Messiah, cf. Isa 11:2. In 1 Cor 1:24 Christ is both the power and the wisdom of God. If the *dotheisa* of Mark 6:2 is the *passivum divinum,* it intensifies the question of "from where."

[76]On secondary literature regarding this Greek term, see Batey, "Is Not This the Carpenter" 257, n.2. He does not deal at all with the Hebrew and Aramaic terminology. See also the entry *tektōn* in BAGD 809.

[77]U. Luz in *Das Evangelium nach Matthäus* 2.385 proposes with some degree of probability that Matthew changes the Marcan phrase "because tradition nowhere else knows anything about Jesus' occupation; it has him travel through the country, teaching, as an itinerant preacher."

[78]BDB 361.

[79]Stolz, *Das erste und zweite Buch Samuel* 73.

interpret the Hebrew phrase as it is now in the MT and the targum,[80] and not as it is changed in the Septuagint.[81]

Yet the same root can also take the form חָרָשׁ, meaning "carpenter." In general it signifies an artisan or craftsman. The term becomes specific when associated with metal (metalworker, smith), stone (mason), or wood (עֵץ). The latter is then a "carpenter," as in 2 Sam 5:11 = 1 Chr 14:1; 2 Kgs 12:12; 22:6 = 2 Chr 34:11; Jer 10:3; Isa 40:20 and 44:13.[82] It has the same meaning in rabbinic Hebrew.[83] The Septuagint often has *tektōn* for *haraš* in the sense of carpenter,[84] and both Philo[85] and Josephus[86] also employ *tektōn* so.

In Judaic sources *haraš* can be taken figuratively to mean a "scholar."[87] If the Jewish Christian author of Mark 6:1-6a had either the Aramaic חרשא or the Hebrew *haraš* for Jesus as the carpenter of 6:3, and the figurative sense of a learned man already prevailed, there might be a double entendre involved. The Nazarites should then have known that Jesus as a "carpenter" (Torah scholar) had wisdom. Their astonishment would then have been unfounded, as they themselves unconsciously indicated by labeling him a "carpenter."

Yet it cannot be shown that the figurative sense of "scholar" for "carpenter" was in use in the early first century C.E. Another connotation of the term "carpenter," however, probably prevailed.

---

[80]Cf., for example, *b. Yoma* 22b (Soncino 103); Saul was overly humble here and should not have held his peace.

[81]The LXX begins 11:1 with: "And it happened after a month that...," corresponding to the Hebrew כְּמַחֲרִישׁ. Daleth and resh were easily confused.

[82]Ezra 3:7 and 2 Chr 24:12 may belong here; cf. BDB 360.

[83]Jastrow, *A Dictionary* 507. For "carpenter" in the Mishnah, cf. *'Arak.* 6:3; *Kelim* 14:3; 16:7; 21:3; *Ohol.* 13:3; and *B. Qam.* 9:3; 10:10. In his Hebrew translation of the NT, F. Delitzsch also has *haraš*. See his *Hebrew New Testament* 71 on Mark 6:3.

[84]Cf. 2 Kgdms 5:11; 4 Kgdms 12:11 (12); 1 Chr 14:1; 22:15; Isa 40:20; and 44:13.

[85]Cf. *Sob.* 35-36; see also *Leg. All.* 1.57.

[86]In *Ant.* 7.66 and 15.390 the carpenter is different from a builder, and in 7.340, 377 and 11.78 from a stonecutter, i.e., mason. Cf. also A. Schlatter, *Der Evangelist Matthäus* (Stuttgart: Calwer, 1929) 455.

[87]See the sources listed in Jastrow, *A Dictionary* 507, and J. Levy, *Neuhebräisches und chaldäisches Wörterbuch* 2.119. Interestingly, the *haraš* as a scholar causes others through his learning to be "like silenced persons," the same phrase as in 1 Sam 10:27. The term נגר, also modern Hebrew for "carpenter," is also used in a figurative sense as "scholar" (Jastrow, *A Dictionary* 876), yet it is not found in the MT in this sense and only later so in Judaic sources. D. Flusser in *Jesus in Selbstzeugnissen und Bilddokumenten* (Hamburg: Rowohlt, 1968) 22 maintains on the basis of the latter terminology that "Tischler" were especially learned at the time of Jesus, who probably himself was one and the son of one. He is followed by R. Pesch, *Das Markusevangelium* (HTKNT 2/A; Freiburg: Herder, 1984⁴) 322. The opposite is true. See below.

Many of the rabbis who were not by heritage well-off supported themselves by practicing a trade.[88] There is even an example of a scholar who was a carpenter, and of one who was the son of a carpenter.[89] Yet a sage normally pursued this only part-time, working enough to support both his family and his studies.[90] The average carpenter, however, had to work full-time, with little leisure to pursue wisdom or Torah.

This state of affairs already prevailed in Palestine in the first quarter of the second century B.C.E. The author of Sirach or Ecclesiasticus wrote in Hebrew in Jerusalem.[91] In 38:24–39:11 he relates how he who devotes himself to the study of the Torah will acquire "wisdom" (sophia, 39:10). Yet the "wisdom" of the scribe depends on the opportunity of leisure; too much business impedes learning (38:24). Along with other craftsmen,[92] for example, the "carpenter" (tektōn) labors night and day (38:27).[93] Wise in the sense of "skillful" in his own work (38:31),[94] a carpenter is not found among those employing parables (38:33 – παραβολή), whose subtleties he cannot penetrate (39:2-3). His pre-

---

[88]See Schürer, The history, 2.328-29, and the secondary literature cited on p. 328, n.24.

[89]Cf. R. Abin as a נגרא in b. Šabb. 23b (Soncino 102). He was probably a fourth generation Palestinian Amora. See Strack and Stemberger, Introduction 103. See also Matya ben (the son of) Ḥarash, a second generation Tanna, if this is the correct vocalization (Introduction 83; Levy, Wörterbuch 2.119).

[90]For remuneration paid to a sage for his teaching, but not his judicial activities, cf. Schürer, The history 2.328-29.

[91]Cf. G. Nickelsburg, Jewish Literature 55-69.

[92]One of these is the "plowman" (38:25-26). The same Hebrew root as found in "carpenter" can be used for the plower (BDB 360-61; Jastrow, A Dictionary 507). For Saul as a plowman, cf. 1 Sam 11:5. In Justin Martyr's "Dialogue with Trypho the Jew" 88, Jesus is described as a carpenter who made (wooden) plows and yokes. In Hebrew, "plow" also is of the same root as "carpenter." See BDB 361 and Jastrow, A Dictionary 764 on מַחֲרֵישָׁה.

[93]Unfortunately the extant Hebrew of this verse is only fragmentary. Cf. F. Vattioni, Ecclesiastico 203. Both Sirach concordances, however, posit ḥaraš here on the basis of the first letter. See The Book of Ben Sira. Text, Concordance and an Analysis of the Vocabulary (Jerusalem: The Academy of the Hebrew Language and the Shrine of the Book, 1973) 149, and D. Barthélemy and O. Rickenbauer, Konkordanz zum hebräischen Sirach (Göttingen: Vandenhoeck & Ruprecht, 1973) 139.

[94]Cf. the expression חָרָשׁ חָכָם in Isa 40:20.

occupation with his trade excludes his acquiring wisdom.[95] This is reserved to those who can afford to take the time to pursue it.[96]

This Palestinian attitude most probably still prevailed at the beginning of the first century C.E. It is the best explanation for the Nazarites' astonishment at the teaching of their earlier home town neighbor, Jesus. They ask, understandably, about the "wisdom" (*sophia* – Mark 6:2) given to a carpenter, who ordinarily had no time whatsoever to study and acquire wisdom. This attitude is reflected in John 7:14-15, where Jesus' fellow Jews marvel at his teaching in the Jerusalem Temple precincts, asking: "How is it that this man has learning, when he has never studied?"

* * *

Excursus on the Messiah as the Eschatological Carpenter, and the (Re-)Building of the Temple

As stated above, it cannot be shown that a *ḥaraš*, carpenter, was used in a figurative sense to mean a scholar, a sage, in the first half of the first century C.E. Yet it seems probable that already at this time, i.e., before the destruction of the Second Temple by the Romans in 70 C.E., the belief existed that the Messiah would be active as a craftsman/artisan/carpenter (*ḥaraš*) in the (re-)building of the Jerusalem Temple.[97]

The motif of the Messiah's (re-)building the Jerusalem Temple is extremely old. Its origin may go back to the Persian Cyrus, whom Second Isaiah, in the middle of the sixth century B.C.E.,[98] calls the Lord's Anointed/Messiah in 45:1. It is he who, after the destruction of the Solomonic Temple by the Babylonian Nebuchadnezzar, shall (re-)build the Lord's city (v 13), which in 44:28 means both Jerusalem and the Temple. Ezra 1:2 states that the Lord had charged Cyrus to (re-)build Him a house at Jerusalem (= 2 Chr 36:23). He therefore encourages the Jews to return home from their exile and to "(re-)build the house of the Lord" (v 3).

---

[95]If not very busy with their work, craftsmen in Babylonia were normally expected to rise (out of respect) before a scholar. See *b. Ḥul.* 54b (Soncino 297). The implication is that they were usually too busy to do so.

[96]This attitude appears to prevail in Philo also. See *Leg. All.* 1.57, where the Alexandrian employs τεκτονικός. D. Lührmann in *Das Markusevangelium* 107 also calls attention to Sirach 38-39, as E. Lohmeyer had done previously in *Das Evangelium des Markus* 110.

[97]This "building" or "rebuilding" presupposes the "tearing down" of the Temple, as Herod the Great did without destroying it (Josephus, *Ant.* 15.389-90, with "carpenters" as opposed to masons), or its actual destruction. For these terms in Hebrew, cf. Str-B 1.1005.

[98]Cf. G. Fohrer, *Das Buch Jesaja* (Zurich and Stuttgart: Zwingli, 1964) 3.2-3.

The main returnee responsible for the rebuilding of the Temple was Zerubbabel (Ezra 2:1). He rebuilt the altar (3:2) and offered there. Since the foundation had not yet been laid, however, he paid masons and "carpenters" *(ḥaraš)* money and procured wood from Lebanon (3:7). Then, under his leadership, they rebuilt the Solomonic Temple (3:10; 4:3; 5:1; Zech 4:9). Since in Judaic tradition the Messiah is a descendant of Zerubbabel,[99] it was understandable that certain rabbinic circles applied the task of (re-)building the final Temple to him.

2 Sam 7:13-15 encouraged them to do so. It states that David's offspring shall build a house for His name; the Lord will be his father, and he shall be His son. The Lord will chasten him with the rod and stripes of men, but His steadfast love will not depart from him, as He took it from Saul. A parallel is found in 1 Chr 17:12-13. The inhabitants of Qumran interpreted this 2 Samuel 7 passage messianically in 4Q Florilegium,[100] showing that Palestinian non-Christian Jews also saw the Messiah as the builder of God's house before the destruction of the Jerusalem Temple in 70 C.E. Targ. Jon. Isa 53:5 (the MT has "with his stripes we are healed") mentions the Messiah, who will build the sanctuary that was polluted and given up because of Israel's transgressions and iniquities.[101] It appears to be dependent on the "stripes" of 2 Sam 7:14.[102]

The prophet Zechariah encouraged Zerubbabel to finish rebuilding the house of God in Jerusalem (Ezra 5:2; 6:14). It is thus also understandable that his words were later applied to the Messiah's (re-) building the final Temple. Targum Jonathan on 6:12-13 reads, for example: "Behold, the man whose name is Anointed will be revealed, and he shall be raised up, and shall build the temple of the Lord. He

---

[99]Cf. 1 Chr 3:19 and 24, where "Anani," he who comes with the "clouds," is interpreted as the messianic "cloud" king of Dan. 7:13 in the sources cited by Str-B 1.67, "q." See also "o" on p. 66. For the Messiah as the "great mountain" before Zerubbabel in Zech 4:7, see the sources in Str-B 1.483. The targum on this verse has the Messiah as the "top stone" (English in K. Cathcart and R. Gordon, *The Targum of the Minor Prophets* 194). *Gen. Rab.* Vayechi, New Version, 97 on Gen 49:8 (Soncino 2.901) has Solomon as the builder of the first Temple, Zerubbabel of the second, and the royal Messiah as (re-)building the (final) Temple. In Matt 1:12-13 and Luke 3:27 the Messiah Jesus is descended from Zerubbabel.

[100]Cf. the analysis of this text in D. Juel, *Messiah and Temple. The Trial of Jesus in the Gospel of Mark* (SBLDS 31; Missoula: Scholars, 1977) 110-111, 180. Juel is not aware of Philo's reference to Zech 6:12 (190), which I cite below.

[101]For the Aramaic and an English translation, see J. Stenning, *The Targum of Isaiah* 180-81. Verse 10 has the Messiah; cf. 52:13.

[102]Against Cathcart and Gordon, *The Targum of the Minor Prophets* 198, n. 13, who in reference to an article by P. Seidelin see it as dependent on Zech 6:12.

shall build the temple of the Lord...."[103] Here the Anointed One/Messiah is the "branch" of v 12, a frequent interpretation.[104] Elsewhere v 12 is interpreted messianically by the rabbis.[105] One important example is *Lam. Rab.* 1:16 § 51 on the "comforter," asking what the name of the King Messiah is. R. Joshua b. Levi, a first generation Palestinian Amora,[106] says it is "branch," as in Zech 6:12. Then the story of the Messiah's birth in Bethlehem, including "swaddling cloths" as in Luke 2:7 and 12, is related. At his coming the Temple was destroyed, and at his coming (again) it will be rebuilt. Here the Messiah is clearly associated with the rebuilding of the Temple.[107] The parallel tradition in *y. Ber.* 2:4, 5a relates this incident in regard to the fourteenth benediction of the "Eighteen Prayer," considered here to be the activity of the future "Son of David": "Who rebuilds Jerusalem."[108]

That Zech 6:12, including the Branch's building the Temple of the Lord, was interpreted messianically in pre-Christian Judaism is shown by Philo in *Conf.* 62-63. The Alexandrian, who elsewhere has almost no eschatological references, here repeats an oracle he has heard from "the lips of one of the disciples of Moses," i.e., a Sage. The man whose name is "rising" ('Ανατολή in the Septuagint for the branch of Zech 6:12)[109] has a most strange title. This being is the incorporeal one who does not differ at all from the divine image. He is the oldest son whom the Father of all "raised up" (ἀνέτειλε). Elsewhere God calls him His "firstborn," who followed the ways of his Father, shaping the different kinds.[110]

Here the Messiah's role at the creation of the world is clearly intended. More importantly, however, this pre-Christian passage shows that the Messiah is the firstborn son of God, who is his Father. The latter "raises" him, as God "raised" Jesus His son on Easter Sunday. The

---

[103] Aramaic in Sperber, *The Bible in Aramaic* 3.485; English in Cathcart and Gordon, *The Targum of the Minor Prophets* 198.

[104] See the sources cited by Cathcart and Gordon, *The Targum of the Minor Prophets* 192, n. 21, on Zech 3:8.

[105] See *Num. Rab.* Korach 18/21 on Numbers 16 (Soncino 6.734); *Pirq. R. El.* 48 (English in G. Friedlander, *Pirke de Rabbi Eliezer* 384); *Midr. Prov.* 19:21 (English in B. Visotzky, *The Midrash on Proverbs* 90; German in A. Wünsche, *Bibliotheca Rabbinica* 33.55); and *Tanḥuma* Korach 12 (Eshkol 2.703). Other rabbinic and pseudepigraphical references to the Messiah's building the Temple are cited in Str-B 1.1003-1005.

[106] Strack and Stemberger, *Introduction* 92-93.

[107] English in Soncino 7.136-37.

[108] English by T. Zahavy in *The Talmud of the Land of Israel*, ed. J. Neusner (Chicago: University of Chicago, 1989) 1.87-89.

[109] Cf. Luke 1:78; Str-B 2.113; and BAGD 62 on *anatolē*.

[110] Cf. the English by F. Colson and G. Whitaker in the LCL edition of Philo's works.

continuation of v 12 regarding the Branch's building the Temple must have been applied to the same eschatological figure, in rabbinic writings the Messiah. Cross-fertilization between Alexandria and Palestine, especially Jerusalem, took place regularly. There was even a synagogue of the Alexandrians in Jerusalem.[111] It seems probable that the "oracle" regarding Zech 6:12, which Philo had already received from an Alexandrian sage, was also known in Palestine. The same type of exchange in fact also took place between Palestine and Babylonia, much further distant.

The above discussion prepares for the rabbinic interpretation of Zech 2:3 (Eng. 1:20). During his first night vision, Zechariah is comforted by the Lord about the seventy years of the Babylonian exile by the Lord's telling him: "My house shall be built in it [Jerusalem]" (1:16). In his second vision the prophet is first shown four horns, which an angel interprets to him as those which have scattered Judah, Israel and Jerusalem (2:1-2; Eng. 1:18-19). Then the Lord shows him four "smiths" (*haraš*) in 2:3 (Eng. 1:20), who come to terrify and cast down the horns of the nations who lifted up their horns against the land of Judah to scatter it (2:4; Eng. 1:21).

The rabbis interpreted these four "artisans/craftsmen" (with wood, "carpenters") as the Messiah, the son of David, also labeled here the royal Messiah and the Great Redeemer; the Messiah the son of Joseph, also called the priest anointed for war; Elijah; and the righteous priest, also termed Melchizedek.[112] I shall now describe the "building" activity of each, culminating in the Davidic Messiah as an eschatological *haraš*, who rebuilds the Temple.

A.

Judaic tradition makes *Shem*, the first son of Noah (Gen 5:32), equal to *the priest Melchizedek* of Gen 14:18.[113] When God tells Noah to make himself an ark out of gopher wood in Gen 6:14, it is assumed that his sons Shem, Ham and Japheth help him in the carpenter work of building it. This is how *Gen. Rab.* Lech Lecha 44/7 on Gen 15:1, after equating

---

[111]See Acts 6:9 and Str-B 2.663-64 on it.

[112]See *b. Sukk.* 52b (Soncino 251); *Num. Rab.* Naso 14/1 on Num 7:48 (Soncino 6.558); *Cant. Rab.* 2:13 § 4 (Soncino 9.125); *Pesiq. Rav Kah.* 5/9 on Cant 2:12 (English in W. Braude and I. Kapstein, *Pesikta de-Rab Kahana* 109); *Pesiq. R.* 15/14-15 on Cant 2:12 (Braude 326); and *Eliyyahu Rabba* 18, p. 96 (English in W. Braude and I. Kapstein, *Tanna debe Eliyyahu* 254).

[113]See the tradition from the school of R. Ishmael in *Lev. Rab.* Kedoshim 25/6 (Soncino 4.319), with a parallel in *b. Ned.* 32b (Soncino 98-99); *Gen. Rab.* Vayera 66/10 on Gen 22:14 (Soncino 1.500); *Num. Rab.* Bemidbar 4/8 on Num 3:45 (Soncino 5.102); and *Midr. Ps.* 76/3 on Ps 76:3 (Braude 2.15).

Shem and Melchizedek, interprets Isa 41:7, "'So the carpenter [*ḥaraš*, RSV 'craftsman'] encouraged': this refers to Shem, who made the Ark."[114]

B.

Elijah is considered a craftsman/carpenter because at the contest with the prophets of Baal on Mt. Carmel, he first "repairs" the altar of the Lord which had been thrown down (1 Kgs 18:30). Then he takes twelve stones corresponding to the number of the tribes of Israel (v 31) and with them "builds" an altar in the name of the Lord (v 32). He then puts the wood in order, cuts the bull offering into pieces, and lays it on the wood (v 33).

Pesiqta Rabbati 4/1-3 deals extensively with this narrative, which is a "haftara" or reading from the prophets.[115] It states that for the sake of the twelve tribes, even the Temple is to be rebuilt.[116] Elijah, the last prophet, is to redeem Israel in the time to come, as Mal 3:23 is interpreted. This redemption from the fourth exile, Edom (Rome), will be an eternal deliverance.[117] Finally, there is an extensive discussion regarding the rebuilding of the House (the Jerusalem Temple) as due to the merit of the twelve tribes. Elijah knew of this and therefore built an altar of twelve stones, representing the twelve tribes of Israel.[118]

Here Elijah's building activity as a carpenter/craftsman (wood and stones) is closely linked to the "re-building" of the Jerusalem Temple. The latter, however, is the direct task of the other two carpenters/craftsmen of Zech 2:3.[119]

The greatest Jewish commentator on Scripture, Rashi (d. 1105 C.E.),[120] noted in regard to the four craftsmen of Zech 2:3 in *b. Sukk.* 52b that they are Shem and Elijah, as above. He then adds: "The two messiahs are called craftsmen because they will build the Temple."[121]

---

[114]Soncino 1.365.

[115]Cf. 4/1 in Braude 1.84.

[116]Also 4/1 (Braude 1.83).

[117]Cf. 4/2 (Braude 1.84-85).

[118]Cf. 4/3 (Braude 1.88-89). In his retelling of the Mt. Carmel incident, Josephus in *Ant.* 8.334 has Obadiah tell Elijah of his zeal for the latter's "fellow craftsmen" (ὁμοτέχνος; LSJ 1228). Elijah's fellow prophets are probably meant, yet it is interesting that Elijah is labeled a "craftsman" here. See Mark 8:28 for Jesus' being considered by some to be Elijah, as well as 9:4-5.

[119]It is certainly not accidental that the narrative of Elijah's building the altar on Mt. Carmel is also related in *Numbers Rabbah* in the same section where the interpretation of Zech 2:3 as four craftsmen occurs (14/1 on Num 7:48 in Soncino 6.563).

[120]Strack and Stemberger, *Introduction* 238.

[121]Translation of Rashi's commentary by Braude and Kapstein in *Tanna debe Eliyyahu* 254, n. 52.

C.

The Priest Anointed for War. The Essene Qumranites, who produced
the pre-Christian Jewish messianic interpretation of 2 Samuel 7 in 4Q
Florilegium, also believed in a second Messiah, the priestly Messiah of
Aaron. H. Ringgren asks, quite correctly, "whether the chief priest in the
War Scroll who plays an important role as leader in the War (ii.1; xv.4;
xvi.13; xviii.5; xix.11) might not also be the priestly messiah."[122] If so, the
rabbis' priest anointed for war, also called the Messiah ben Joseph, might
be connected in their interpretation of Zech 2:3 to the dual messianism of
Qumran, a branch of Judaism intensely interested in restoring the
Temple in Jerusalem.[123]

D.

Finally, the OT passages discussed extensively above, primarily 2
Sam 7:13 and Zech 6:12-13,[124] are interpreted in Judaic tradition of the
Davidic Messiah's "rebuilding" the Temple.

* * *

The above tradition of the Davidic Messiah as one of the four
craftsmen/carpenters of Zech 2:3 is now related by rabbis from the
beginning of the third century C.E.[125] Yet the fact that it is found in so
many different sources and variants shows that it was important in a
number of different Palestinian circles. I suggest that at least the
identification of the Davidic Messiah as a craftsman/carpenter from
Zech 2:3 already prevailed when a Palestinian Jewish Christian
composed Mark 6:1-6a. This would mean that the Nazarites'
identification of Jesus as "the carpenter" *(tektōn, haraš)* in v 3 is a fine
example of the author's irony. The inhabitants of Jesus' home town are
astonished at his wisdom and ask how it can derive from "the carpenter"
they know so well from before. They take offense at him and refuse to
recognize him as the Davidic Messiah, "the carpenter." Therefore Jesus
can only marvel at their unbelief. The original hearers of this narrative
would have understood the double meaning of "carpenter" in Aramaic.

---

[122]See his *The Faith of Qumran. Theology of the Dead Sea Scrolls* (Philadelphia:
Fortress, 1963) 179, in a discussion of the messiahs of Aaron and Israel (176-182).
[123]Cf. for example the Temple Role in J. Maier, *Die Tempelrolle vom Toten Meer.*
See also Deut 20:2 and the Anointed for Battle in *m. Soṭa* 8:1 (English in H. Danby,
The Mishnah 301-302). *Pesiq. R.* 8/4, in an interpretation of Zech 4:3 (Braude
1.152), has both the priest anointed in a time of war, and the king anointed to rule
over Israel.
[124]See also Zech 4:3 and 14 for two anointed ones.
[125]They are R. Isaac (II) the Smith, a third generation Palestinian Amora (Strack
and Stemberger, *Introduction* 98) in the *Cant. Rab., Pesiq. R.,* and *Pesiq. Rav Kah.*
passages, and R. Simeon the Pious, ca. 210 C.E. (Str-B 5/6.133) in *b. Sukk.* 52b.

It was unfortunately lost when the episode was translated into Greek and later incorporated by Mark into his gospel.[126]

11. Mighty Works Through One's Hands.

A. *Mark.*

In 6:2 the Nazarites are astonished at Jesus' teaching in their synagogue and ask not only where he gets these things, but also: And what (from where) is the wisdom given this man "so that even mighty works (δυνάμεις)[127] are performed through his hands?"[128] The latter phrase, "through his hands," is a Semitism. For διὰ τῶν χειρῶν normal Greek would simply have διά.[129] Verse 5 states that Jesus could not "do" (ποιέω) a single "mighty work" *(dynamis)* there (in Nazareth). The latter lack of power on the part of the Son of God was so shocking to a later, post-Marcan redactor or copyist, that he mollified it by adding: "except that he laid his hands upon a few sick people and healed them."[130] The term for "sick people," ἄρρωστος, is found in Mark only here and in v 13,[131] where the disciples sent out by Jesus anoint with oil many that are "sick" and heal them. From there the redactor or copyist appropriated the term and transferred it back to the nearby v 5.

The remark about the "mighty works" done by Jesus in 6:2 seriously disrupts the context. First, the real contrast is between the great wisdom just displayed by Jesus while teaching in the Nazarite synagogue, and his being the (simple, lowly) carpenter the inhabitants know so well from

---

[126]It should also be noted that Jesus, the messianic *ḥaraš*, healed the "deaf and dumb" (Mark 7:37; 9:25). The latter is also expressed by *ḥērēš*, so a word play occurs. Cf. BDB 361; Jastrow, *A Dictionary* 507; and Levy, *Wörterbuch* 2.118, who notes *m.* Ter. 1:2 (Danby 52): "The *ḥērēsh* of which the Sages have spoken is always one that is both deaf and dumb."

[127]The expression *dynamis* in the sense of "mighty work" is found in Mark elsewhere in 9:39, and possibly in 6:14. The NRSV now has "deed(-s) of power" in 6:2 and 5. According to Isa 11:2 (cf. n. 75 on "wisdom"), the spirit of "might" (MT גבורה, LXX ἰσχύς) is to rest upon the Messiah.

[128]Cf. the KJV: "that even such mighty works are wrought by his hands." The RSV transforms the *hina* clause into a direct question. "What mighty works are wrought by his hands?" Variants are found in the apparatus of *The Greek New Testament*, ed. K. Aland, et al. 141, yet *hina* with the subjunctive remains the best reading.

[129]Cf. BDF § 217 (p. 117), citing this verse. The Hebrew would be בְּיַד. J. Wettstein had already called this a "Hebraism" in 1752. See his *Novum Testamentum Graecum* 1.576.

[130]Cf. Grässer, *Jesus in Nazareth* 26, and most of the commentators. I doubt that Mark himself made the addition. He also left 13:32 standing, without weakening it.

[131]In the NT elsewhere only in Matt. 14:14 and 1 Cor. 11:30.

before (v 3). Secondly, Jesus has not just performed mighty works in Nazareth,[132] so that this remark must refer to an earlier period. In the present context the raising of Jairus' daughter from the dead in Capernaum (5:22-24, 35-43), and the healing of the woman with a hemorrhage (5:25-34; in v 30 power – *dynamis* – goes forth from Jesus and heals her), are the most immediate examples of Jesus' "mighty works." The Jewish Christian author of 6:1-6a has rather clumsily inserted the last clause of v 2, inspired by his own mentioning of no "mighty work" in v 5a.

I propose that both the motif of "mighty works" and the Semitic phrase "doing 'by the hands of'" are based on the Jewish Christian author's interpretation of 1 Samuel 10.

B. Saul.

In 1 Sam 10:1 the original Hebrew most probably had what is now inserted into the RSV from the Septuagint. Samuel informs Saul, after anointing him prince, of a "sign" (σημεῖον) to this effect. It is spelled out in vv 2-6, including the spirit of the Lord coming mightily (lit. "leaping, rushing") upon Saul and his prophesying in his home town of Gibeah (v 6). Verse 7 continues: "Now when these 'signs' (אֹתוֹת; LXX σημεῖα) meet you, do (עֲשֵׂה; LXX ποίει) what your hand (יָדְךָ; LXX ἡ χείρ σου) will find, for God is with you." Verse 10 then relates that all these "signs" (אֹתוֹת; LXX σημεῖα) come to pass that day. The spirit of God comes mightily upon Saul, he prophesies, and the people ask what has come over the son of Kish.   This leads to the proverb, "Is Saul also among the prophets?" (vv 11-12).

In his commentary on 1 Samuel, P. McCarter, Jr. notes that the "signs" of vv 7 and 9 mean "wondrous things," "as in the hendiadytic combination *'ôtôt ûmôpetîm*, 'signs and wonders' = 'wondrous signs'...."[133] The same phrase is found in Mark 13:22 – σημεῖα καὶ τέρατα. In the Saul narrative, one of the signs is that the spirit of God will come mightily upon him. Here it is meant of his prophesying, but usually it means his valiance in war. The result of 1 Sam 11:6, for example, is the great victory of vv 11-12. McCarter speaks here of "the

---

[132]It was probably known to the author of Mark 6:1-6a that Jesus had done no "mighty works" in his home town Nazareth, for whatever reason. A "Q" tradition notes that most of them were performed in three towns on or near the north shore of Lake Tiberias: Chorazin, Bethsaida and Capernaum (Matt 11:20-24; Luke 10:13-15). There they had no positive effect, however, in the opinion of Jesus.

[133]Cf. his *I Samuel* 183. BDB 68 on מוֹפֵת 1, has: "'wonder,' as special display of God's power." See its frequent association with "signs" there.

invigorating power of God" involving "an explosive surge of strength."[134]

I suggest that the Jewish Christian author of Mark 6:1-6a employed the term "wonder" (מוֹפְתָא or מוֹפֵת)[135] of Jesus' "mighty works" in vv 2 and 6 because it was almost automatically associated with the "signs" found in 1 Sam 10:1, 7 and 9.

When Josephus retells the Saul narrative, he notes in *Ant.* 6.57 on 1 Sam 10:7, after relating the astonishment, marveling, and the question of *pothen*: "And when these *signs* are come unto thee, know thou that God is with thee; and go and salute thy father and thy kinsfolk."[136] The first phrase in Greek is ὅταν δέ σοι ταῦτα γένηται τὰ σημεῖα. It does not follow the LXX at this point, which has ὅταν ἥξει, and the verb γίνομαι is the same as in Mark 6:2 – ἵνα καὶ δυνάμεις διὰ τῶν χειρῶν αὐτοῦ γίνωνται.

Josephus' phrase "and go and salute thy father and thy kinsfolk" is a haggadic interpretation of "do what your hand will find" in 1 Sam 10:7, right after "Now when these signs meet you." I suggest that the Jewish Christian author of Mark 6:1-6a also interpreted the same difficult phrase in a different direction.[137] He moulded the terms "do" and "hand" into the phrase "so that even mighty works are *performed* through his *hands*" in v 2. As in Josephus, *ginomai* is employed in the present Greek clause for *'śh*, not the Septuagint's *poieō*. Finally, "through his hands" is Semitic, as indicated above.

For these reasons I consider it probable that the terms "mighty works" and "through his hands" in Mark 6:2 and 5 also derive from the Saul narrative.

12. Rejection.

A. Mark.

Although the term "rejection" occurs nowhere in 6:1-6a, all editions of the bible with pericope headings label this narrative Jesus' rejection at Nazareth. This is certainly correct, for the unit deals with the refusal of the inhabitants of Jesus' home town to acknowledge him as being someone very special. In the Gospel of Mark the demons call him the

---

[134]*Ibid.*, 182.

[135]Jastrow, *A Dictionary* 746 as "miracle." A passage from *Sifre* cited by him distinguishes between heavenly "signs" and earthly "miracles."

[136]Translation by Thackeray and Marcus in the LCL edition.

[137]The targum, for example, has: "prepare for yourself the instruments of kingship, for the Memra of the Lord is at your aid" (Harrington and Saldarini, *Targum Jonathan of the Former Prophets* 119, with n. 14). It, too, felt forced to interpret the difficult Hebrew.

Holy One of God (1:24), the Son of God (2:12), Son of the Most High God (5:7). The reader also knows from the first words of the Gospel that Jesus is (the) "Christ, the Son of God" (1:1). Yet those in Jesus' home town, because they have no faith in him (6:1), cannot accept his special relationship to God.[138] Because of their lack of faith, in contrast to others',[139] he cannot do a single mighty work, demonstrating the power of God as active through him. The Nazarites intentionally refuse to ask who his father is because that would necessitate a confrontation with the question of his true Father.

The Jewish Christian author of 6:1-6a, composing his narrative before the Gospel of Mark, knew of the rejection of Jesus by the leaders of the Jewish people in Jerusalem at the end of Jesus' life.[140] Tradition informed him that the chief priests and scribes mocked Jesus on the Cross as "the Christ, the King of Israel" (15:31-32). Those crucified with him also reviled him (v 32). Only a Gentile, the Roman centurion at Jesus' Cross, acknowledged him as "the Son of God" (v 39).

This final rejection of Jesus, leading to his crucifixion, was projected backwards by the early church into the time of his public ministry. In the earliest Jewish Christian communities, Jesus was described in Jerusalem as the stone which the builders "rejected" (ἀποδοκιμάζω). Yet it became the head of the corner (Ps 118:22 in Mark 12:10).[141] After Peter's confession near Caesarea Philippi of Jesus as the Anointed One/Messiah,

---

[138]Cf. John 1:11 ("He came to his own home, and his own people received him not"), which is contrasted to those who "believe in his name" in v 12.

[139]Cf. Mark 1:40; 2:5; 5:23, 28, 34, 36 and other passages where the fact that people bring the sick to Jesus to be healed, implies their belief in his ability to do so.

[140]Jesus was sentenced to death by a Roman, Pontius Pilate, because he was considered by him to be a political insurgent ("The King of the Jews" – 15:26). That Pilate received aid in this matter from a very small number of the self-serving Jerusalem priesthood and aristocracy is acknowledged by most Jewish scholars today. Cf., for example, P. Winter, *On the Trial of Jesus* (Berlin: de Gruyter, 1974²) 192.

[141]This verse is interpreted of Samuel's anointing David king of Israel after God "rejects" Saul in 1 Sam 16:1, as well as Jesse's seven other sons (vv 6-10), in *b. Pesaḥ.* 119a (Soncino 615) in the name of R. Jonathan (ben Eleazar), a first generation Palestinian Amora (Strack and Stemberger, *Introduction* 92). See also *Exod. Rab.* Tetzaveh 37/1 on Exod 28:1 (Soncino 3.442) with the "cornerstone" of Zech 10:4, as well as Targ. Ps 118:22 (translated in Str-B 1.876, who also notes the messianic interpretation of this psalm verse by Rashi on Mic 5:1). Psalm 118 concludes the Hallel (113-118), spoken at Passover, the pilgrimage festival of Israel's redemption, as in Mark 14:26 (part of the Jewish day on which Jesus was "rejected" by the leaders of his people). Already at a very early time Ps 118:21-29 were repeated. See *b. Pesaḥ.* 119b (Soncino 615 and n. 13), as well as *b. Sukk.* 38a (Soncino 172 and n. 2). Ps 118:26 is employed to describe Jesus' entry into Jerusalem in Mark 11:9, on "Palm Sunday."

Jesus teaches the disciples the necessity of his suffering and being "rejected" *(apodokimazō)* by the elders, chief priests and scribes, and being killed (8:29, 31). This first passion prediction is now followed in Mark by two others (9:31 and 10:33-34).

Jesus' rejection by the people of his own country was traced back even further by the earliest Christians. Although it was known that after Jesus' Resurrection appearances his brothers became missionaries, propagating belief in him,[142] earlier stories of his own family members' wanting to seize him because he was "beside himself" were nevertheless preserved (3:21, 31-35). During the time of his public ministry they did not believe in him yet as the Anointed One/Messiah, as the Son of God.[143]

The Jewish Christian author of Mark 6:1-6a filled what he considered to be a gap between Jesus' final rejection in Jerusalem by the leaders of the nation, and Jesus' first rejection by his immediate family. He did so by composing the narrative of Jesus' also being rejected by the inhabitants of his home town, Nazareth, in their synagogue.[144] By including mention of Jesus' family members, it connects with the earlier rejection. By raising the motif of rejection to a higher level, it prepares for Jesus' final rejection by the leaders of the entire nation.[145] To this extent it is typical of Judaic haggadah, which tends to fill in what was later considered to be a gap in a narrative. As I have indicated elsewhere, another early Jewish Christian knew of John the Baptist's being executed by Herod Antipas. With great literary skill he created what is now the extensive narrative of John's beheading in Mark 6:17-29.[146] The Jewish Christian author of 6:1-6a did basically the same thing.

He may have known from his own community that Jesus, as an historical fact, was not accepted by the inhabitants of his own home town. Or, more probably, like Mark later he knew that members of Jesus' family who had moved to Capernaum at this point considered him "out of his mind." This he developed into a new narrative of Jesus' rejection in Nazareth, linking the rejection motif to earlier times, and preparing for Jesus' final rejection. To do so, just as Pseudo-Philo and Josephus retold the story of Saul's anointing in a haggadic manner in the

---

[142]Cf. 1 Cor 9:5 and Acts 1:14.

[143]See also John 7:5.

[144]It is important to note that for Mark, although Jesus preached in synagogues throughout all Galilee (1:39), this is his last appearance in a synagogue. The transition of the Christian message from Jews to Gentiles is hinted at here.

[145]In this regard Luke acts against the intention of the creator of Mark 6:1-6a by placing his version of the narrative at the *outset* of Jesus' ministry, directly after the baptism and temptation (4:16-30).

[146]Cf. my study mentioned in n. 3.

first century C.E.,[147] he borrowed extensively from the Hebrew Bible and Judaic interpretation of it regarding Saul, the first anointed king of Israel, himself soon to be rejected and killed.

B.   *Saul.*

In the only two occurrences of the verb "to reject" *(apodokimazō)* in Mark, Jesus is the stone which the builders "reject," but which becomes the head of the corner, a quotation of LXX Ps 117 (118):22 in Mark 12:11. Jesus is also he who is to suffer many things, be "rejected" by the elders, chief priests and scribes, and be killed (8:31). This Greek verb in the Septuagint is always a translation of the Hebrew מָאַס.[148] A major cluster of occurrences of this Hebrew verb (eight times) is found in 1 Samuel regarding the anointing of Saul.

The Israelites ask Samuel to give them a king to govern them (8:6). The Lord informs the prophet that they have not "rejected" him, but have "rejected" the Lord from being king over them (8:7). Nevertheless, Samuel is to give them a king, and the anointing of Saul occurs (10:1), connected with the proverb incident in his home town of Gibeah analyzed above. The "Late Source" in 10:19 repeats the motif of Israel's "rejecting" the Lord on this day. Because of Saul's independently offering in 13:7b-15a, and his neglect to utterly destroy all the Amalekites in chapter fifteen, the Lord "rejects" him from being king (15:23, 26; 16:1). In addition, he had caused the priests of Nob to be massacred.[149]

The motif of Saul's rejection in 1 Samuel 10 is intensified just before the occurrence of the root *ḥrš* in v 27, important in regard to the term

---

[147]For Josephus, cf. n. 25. On Pseudo-Philo, see chapters 56-58 in *OTP* 2.370-72. Interestingly, the term "stumbling block" is associated with Saul in 58:3, 4 and 65:4; see Mark 6:3. D. Harrington considers this writing to have been composed in Hebrew in Palestine around the time of Jesus (2.298-300). If the community in which the Jewish Christian author of Mark 6:1-6a lived knew of Jesus' "Q" saying now found in Matt 11:6 and Luke 7:23, where Jesus blesses him who "takes no offense" at him after performing the mighty works mentioned directly before, it would help to understand the Nazarites' being "offended" by Jesus in Mark 6:3 as the exact opposite of this blessing. It may also be noted that the son of David (= Messiah) is described as the stone of "stumbling" (מִכְשׁוֹל; *skandalon* in Aquila, Symmachus and Theodotion) of Isa 8:14 in *b. Sanh.* 38a (Soncino 238). This is spoken to Rabbi, Judah the Prince, a fourth generation Tanna (Strack and Stemberger, *Introduction* 89-90). On the messianic interpretation of this verse in the NT, see also Luke 2:34, Rom 9:32 and 1 Pet 2:8. The same Hebrew term for "stumbling" is associated with *ḥrš* in Lev. 19:14.

[148]There are six such LXX passages, including Ps 118:22.

[149]Cf. Josephus, *Ant.* 6.262-68, for a negative appraisal of Saul's behavior. In 6.343-50, however, the Jewish historian offers a positive appraisal, primarily because of Saul's heroism in war. Only such a man is valiant and "wise" (σώφρων – 346).

"carpenter." Here worthless fellows "despise" (בזה) him. As pointed out above, the Septuagint here has *atimazō*, employing the same Greek root as a prophet's being "without honor" in Mark 6:4. When Josephus retells this incident in *Ant.* 6.67, he notes that Saul is given the τιμή appropriate to a king by "many" good people. Nevertheless, even more malicious people "despise" (καταφρονέω; cf. 6.80) him and "scoff at" (χλευάζω) the others. This occurs in connection with Gibeah, where Saul grew up, just as Samuel returns to Ramah, his home town *(patris)*.

Judaic comment on Saul's becoming king thus amplifies the motif of his "rejection" in connection with his home town. This was a main reason the Palestinian Jewish Christian author of Mark 6:1-6a drew upon it for his description of Jesus' rejection in his own home town of Nazareth. He intensified the rejection by not having "some" (MT) or "more" malicious people (Josephus) despise Jesus, as they had Saul. For him, "and they took offense at him" (v 3) means that all the Nazarites did so.[150]

* * *

The above twelve similarities in motifs, verbal expressions, and a question structure between Mark 6:1-6a and the anointing of Saul by Samuel to become king of Israel may be questioned individually. Nevertheless, cumulatively they present a very solid argument for the proposal that the Jewish Christian author of Mark 6:1-6a creatively drew upon the Saul narrative, especially in Judaic tradition, for motifs, verbal expressions, and a question structure he employed in his own narrative of Jesus' rejection in his home town of Nazareth.

III
The Original Narrative, and Mark's Redactional Work

According to the results obtained in section II above, the Jewish Christian author of Mark 6:1-6a originally composed the following narrative:

> Jesus came to his home town, and his disciples followed him. When the Sabbath arrived, he began to teach in the synagogue. Many who heard him were astonished and said: "From where does 'this man' get these things? And what wisdom is given to 'this man' so that even mighty works are done through his hands? Is 'this man' not the carpenter, the son of Mary and brother of James and Joses and Judas and Simon, and are not his sisters here among us?" They took offense at him. Therefore Jesus said to them: "A prophet is not without honor except in his home

---

[150]The author of the parallel incident in Luke 4:28-29 intensifies it even more by having the Nazarites become full of wrath and attempt to murder Jesus.

town and among his relatives and in his own family." He was not able
to do a single mighty work there. He marveled at their lack of belief.

This reconstruction means that the original narrative is much more
extensive that modern redactional critics and most of the commentators
maintain. Mark certainly created the introductory words "And he
departed" in 6:1a to link the narrative to the preceding story of the
raising of the daughter of Jairus, a ruler of the synagogue (in
Capernaum). Yet, as pointed out at the end of section II 2B above, "and
he comes from there to" derived from the Saul episode. The author also
omitted the name "Jesus," which must have stood at the beginning of the
original story. My argument for retaining the clause with the disciples in
6:1b is found above in section II 3A.

A later redactor of Mark or a copyist added 6:5b, borrowing
terminology from 6:13 in order to do so, as I indicated in section II 11A
above.

These are the only redactional changes made by Mark or a later
editor or copyist. In contrast to other analyses, for example that of
Grässer, they are astonishingly few.

* * *

In its present context, 6:1-6a is first of all a striking contrast to Jesus'
mighty work just performed for the ruler of the (Capernaum) synagogue.
He is confident that Jesus can heal his daughter, who is at the point of
death (5:23). When people then come from his house and inform Jairus
that his daughter has died, Jesus tells him not to fear, only to believe (v
36). When he maintains the child isn't dead, but merely sleeping, those
gathered there "laugh at" Jesus (v 40). Yet he raises her from the dead.

The motif of "belief" in Jesus' ability to heal is greatly emphasized
here. It is coupled with that of those present at Jairus' house "laughing
at" Jesus, considering him incapable of raising someone from the dead.
Yet like the prophet Elijah, who restored the son of the Zarephath widow
to life (1 Kgs 17:17-24), and like the prophet Elisha, who acted similarly
(2 Kgs 4:18-37), the prophet Jesus does have the power to perform such a
mighty work when belief on the part of the person requesting aid is
present. The Nazarites, however, refuse to place such confidence in their
"home town boy." Therefore Jesus cannot perform such a mighty work
for them. Mark purposely places 6:1-6a at this point in his Gospel in
order to contrast the two reactions to Jesus: faith, and lack of faith.

Secondly, Jesus' commissioning and instructing his twelve disciples
in 6:7-13 refers back to motifs in 6:1-6a. Jesus gives his disciples
authority

over unclean spirits (v 7), and this they put into practice by casting out many demons (v 13). They thus receive the power to do so from him who elsewhere does mighty works (6:2).

Finally, when people refuse to receive them as his disciples, they must learn to come to terms with it (6:10-11). Their rejection will not differ from the rejection their master experienced in their presence in Nazareth. For the reader, this signifies that the Christian missionaries as successors of Jesus' disciples may at times share the same fate which he and they had.

IV
The Original Language

There are no clear indications in Mark 6:1-6a that the author was acquainted with the Septuagint form of Saul's becoming king. The opposite is rather the case. He definitely shows familiarity, however, with the Hebrew text, as in the root *ḥrš* in 1 Sam 10:27 for "carpenter." He also may have been acquainted with an earlier form of the present targumic text. Its emphasis on "teacher/scribe" instead of prophet in the Saul narrative, for example, probably caused him to have the prophet Jesus "teach" in the Nazareth synagogue.

The author in addition made use of specific terminology and motifs from Palestinian Judaic interpretation of the Saul episode. This is shown above all in the retelling of the narrative by Josephus. Examples are astonishment, marveling, lack of honor, unbelief, and more people despising/rejecting Saul in connection with his "home town." Finally, "through his hands" is definitely a Semitism. The same is true for the consecutive use of καί at the beginning of the author's sentences.[151] I therefore omit most of them in the English translation above in section III.

These observations make it very probable that the author of Mark 6:1-6a composed his narrative in Aramaic or Hebrew. Hebrew is possible, just as the section on Saul in Pseudo-Philo, with many haggadic developments, was written in the language of the entire work, Hebrew.

Yet Aramaic is more probable. I proposed above that the narrative was composed by a Palestinian Jewish Christian to link the rejection of Jesus by his own family to the final, major rejection at the end of his life in Jerusalem. If so, it was created in an Aramaic-speaking Jewish Christian community in Palestine (or possibly Syria) in order to

---

[151]This corresponds, for example, to the waw of the Hebrew and Aramaic texts of 1 Samuel 10. See *Biblia Hebraica ad loc.*, and Sperber, *The Bible in Aramaic* 2.111-113. For this as Semitic style in Greek, especially in Mark, see BDF § 458 (p. 239) and § 442,2) (p. 227).

emphasize the motif of Jesus' rejection by his own people, so important in the earliest preaching. By its providing one more specific example of this motif for the purpose of proclamation, the members of the addressed Christian community now also had even one more impetus to missionize not only among their fellow Jews, but also among non-Jews. For this purpose the episode was translated at an early stage into Greek, perhaps in a bilingual environment such as Syria.[152] As such it became available to Mark. There is no evidence that the author of our first gospel himself knew either Aramaic or Hebrew.

If the original language of Mark 6:1-6a was Aramaic,[153] this excludes its origin in a Hellenistic Gentile Christian or Jewish Christian community. It has been proposed that the Nazarites' response to Jesus' teaching is based on the model of a Hellenistic epiphany narrative, and that the cluster of Spirit, teaching and power derive from a Hellenistic Jewish area with the idea of a divine man ($\theta\epsilon\hat{\iota}os$ $\dot{\alpha}\nu\dot{\eta}\rho$).[154] As shown above, they rather derive from Palestinian Judaic interpretation of the Saul narrative.

V
The Historicity

Earlier, scholars mostly considered Mark 6:1-6a to be historical because of its concrete individual points.[155] These, however, are typical of Judaic and Jewish Christian haggadah and do not guarantee historicity.[156] The names of Jesus' brothers are probably historical.[157]

---

[152]Palestine should not be excluded, however, for there were many Greek-speaking cities there. Cf. the many Hellenistic cities in Palestine described in Schürer, *The history* 2.85-183.

[153]Interestingly, W. Grundmann, relying on Schlatter and Violet, states regarding Luke 4:16-30: "The strong Aramaic influence on the language of the entire pericope points to its origin in Special Luke" (*Das Evangelium des Lukas;* 119). If this is true, it corroborates the above proposal regarding Mark 6:1-6a, which it develops in a different direction – within an Aramaic-speaking community. J. Wellhausen in *Das Evangelium Lucae* (Berlin: Reimer, 1904) 10-11 had already pointed to a confusion of ארמיא and ארמלא in Luke 4:26. He also viewed εἰ μή in v 27 as the Aramaic *ella*, adversative, not as making an exception. For this reason he advocated a written Aramaic source for vv 25-27.

[154]Grässer, *Jesus in Nazareth* 20-21.

[155]See the summary discussion in Grässer, *op. cit.,* 1-2. The statement by S. Johnson in "The Gospel According to St. Matthew" in *IB* (1951) 7.423 is typical: "Certainly the early church loved to develop the theme that Jesus 'was despised and rejected of men' [the Suffering Servant of Isa 53:3], but there is no reason to doubt that this story is historical."

[156]Cf. the remarks by I. Heinemann in Strack and Stemberger, *Introduction* 260.

[157]Cf. the discussion in Grundmann, *Das Evangelium nach Markus* 157.

Grundmann proposes that Jesus was the (only) *tektōn* of Nazareth,[158] which is pure speculation. Indeed, in light of the discussion above of the Messiah as a *haraš* who will (re-)build the Temple, it must be questioned whether Jesus' earlier occupation was known at all. According to Judaic interpretation of Zech 2:3, the Messiah was to be a *tektōn;* therefore Jesus was presented by the Palestinian Jewish Christian author of Mark 6:1-6a as such.[159] Gnilka believes the *sui generis* form of the narrative is best explained by its retaining an historical reminiscence of a concrete rejection of Jesus in his home town.[160] This may, of course, be the case. Yet it is more probable that the author based his narrative on the information he also had access to, which is now found in Mark 3:21, 31-35. He very creatively composed a narrative designed primarily to emphasize Jesus' rejection, providing yet one more example of this theme. This example lay between Jesus' rejection by his own family in Capernaum, and his rejection in Jerusalem. The expression "home town," from Judaic tradition on the Saul narrative, caused him to set his story in Nazareth, historically Jesus' home town where he grew up.

Almost the entire content of Mark 6:1-6a is derived by its author from the Saul narrative, especially in Judaic tradition. Its lack of historicity does not mean, however, that it is not true in a religious sense. The first hearer of the episode, like the present reader of the Gospel of Mark, was forced to ask him- or herself if he or she knows the origin of Jesus' wisdom and mighty deeds. Does the hearer/reader acknowledge him as the carpenter/Messiah, i.e., "believe" in him? If not, he or she is like the Nazarites, who rejected their own native son. The main question was and remains: Does the hearer/reader acknowledge who Jesus' true Father is, and believe in His Son?

VI
What the Narrative Is Not

To highlight the narrative of Jesus' rejection in Nazareth, it is helpful to state what is not true of the episode. This aids in defining the contours of the story. In addition to the points noted above (it was not composed in Greek; it does not derive from Hellenistic Gentile or Jewish Christianity; it is not historical), the following ten statements are appropriate.

---

[158]*Ibid.,* 156.

[159]A similar phenomenon is the placing of Jesus' birth in Bethlehem because the Messiah was to be born there (Mic 5:1, Eng. 2). In all probability Jesus was born and raised in Nazareth, for he is always "Jesus of Nazareth."

[160]*Das Evangelium nach Markus (1-8,26)* 229. See also p. 233, as well as E. Haenchen, *Der Weg Jesu* (Berlin: de Gruyter, 1968[2]) 220.

1) The pre-Marcan form of the episode did not have primarily an apologetic purpose. It was not conceived to explain Jesus' lack of success in his place of origin, Nazareth, and with his relatives, which purportedly was a burden for the early Christian community.[161] Rather, it accentuated the general motif of Jesus' rejection by providing a middle link between that of his relatives and his final rejection in Jerusalem.

2) Mark 6:1-6a is not composed of two different original accounts, one dealing with a successful encounter of Jesus in Nazareth, and another from a later time, which reported the opposite.[162] Rather, only one narrative obtains, almost completely based on motifs, expressions, and a question structure from the Saul episode.

3) Jesus' appearance in the synagogue of Nazareth is not described in terms of Mark 1:21-22.[163] As proposed above, the opposite is probably the case.

4) The contents of Jesus' teaching in the Nazareth synagogue are not given in Mark 6:2. This is not due to the redactor Mark,[164] but to the fact that the author's source, 1 Samuel 10, also did not relate the contents of Saul's prophesying.

5) It cannot be asserted that before Jesus' public ministry he was a carpenter/cabinetmaker/wheelwright/construction worker, as *tektōn* is variously translated. The "carpentry" imagery Jesus ostensibly uses elsewhere in the gospels is actually sparse.[165] Nor did his father Joseph pass his own trade on to his first son.[166]

Rather, Jesus is characterized as "the carpenter" in 6:3 because he was considered to be the Messiah, the son of David, who as one of the two messianic "carpenters" of Zech 2:3 (Eng. 1:20) will (re-)build the Jerusalem Temple.

---

[161]Against Grundmann, *Das Evangelium des Markus* 155.

[162]Against K.L. Schmidt, *Der Rahmen der Geschichte Jesu* (Berlin, 1919; reprint Darmstadt: Wissenschaftliche Buchgesellschaft, 1964) 155-56, as well as R. Bultmann, *The History of the Synoptic Tradition* 31.

[163]Against Gnilka, *Das Evangelium nach Markus (Mk 1-8,26)* 228, agreeing with Wendling (n. 8).

[164]Against Grässer, *Jesus in Nazareth* 19.

[165]Against Batey, "Is Not This the Carpenter?" 255. According to this type of argumentation, Jesus could have had a number of different occupations.

[166]Against Gnilka, *Das Evangelium des Markus (Mk 1-8,26)* 233, and J. Lightfoot, *A Commentary on the New Testament from the Talmud and Hebraica* (Peabody, Massachusetts: Hendrickson, 1989, original 1859) 2.415. Cf. also the remark by U. Luz in n. 77.

6) Although Joseph is not mentioned, there is no allusion to the virgin birth in Mark 6:3.[167] The question of who Saul's "father" is in the narrative of Saul's prophesying in the MT and Judaic interpretation of 1 Samuel 10 is rather of central importance. It is reflected in the question of "from where" in Mark 6:2, which is also of central importance. It requires the hearer/reader to confront the issue of whether God is Jesus' true Father, the source of his wisdom and power.

7) Early Jewish sayings adduced up to now are irrelevant as so-called "parallels" to Jesus' proverb in Mark 6:4.[168] I know of only one general saying of relevance: "It is the manner of human beings to revere those distant more than those near."[169] The English adage, "familiarity breeds contempt," is crasser but similar. Yet Jesus' proverb in Mark 6:4 is very specific, and *all* its elements have been shown above to derive from Judaic interpretation of the episode of Saul's becoming the anointed one in 1 Samuel 10.

8) Jesus' proverb in Mark 6:4 is not a bundling of the negative experiences of itinerant Jewish preachers, who could be called prophets.[170] Rather, it was formed by a Jewish Christian on the basis of the Saul episode.

9) A number of Hellenistic sayings relevant to the content of Jesus' proverb have been known since J. Wettstein.[171] None of them, however, deals with a prophet's lack of honor in his home town, among relatives and family. These, however, are all found in Judaic interpretation of Saul's anointing in 1 Samuel 10.

10) Finally, the oldest form of Jesus' proverb in Mark 6:4 is not found in Papyrus Oxyrhynchus 1:5, which reads: "A prophet is not accepted in his home town; a physician does not perform cures

---

[167]Against F. Grant, "The Gospel According to St. Mark" in *IB* 7.727; E. Klostermann, *Das Markusevangelium* (Tübingen: Mohr, 1950⁴) 55; and Gnilka, *Das Evangelium des Markus (Mk 1-8, 26)* 232.

[168]Cf. Str-B 1.678.

[169]Cf. *Mek. R. Ish.* Shirata 8 on the "fearful in praises" of Exod 15:11. See the edition of J. Lauterbach, *Mekilta de-Rabbi Ishmael* 2.63.

[170]Against O. Steck, *Israel und das gewaltsame Geschick der Propheten* (WMANT 23; Neukirchen-Vluyn: Neukirchener, 1967) 214.

[171]See his *Novum Testamentum Graecum* 1.409, as well as Grässer, *Jesus in Nazareth* 7, n. 28; Gnilka, *Das Evangelium des Markus (Mk 1-8,26)* 232, n. 27; and Luz, *Das Evangelium nach Matthäus* 2.385, n.16.

for those who know him."[172]   This is rather a further development of the Lucan form. The tradition behind the Third Evangelist made Mark 6:4 into a double proverb by adding in Luke 4:23, "Physician, heal yourself."[173]   Later tradition appropriated the term "physician" from here and made a saying out of it parallel to the Lucan version of the prophet saying.[174]

Matthew's version of the prophet proverb omits only Mark's "and among his own relatives" (13:57).   Luke omits both relatives and house/family (4:24).   John 4:44 also has the abbreviated form: "a prophet has no honor in his own home town/country."   "Relatives" and "house/family" seemed redundant to Matthew, therefore he leaves out one of these expressions. Luke intentionally omits the names of Jesus' family members except for Joseph at 4:22. He therefore sees no need to mention relatives and house/family in v 24.   In the Johannine setting, the region of Galilee is dominant, with no mention of Jesus' relatives at this point (4:43-45). The author understands *patris* as "native region," not as the other legitimate translation of "home town" in connection with a city, town or village. Here, too, there was no reason for him to mention relatives and house/family.

The long form of Jesus' proverb in Mark 6:4 is indeed the earliest, not connected with a similar saying with a physician, but with relatives and house/family.   The Palestinian Jewish author of 6:1-6a found *all* the present elements in v 4 in the MT and Judaic traditions on the anointing of Saul as king in 1 Samuel 10.   From there he appropriated them and very creatively formed them into the present prophet proverb.

---

[172]Bultmann, *The History* 31. See now also the Gospel of Thomas 31, which has: "No prophet is accepted in his own village; no physician heals those who know him." English in J. Robinson, *The Nag Hammadi Library* 122. Cf. Haenchen, *Der Weg Jesu* 216, n. 4.

[173]The combination of honor and physician in Sir 38:1 (cf. also vv 3 and 12) may have contributed to this. The LXX has here Τίμα ἰατρόν; the available Hebrew רעי רופה. For the latter verb, see Jastrow, *A Dictionary* 1486 II in the sense of "welcome, accept." See Vattioni, *Ecclesiastico* 199, with variants and rabbinic sayings in the apparatus with "honor." Cf. also I. Lévi, *The Hebrew Text of the Book of Ecclesiasticus* 44.

[174]See J. Fitzmyer, *The Gospel According to Luke (I-IX)* 528: "Since the Oxyrhynchus saying uses *dektos* and contains the double proverb, which is found in the canonical tradition only in Luke, it is certain that the Oxyrhynchus form of the saying is dependent on Luke."

* * *

The above ten negative statements, coupled with those regarding the original language and historicity, are directed against what previous scholarship has falsely maintained about Mark 6:1-6a. They help to capture the light of the narrative's real content and intention by also pointing out its shadows.

3

The Prodigia at Jesus' Cruxifixion
(Matt 27:51b-53; Mark 15:33 & 38 Par.),
The Repentant Criminal (Luke 23:39-43),
The Ascension of Jesus' Soul from the Cross,
and
Judaic Interpretation of 1 Samuel 28

Introduction

In May of 1992 more than 400 Orthodox Jews from all over the world protested against a supermarket's being built in Hamburg-Ottensen upon land which previously had been used as a Jewish cemetery. The chief rabbi of Jerusalem, Itzchak Kulitz, was asked to come to Hamburg from Israel in order to mediate in the case, which for the Ultra-Orthodox involved "disturbing the peace" of the deceased.[1] To me, this recalled a similar incident I experienced in September of 1981 in Jerusalem. Archaeologists had received an official license from the Israeli government to conduct excavations for the city of David from the 11th century B.C.E. Ultra-Orthodox Jews nevertheless besieged the site of the dig, and in the end they had to be chased away by mounted police. The protesters, including one of Israel's chief rabbis of the time, Shlomo Goren, maintained they had found bones at the site. In their opinion this definitely showed that it was earlier a cemetery. For their contention that the graves may not now be "disturbed," they cited 1 Sam 28:15. After the medium/witch of Endor raises Samuel for Saul's sake from the dead, the

---

[1] Cf. the Berlin "Tagesspiegel" of May 7, 10 and 22, and December 12, 1992.

prophet asks the king reproachfully: "Why have you *disturbed* me by bringing me up?"[2]

It is precisely this biblical verse, along with the material surrounding it, which in Judaic tradition forms much of the background for the prodigia at Jesus' Crucifixion in the Synoptics, as well as for Luke 23:39-43.

After a description of Saul's encounter with the deceased Samuel, raised up by the medium of Endor in 1 Samuel 28 (I), as well as a discussion of the very early dating of many Judaic traditions on this incident (II), I shall analyze the prodigia at Jesus' Crucifixion (III): A. An earthquake, and the raising/rising of saints from their tombs in Matt 27:51b-53; B. The sun's eclipse in Mark 15:33 par.; and C. The tearing/rending of the Temple curtain in Mark 15:38 par. Related to these is D., Jesus' promise to the repentant criminal crucified with him of participation in Paradise on the same day (Luke 23:39-43). Finally, on the basis of the results obtained in I-III, I propose that Matt 27: 51b-53 and Luke 23:39-43 have preserved a very early Palestinian Jewish Christian tradition, according to which Jesus' soul ascended to heaven directly from the Cross (IV).

I
Saul, the Deceased Samuel, and the Medium/Witch of Endor

A brief description of 1 Sam 28:3-25 is helpful at the outset in order later to appreciate expressions and motifs from Judaic interpretation of this episode which are of relevance to the prodigia at Jesus' Crucifixion, and to Jesus' words to the repentant criminal crucified with him.

This "thrilling story,"[3] called by G. Caird a "pathetic tale,"[4] begins by recalling the fact that all Israel had recently "mourned" (ספד; see also 25:1) for the prophet Samuel, who was buried in his home town of Ramah. In his zeal to enforce the Torah's requirement of prohibiting mediums and wizards,[5] Saul had put them out of the land (v 3). Unfortunately, Israel's major enemy, the Philistines, now assemble for

---

[2]On this incident in Jerusalem, cf. *Time* of September 7,1981, p. 18.
[3]So H. Hertzberg, *I & II Samuel* 217.
[4]Cf. his "The First and Second Books of Samuel" in *IB* (1953) 2.1026.
[5]Cf. Lev 19:31 and 20:27, as well as Deut 18:11. In contrast to evil King Manasseh (2 Kgs 21:6), King Josiah later followed Saul's positive example (2 Kgs 23:24). A special study of the divination practiced in 1 Samuel 28 is the short 1955 Vienna dissertation of W. Beilner, *Die Totenbeschwörung im ersten Buche Samuel (1 Sm 28, 3-25)*. Unfortunately, he labels rabbinic views of this phenomenon "absurd, phantastic and quite artificial" (44), and denies the relevance of 1 Samuel 28 to the NT (119). The main merit of this study is its discussion of the relevant phenomena.

battle at Shunem, on the edge of the Valley of Jezreel.[6] As Israel's
military leader, King Saul gathers his own forces at Mount Gilboa, some
15 kilometers or 9 miles south-southeast of Shunem.   Viewing the
Philistine army, Saul becomes afraid, and his heart "trembles" greatly (v
5).[7] Because Saul had been rejected by the Lord, had killed the priests of
Nob, and had spared the enemy Amalek in spite of the prophet Samuel's
injunction not to do so,[8] no revelation is now available to him from these
three sources (v 6). In his desperation to know the outcome of the battle
the next day, Saul tells his servants to seek a female medium for him,
someone he himself had banned. They inform him of one at Endor (v 7),
7 kilometers or 4 miles southwest of Mount Tabor, or 22 kilometers (= 13
miles) southwest of Lake Tiberias. Shunem lay only 6 kilometers or 3.5
miles southwest of Endor.[9]

The Israelite king disguises himself and goes there by night with two
servants. He requests the woman to divine for him by a spirit and to
"raise/bring up/cause to ascend" (hiphil of עלה) the person he names (v
8). The medium is at first very hesitant, but Saul assuages her with an
oath (vv 9-10). She asks him whom she should "raise" for him, and he
requests her to "raise" Samuel (v 11). This she does, informing Saul that
she sees אֱלֹהִים "rising" (עלה) from the earth (v 13). When asked regarding
Samuel's appearance, she replies: An old (זקן) man is "rising" (עלה),
wrapped in a robe. Knowing that this is Samuel,[10] Saul bows and does
obeisance before him (v 14).

At this point the prophet asks Saul: "Why have you 'disturbed'
(hiphil of רגז) me by 'raising' (hiphil of עלה) me?" Saul explains his
situation of dire distress, God having abandoned him. He therefore calls
upon Samuel to inform him what to do (v 15). The prophet reproves the
king, emphasizing that the Lord has "torn" (קרע) the "kingdom" (ממלכה)
from his hand and given it to David (v 17). He enumerates again the
grounds of Saul's guilt and prophesies from the dead that the Lord will

---

[6]For a description of the site, see the art. "Shunem" by G. Van Beek in *IDB* 4.341-
42.

[7]The verb חרד can also be used of a mountain's "trembling" or "quaking." Cf.
BDB 353. In 1 Sam 14:15 and Isa 32:11 (in a context of mourning) it is parallel to
רגז, important in 1 Sam 28:15.

[8]Cf. 1 Sam 13:7b-15a; 15; 22:11-19.

[9]Cf. the art. "En-dor" by W. Reed in *IDB* 2.100.

[10]Cf. the robe of Samuel in 1 Sam 2:19 and 15:27. Judaic tradition maintained it
was the robe which Samuel tore and in which he was buried, and that the dead
rise in their last garments. See for example *Pseudo-Philo* 64:6 (*OTP* 2.377, with n.
"h"); *b. Ketub.* 111b (Soncino 720); and *Pirq. R. El.* 33 (Friedlander 245-46, with
notes).

also give Israel into the hand of the Philistines. Then he states: "And tomorrow you and your sons [will be] with me" (v 19).

At this point Saul falls full "length" (קוֹמָה, from the root קוּם, "to rise") to the ground, greatly afraid because of Samuel's words, and exhausted because of not having eaten anything all day and night (v 20). The female medium at Endor then graciously prepares a meal for him and his servants. Saul "arises" (קוּם) from the earth and sits upon the woman's bed (v 23). Having partaken of the meal, the king and his servants "rise" (קוּם) and depart that same night (v 25).

Samuel's prophecy from the dead is then fulfilled when Saul and three of his sons die the next day in battle on Mount Gilboa (chapter 31). When David hears this terrible news, he "tears" (קָרַע) his clothes, mourns (סָפַד), weeps and fasts (2 Kgs 1:11-12) over the Lord's "anointed one" (מָשִׁיחַ: vv 14, 16), even composing a lament for this tragic occasion (vv 17-27).

* * *

I propose that the above narrative, especially in Judaic tradition, provided the background for a Palestinian Jewish Christian (or possibly Christians), who composed the prodigia at the death of Israel's "Anointed One" or Messiah, Jesus, on the Cross. These include the earth's "shaking," rocks being split, and the appearance of many saints in Jerusalem after they have been "raised" (Matt 27:51b-53); the eclipse of the sun (Mark 15:33 par.); and the "tearing" in two of the Temple curtain (Mark 15:33 par.). Finally, it also provided a Palestinian Jewish Christian with the background for the words of Jesus to the criminal crucified with him: "today you will be with me in Paradise" (Luke 23:43).

II
The Early Dating of Judaic Traditions on 1 Samuel 28

Before discussing III.A-D, it is appropriate to address the question of how old Judaic traditions on 1 Samuel 28 are. It can be maintained with assurance that the narrative of Saul's encounter with the medium of Endor, including the raising of the prophet Samuel from the dead, was very popular in Judaic tradition from a very early time onwards. This is shown, for example, in the Septuagint, Sirach, Pseudo-Philo and Josephus.

1) The Septuagint.

It is very probable that the Septuagint read in 1 Sam 28:14 not the אִישׁ זָקֵן, "old man," of the MT, but אִישׁ זָקֵף, an "upright/erect man": ὄρθιος.[11] This very early tradition, at least from the second, perhaps from the third century B.C.E.,[12] was the basis for the later rabbis' contention that the medium of Endor suddenly knew that she was dealing with Saul (28:12): for an ordinary person a spirit ascends with its head down and its feet up. For a king, however, it ascends with its feet down and its head up.[13] Although the rabbinic sources on 1 Samuel 28 in their present form are only from the Common Era, this example shows that at times they retained very old material.

Secondly, the Septuagint at 1 Sam 28:19 states regarding Saul: "And tomorrow you and your sons, with you they shall fall" (3rd per. pl.). This differs basically from the MT noted in section I above, which has no "falling," but "[being] with me," Samuel. This is important to note in regard to the definitely Semitic background of Luke 23:43, described in section III.D below.

2) Sir 46:20.

Ben Sira wrote Sirach or Ecclesiasticus in Hebrew in Jerusalem sometime between 198-175 B.C.E.[14] In a list of famous men in chapters 44-50, the author in 46:13-20 recalls the career of Samuel, "beloved by his Lord." His final sentence regarding the great Israelite states: "Even after he had fallen asleep, he prophesied and made known to the king his death, and lifted up his voice from the ground in prophecy...."[15]

This clearly alludes to 1 Sam 28:15-19, Samuel's words from the dead to King Saul when the latter has the medium of Endor raise him. It shows that Samuel's singular prophesying from the dead to Saul was a motif which interested Palestinian Jews in a major way at least 250 years

---

[11]Cf. the apparatus of *Biblia Hebraica*, ed. R. Kittel, et al., and Jastrow, *A Dictionary* 409-410 on the passive participle of זָקֵף. L. Ginzberg had also suggested this in *Legends* 6.236, n. 75.

[12]Cf. O. Eissfeldt, *The Old Testament. An Introduction* (Oxford: Blackwell, 1966) 702-03, 605.

[13]Cf., for example, *Lev. Rab.* 'Emor 26/7 on Lev 20:27 in Soncino 4.332, and J. Neusner, *Judaism and Scripture. The Evidence of Leviticus Rabbah* 458.

[14]Cf. G. Nickelsburg, *Jewish Literature Between the Bible and the Mishnah* 64.

[15]NRSV. The Greek is found in J. Ziegler, *Sapientia Iesu Filii Sirach*, Septuaginta 345. Unfortunately the available Hebrew does not have the very end of the verse. See F. Vattioni, *Ecclesiastico* 255. For Samuel in another list of OT heroes, see Heb 11:32.

before the writing of the Synoptic Gospels. The earliest of the latter, Mark, was probably composed shortly before or after 70 C.E.[16]

The very end of Sir 46:20, not cited above, is also of relevance to the motif of gaining atonement through one's own death in Luke 23:39-43 (see section III.D below).

3) Pseudo-Philo.

The present Latin of this writing, probably from Palestine, is from a Greek translation of the original Hebrew. It most probably stems from approximately the time of Jesus.[17] In chapter 64 it contains very many haggadic developments of 1 Samuel 28, such as Saul's removing the magicians from Israel for the sake of his own later reputation (v 1); the name of the medium of Endor as "Sedecla, the daughter of Debin the Midianite" (v 3);[18] her having already raised up the dead on behalf of the Philistines for forty years (v 5); and two angels' leading Samuel up from the dead, clothed in a white robe (v 6).

I shall also point out below the relevance of Pseudo-Philo's description of Samuel's rising from the dead (v 7), and Saul's death as an atonement for his iniquities (v 9). The first four passages, however, show how popular the episode of 1 Samuel 28 already was in Palestine even before the time of Jesus, for it certainly took some time for these haggadic motifs to develop.[19]

4) Josephus.

A native of Jerusalem whose mother tongue was Aramaic, Josephus completed his "Antiquities" ca. 93-94 C.E.[20] In 6.327-42 he retells Saul's visit to the "witch" of Endor in 1 Samuel 28. He, too, incorporates so many haggadic elements in his narrative that it is extremely improbable he himself invented them. Rather, he is dependent on Palestinian tradition here. Three examples are the medium's summoning Samuel from Hades (332); Saul's also asking about the dress and age of the man

---

[16]Cf. J. Gnilka, *Das Evangelium nach Markus (Mk 1–8,26)* 34-35 as well as W. Kümmel, *Einleitung in das Neue Testament* 70.

[17]Cf. D.J. Harrington in *OTP* 2.299-300; chapter 64 is on pp. 376-77. For the Latin, see his Pseudo-Philon, *Les Antiquités Bibliques.* Tome I.

[18]L. Ginzberg in *Legends* 6.236, n. 74 plausibly interprets this as צדק לא = "the unrighteous one."

[19]Philo of Alexandria himself spoke of Samuel as "the greatest of kings and prophets," whose "place has been ordered in the ranks of the divine army..." (*Ebr.* 143 in the LCL translation of F.H. Colson and G.H. Whitaker). It appears that he imagined him as already somewhere next to God in heaven. Philo was probably born ca. 20 C.E. See LCL 1.ix.

[20]Cf. *Ant.* 20.263 and 267; *Vita* 7; *Bell.* 1.3; and *Cont. Ap.* 1.50.

ascending (333); and the medium as having only one calf, she being a working woman who has to be content with it as her only possession (339).

Josephus, writing only a few decades after the earliest gospel, is thus one more witness to the early and extensive Palestinian haggadic development of 1 Samuel 28.[21]

* * *

The Septuagint, Sirach, Pseudo-Philo and Josephus all attest extensive pre-Christian and first century C.E. Judaic development of the story of Saul's encounter with the deceased Samuel via the medium of Endor. As noted above, this should be borne in mind when later rabbinic interpretations of the same episode are considered. While some are patently late, others go back to a much earlier time, although in their present context they are frequently late or even undateable.

In light of the relatively large amount of early Judaic haggadic material on 1 Samuel 28,[22] due to the great popularity of the narrative, it is also understandable that a Palestinian Jewish Christian could employ expressions and motifs from this episode to describe the prodigia accompanying the death of his own hero, Jesus, on the Cross, from which he ascended to his Father. The same is true of Jesus' words to the repentant criminal crucified with him: he would be with him today in Paradise (Luke 23:43).

III
The Three Prodigia at Jesus' Crucifixion, and His Promise to the Repentant Criminal

The Gospel of John knows of no prodigia at the death of Jesus (19:30). All three Synoptics, however, have at least two: a three-hour eclipse of the sun (Mark 15:33 par.), and the tearing/rending into two of the Temple curtain (Mark 15:38 par.). In addition, Matthew's special material adds in 27:51b-53 that the earth shook, rocks split, tombs were opened, and many bodies of the deceased saints were raised. The latter entered Jerusalem and appeared to many. Finally, Luke's special material adds in 23:39-43, just before the eclipse and the tearing of the Temple curtain, the words of one repentant criminal to his fellow crucified criminal and to Jesus, and the latter's reply.

---

[21]The relevance to Jesus' Crucifixion of Josephus' description of Samuel's rising from the dead (334), and of Saul's later being with Samuel (336), will be pointed out below.

[22]For an almost encyclopaedic treatment of Judaic sources on Saul's encounter with Samuel via the medium of Endor, cf. Ginzberg, *Legends* 4.70-72, and the relevant notes in 6.235-239.

In the following I shall point out how all four of these ultimately derive from Judaic interpretation of 1 Samuel 28.

A. An Earthquake and Saints Rising from the Dead

Very disparate opinions prevail concerning the short two and one half verses of Matt 27:51b-53. W. Schmauch, for example, calls the episode a "small and profound...legend."[23] E. Haenchen describes it as the "unsuccessful introduction of a tradition gone wild."[24] In contrast, K. Stendahl thinks it "must have been a piece of a primitive Christology."[25] Finally, J. Jeremias also considers it "a very old tradition," "a piece of the tradition's bedrock (Urgestein)," which has retained something of the mood of the first days of the new era.[26] I shall deal with the date of the episode below in section 4.

1. Vocabulary and Grammar.

The vocabulary and grammar of 27:51b-53 show that the Evangelist has most probably appropriated the pericope from elsewhere. In v 51b the earth "quakes/trembles" (σείω, pass.). While Matthew labels this an "earthquake" (σεισμός) in v 54, and himself emphasizes the same motif with the noun and verb in 28:2 and 4, the verb in 51b derives from his source, as I indicate below.

This earthquake causes rocks (πέτρα) to be "split" (σχίζω, pass., v 51b), the same verb as employed for the Temple curtain's being "torn" in v 51a (appropriated from Mark 15:38). This verb only occurs here in Matthew. The association of rock and tomb (μνημεῖον) is also found in 27:60, yet there it is borrowed from Mark 15:46.

In v 52 the splitting of the rocks leads to the tombs' being "opened" (ἀνοίγω, pass.). Except for the "tombs" in vv 52-53, all other occurrences of this noun in Matthew derive from Mark or "Q."

The term "bodies" (σῶμα) in v 52 only occurs here in Matthew with "many" (πολλός). The "saints" (ἅγιος) in the same verse is only found here in Matthew in the plural. "Who had fallen asleep" (= died: κοιμάομαι) is also only found here in Matthew in this sense.[27] In v 53 the noun "raising" (ἔγερσις) is employed, singular in the entire NT. Here

---

[23]*Das Evangelium des Matthäus* (Meyer; Göttingen: Vandenhoeck & Ruprecht, 1962³) 397.

[24]*Der Weg Jesu* 531.

[25]*Peake's Commentary on the Bible,* ed. M. Black and H. Rowley (London: Thomas Nelson and Sons, 1962) 797.

[26]*Neutestamentliche Theologie* (Gütersloh: Mohn, 1971) 293-94.

[27]In Matt 28:13 it is employed of actual sleep, as in Luke 22:45. For the sense of "having died," see John 11:11-14; Acts 7:60; 13:36; 2 Pet 3:4; and always in Paul (nine times).

the "holy city" (ἄγια πόλις) also occurs, Jerusalem,[28] as in 4:5.[29] As I note below, the "holy" aspect of those who arise (the saints) and the city is probably triggered by another OT text, Zech 14:5. Finally, the only occurrence of ἐμφανίζω in the Synoptics is in Matt 27:53. The form here is passive, as in Heb 9:24.

Only one element in the present text of 27:51b-53 must be emended. Since it became standard practice in the early Christian communities to view Christ after Easter Sunday as the "first fruit" of the resurrection, of all those who had fallen asleep (1 Cor 15:20, 23; cf. Col 1:18), a later editor or copyist of Matthew for reasons of piety changed "after *their* (αὐτῶν) raising/being raised" in 27:53 to "his" (αὐτοῦ). That is, the dead saints were now raised *after* Jesus on Easter Sunday and not together with him on Good Friday. Other scholars believe the whole phrase is a gloss, added at a date so early that there are now almost no variants in the textual tradition.[30]

The fact that each of the four verbs in 27:51b-53 is in the passive is highly unusual and certainly not typically Matthean. The form is the *passivum divinum.* God stands behind each step of the crescendoing action, which culminates in the dead saints' being "raised"/rising and entering Jerusalem.

In light of the peculiar terminology and grammar of 27:51b-53, it is thus most probable that Matthew appropriated this small pericope from elsewhere.

2. *The Physical Setting, Zechariah 14, and Ezekiel 37.*

Someone visiting modern-day Jerusalem for the first time is struck by the many graves on the western or Jerusalem side of the Mount of Olives. In reference to Zech 14:1-14, a popular guide to Israel, Z. Vilnay, states:

> On the slope of the Mount of Olives facing Mount Moriah – the Temple area, lies the largest and oldest Jewish cemetery in the world. It dates back to biblical times. It is believed that here will take place the Resurrection of the dead at the end of time.[31]

---

[28]Cf. the various early sources cited in Str-B 1.150.

[29]Matthew most probably found "holy city" in "Q" at 4:5. Luke 4:9 has Jerusalem, but this is probably an explication of Q for his non-Jewish readers.

[30]Cf. E. Klostermann, *Das Matthäusevangelium* (HNT 4; Tübingen: Mohr, 1927²) 225; W. Grundmann, *Das Evangelium nach Matthäus* (THKNT 1; Berlin: Evangelische Verlagsanstalt, 1975⁴) 562-63; and R. Schnackenburg, *Matthäusevangelium 16, 21–28, 20* (EB 1; Würzburg: Echter, 1987) 282. It cannot be excluded that Matthew himself changed the "their" of his source to "his" in v 53, yet this seems improbable.

[31]Cf. his *Israel Guide* 131 and 133.

Judaic interpretation of Zechariah 14 substantiates this. When the Lord gathers all the nations against Jerusalem to battle (the forces of Gog and Magog: Ezekiel 38-39), His feet will stand on the Mount of Olives east of Jerusalem. The latter will be "split in two" (נבקע מחציו; the Septuagint has the pass. of σχίζω), causing a very wide valley east to west (v 4). After reference to an earthquake (רעש; LXX σεισμός) in the days of the Judean King Uzziah, the prophet relates in v 5 that then the Lord will come with all His "holy ones" (קדשים; LXX οἱ ἄγιοι).[32] The Septuagint then interprets the difficult Hebrew of v 6 as: "In that day there shall be no light...," and v 7 notes that "at evening time there shall [again] be light." This is when the Lord will become King over all the earth (v 9).[33]

As in the Matthean description of Jesus' Crucifixion, including 27:51b-53, there are here references to an earthquake, a splitting/tearing (of the mountain's rocks), and holy ones/saints. In addition, there is darkness on this day, as at the Crucifixion. When v 53 also speaks of the saints coming out of their tombs, entering the holy city (of Jerusalem) and appearing to many, it can only mean their proceeding from the nearby Mount of Olives.

---

[32]I follow here the Greek, Syriac, Vulgate and Targum against the Hebrew of v 5. It is interesting in regard to the combination of an earthquake and the curtain of the Temple being torn in two in Matt 27:51 that Josephus in *Ant.* 9.225 relates regarding Uzziah's becoming leprous in the days of Zechariah (2 Chr 26:5): a great earthquake shook the earth, and the Temple was split open. *'Abot R. Nat.* A 9 (Schechter 42, Goldin 56-57) has R. Simeon b. Eleazar, a fourth generation Tanna (Strack and Stemberger, *Introduction* 88), state that at this time the Temple was split open (נבקע), twelve miles in one direction and twelve in the other. *Tanhuma* Noah 13 on Gen 9:20 (Singermann 68) has a parallel to the latter tradition.

[33]To my knowledge, only Stendahl (Peake's 797) and E. Schweizer in *Das Evangelium nach Matthäus* (NTD 2; Göttingen: Vandenhoeck & Ruprecht, 1973[13]) 337 call attention to the Mount of Olives here. It may also be noted that Judaic tradition locates the grave of Zechariah the son of Berechiah (Zech 1:1) at the base of the Mount of Olives. According to the "Lives of the Prophets" 15:6, he was buried near Haggai, who in turn "was buried near the tomb of the priests" (14:2, in *OTP* 2.394, with n. "c"). This writing is most probably Palestinian and from the beginning of the first century C.E. (2.380-81). The tomb of the priestly House of Hezir (Neh 10:21, Eng. 20), with an inscription to that effect, is located in the Kidron Valley on the western side of the Mount of Olives (Vilnay, *Israel Guide* 158). If the site of Zechariah's grave was also known in the first century C.E., as seems probable, it would have reinforced the association of Zechariah 14 and the Mount of Olives as the site of the final resurrection, important for Matt 27:51-53. See also the discussion of the grave site in J. Jeremias, *Heiligengräber in Jesu Umwelt (Mt. 23, 29; Lk. 11, 47)* (Göttingen: Vandenhoeck & Ruprecht, 1958) 73.

R. Eleazar of Modiim, an older second generation Tanna,[34] interprets Zech 14:2 as the generation of the Messiah in *Cant. Rab.* 6:10 § 1.[35] The Lord's standing on the Mount of Olives in Zech 14:4 is viewed as His judging His world in the time to come in *Exod. Rab.* Bo 17/4 on Exod 12:23.[36] In reference to Zech 14:1, R. Samuel bar Naḥmani, a third generation Palestinian Amora,[37] states that the nations will come to Jerusalem on the "day of the Lord" because "Gehenna is set in Jerusalem, where the Holy One will sit in judgment upon them, declare them guilty, and send them down to Gehenna." His proof for Gehenna's being located in the city is Isa 31:9 – "the Lord, whose fire is in Zion, and whose furnace is in Jerusalem."[38]

Already in Tannaitic times it was believed in regard to the land of Israel: "It is a land, the dead of which will be the first to come to life in the messianic era."[39] R. Ilai, a second generation Tanna,[40] states that the righteous who are buried outside the land of Israel (will proceed there at the resurrection of the dead) "by rolling."[41] God will make underground passageways for them, in which they roll until they arrive under the Mount of Olives. At this time it will be split open for them, and they will come up out of it.[42] In *Gen. Rab.* Vayechi 96/5 on Gen 47:29 this is based

---

[34]Strack and Stemberger, *Introduction* 78.
[35]Soncino 9.269. Cf. also R. Jonathan, a third generation Tanna (Strack and Stemberger, *Introduction* 83), in *Ruth Rab.* 5/6 on Ruth 2:14 (Soncino 8.64). It may also be noted that an Egyptian "false prophet," certainly a Jewish messianic pretender, led some 30,000 people to the Mount of Olives, from which he planned to enter Jerusalem, defeat the Romans, and himself rule. This was quelled by the procurator Felix some time after 54 C.E. See Josephus, *Bell.* 2.261-263 and *Ant.* 20.169-172; Acts 21:38; and Schürer, *The history* 1.464. It shows the importance of the Mount of Olives for the final, messianic time. See also the Slavonic addition regarding Jesus' activity on the Mount of Olives, inserted after *Bell.* 2.174 (in LCL 3.649).
[36]Soncino 3.214.
[37]Strack and Stemberger, *Introduction* 97.
[38]Cf. *Pesiq. Rav Kah.*, Suppl. 2/2 (Braude and Kapstein 463). Later this judgment is described in terms of Joel 4:12 (Eng. 3:12 – the valley of Jehoshaphat, the valley of decision, in which the sun will be darkened and the earth will shake [vv 14-16]), Ps 2:2 with the Lord's Anointed, and Zech 14:6, with no light on that day (p. 465). For Gehenna as the Valley of Hinnom directly south of Jerusalem, cf. the art. "Gehenna" by T.H. Gaster in *IDB* 2.361-62.
[39]Bar Qappara, a fifth generation Tanna (Strack and Stemberger, *Introduction* 90-91), says this in regard to Gen 47:30 in *y. Kil.* 9:3, 32c (Neusner 4.277; English by I. Mandelbaum). He bases this on Isa 42:5.
[40]Strack and Stemberger, *Introduction* 80.
[41]Cf. *b. Ketub.* 111a (Soncino 717-18).
[42]See *Pesiq. R.* 31/10 (Braude 617), with Zech 14:4.

on Ezek 37:12 and 14,[43] frequently and correctly considered part of the background of Matt 27:51b-53.[44]

Chapters 38-39 of Ezekiel were intimately connected to the Lord's final battle against the nations in Zech 14:2-3.[45] The chapter directly before this, Ezekiel's vision of the dry bones in thirty-seven, was also the "haftarah" or prophetic reading for the second day of Passover in Babylonia.[46] Since Jesus was crucified at Passover (Mark 14:12-16, 26 par.), it is understandable that a Palestinian Jewish Christian could have made the same association with Ezekiel 37, and could have described one prodigium at Jesus' death partly in terms of this chapter. There the Lord God will "open" and "raise" Israel from their "graves" and put His spirit within them, and they will live (again): vv 12-14. Precisely these three terms are also employed in Matt 27:52-53.

In light of this description of the physical setting of Matt 27:51b-53, including the influence of Zechariah 14 and Ezekiel 37, the application to Jesus' Crucifixion of Judaic interpretation of 1 Samuel 28 as the Day of Judgment, involving the premature rising of many deceased righteous, becomes more understandable.

3. 1 Samuel 28 in Judaic Tradition.

In section I above, I pointed out the great emphasis in this chapter on "rising" (עלה and קום) and "raising" (from the dead – the hiphil of עלה). It thus was easily associated with the final "resurrection" of the dead, immediately preceding the Final Judgment, as in Matt 27:51b-53.

Speaking with the deceased, necromancy, a form of sorcery/divination/witchcraft, was never entirely blotted out in Israel, in spite of the Pentateuchal prohibitions. This is shown in numerous

---

[43]Soncino 2.889, with Isa 42:5.

[44]Cf. C.G. Montefiore, *The Synoptic Gospels* (New York: Ktav, 1968[2], original 1927) 2.349; R. Gundrey, *Matthew. A Commentary on His Literary and Theological Art* (Grand Rapids, Michigan: Eerdmans, 1982) 576; N.A. Dahl, "Die Passionsgeschichte nach Matthäus" in *NTS* 2 (1955-56) 28, with reference to H. Riesenfeld and the Dura-Europos paintings; M. Riebl, *Auferstehung Jesu in der Stunde seines Todes?* Zur Botschaft von Mt 27, 51b-53 (SBB; Stuttgart: Katholisches Bibelwerk, 1978) 43-45; and D. Senior, "The Death of Jesus and the Resurrection of the Holy Ones (Mt 27:51-53)" in *CBQ* 38 (1976) 321.

[45]Cf. the eschatological battle against Gog and Magog in *Sifre* Behaalotekhah § 76 on Num 10:1-10 (Neusner 2.47); *Esth. Rab.* 7/23 on Esth 3:12 (Soncino 9.101-102), with parallels in *Lev. Rab.* 'Emor 27/11 on Lev 22:28 (Soncino 4.355) and *Pesiq. Rav Kah.* 9/11 (Braude and Kapstein 183); and *Midr. Ps.* 17/10 (Braude 1.215).

[46]Cf. *b. Meg.* 31a (Soncino 189). It should also be noted that in 1 Sam 28:24 the medium of Endor hastily bakes "unleavened bread" for Saul and his servants, which is reminiscent of Passover (Exod 12:15-20; Deut 16:3-4).

rabbinical examples,[47] including the sages' personal encounters with the dead.[48] Thus their own dealing with Samuel's rising from the dead in 1 Samuel 28 was not repulsive to them.

A baraitha or non-Mishnaic Tannaitic teaching states that it was possible for the medium of Endor to raise Samuel because it was within twelve months of his death.[49] During this period the body was thought to be still in existence, and the soul ascends and descends.[50]

In 28:13 the medium of Endor informs Saul: "I see (lit. 'saw') אֱלֹהִים rising from the earth." This is Samuel. The usual translation of this plural Hebrew form is the singular "god," as in the RSV, although the Septuagint also has the plural (θεούς). Josephus in *Ant.* 6.332 says at this point, Samuel is "godlike" (θεοπρεπής), in 333 "having a form like a (lit. 'the') god." Since אלהים can also be angels in the MT, the Targum interprets the Hebrew noun here as an "angel."[51] Writing in Hebrew, probably in Palestine at about the time of Jesus, Pseudo-Philo speaks here (64:6) of "divine beings" *(diis).*[52] He combines this with the tradition still found in the Targum, however, by stating that "two angels *(angeli)* are leading him [Samuel]."[53] Samuel then asks Saul (28:15): "'Why have you disturbed me by raising me up?' I thought that the time for being rendered the rewards of my deeds had arrived" (64:7).[54]

This time is definitely the Day of Judgment, preceded by the resurrection of all the dead.[55] Pseudo-Philo thus shows that 1 Sam 28:15 was already interpreted in a Palestinian pre-Christian Judaic source as Samuel's believing the Final Judgment had arrived. For this reason the prophet now rose from the dead.

Rabbinic sources corroborate this thought. Typical is *Lev. Rab.* 'Emor 26/7 on Lev 20:27, where Samuel objects to Saul's making an idol out of him. He then adds: "Since I thought that it was the Day of Judgment (יום הדין), I brought up (hiphil of עלה) Moses with me." Although of excellent character, Samuel now prefers having legal assistance from Israel's first redeemer and great lawgiver, Moses. He

---

[47]Cf. *b. Ber.* 21b (Soncino 128, a baraitha); 59a (Soncino 367); and *b. Sanh.* 65b on m.7:7 (Soncino 445-46). See also *Midr. Ps.* 19/1 on Ps 19:1-2 (Braude 1.271).

[48]Cf. for example *Gen. Rab.* Bereshith 11/5 (Soncino 1.83-84), and *b. Šabb.* 152b (Soncino 779-80).

[49]Based on the four months of 1 Sam 27:7, *Seder 'Olam* 13 states that "Samuel died four months before Saul" (Milikowsky, Hebrew 298, English 487).

[50]Cf. *b. Šabb.* 152b-153a (Soncino 780).

[51]Aramaic in Sperber 2.152; English in Harrington and Saldarini 155.

[52]Latin in Harrington, *Les Antiquités Bibliques* 1.384; English in *OTP* 1.377.

[53]*Ibid.*

[54]*Ibid.*

[55]Cf. Harrington's note "j" in *OTP* 1.377.

would attest that Samuel had fulfilled everything in the Torah.[56] The author of the midrash then continues by stating that if Samuel, the master of the prophets, was afraid of the Day of Judgment, how much more so should all other people be.[57]

This view of the occasion as the Day of Judgment is emphasized by Rabbi (Judah the Prince), a fourth generation Tanna.[58] When he came to 1 Sam 28:15, he would weep. He connected the verse to others dealing with the Judgment, the day of the wrath of the Lord, when everything, including the smallest details "written down in a man's [heavenly] account-book," will be "read out to him at the time of his death."[59] The latter indicates that God's judgment can be thought of as occurring directly after death, also implied in Luke 23:43, to be treated in section D below.

1 Sam 28:15 has Samuel ask Saul why he has "disturbed" him. This verb is the hiphil of רגז, which in the qal can mean "quake, tremble, shake."[60] It is frequently employed of the earth's quaking/trembling/shaking.[61] This, too, may form part of the background of the first

---

[56]Cf. *b. Ḥag. 4b* (Soncino 16-17). Interestingly, it is not stated in Mark 9:4 par. where Moses comes from at Jesus' transfiguration, nor where he returns afterwards. It must be assumed, however, that he comes from the same place as he and Samuel do in Judaic comment on 1 Samuel 28: the division (of heaven) for the righteous under the throne of God. On this, see below.

[57]The Hebrew is found in *Leviticus Rabbah: Midrash Wayyikra Rabbah*, ed. M. Margulies, 603-604. English in Neusner, *Judaism and Scripture* 457 and Soncino 4.334. The Soncino translation is based on a text which also cites Exod 7:1 here, where the Lord says to Moses: "See, I make you as אלהים to Pharaoh." For Samuel's believing it was the Day of Judgment, see also *Tanḥuma* 'Emor 2 (Eshkol 599); *Tanḥuma B* 'Emor 4 (Bietenhard 2. 119-120, based on Vaticanus Ebr. 34, in many points different from the Oxford Opp. 20 MS Buber follows in his *Midrasch Tanchuma* 2.82-83); *Midrash Haggadol* 'Emor on Lev 21:1 (Kook 591); *Midrash Aggadah* 'Emor 4 on Lev 21:1, where "our rabbis" relate a whole dialogue between Samuel and Moses on the Day of Judgment (Buber 51); and *Midrash Samuel* 24/5 (Buber 120; German in Wünsche, *Aus Israels Lehrhallen*, 5.134).

[58]Strack and Stemberger, *Introduction* 89-90. He is thought to have edited the Mishnah.

[59]I prefer here the printed text, translated in Soncino 4.333. Neusner in *Judaism and Scripture* 459 follows Margulies, who omits the latter remark (*Leviticus Rabbah* 603), relegating it to his apparatus. For parallel passages, see G. Wewers, *Hagiga*. Übersetzung des Talmud Yerushalmi 33, n. 10, on 2:1, 77a.

[60]BDB 919.

[61]Cf. 1 Sam 14:15; Joel 2:10 (associated with a solar eclipse); Amos 8:8 (also associated with a solar eclipse in v 9); Ps 77:19 (Eng. 18); Prov 30:21; as well as the hiphil in Isa 14:16 and Job 9:6. The earth's shaking in Matt 27:51b is associated with the rocks (of the Mount of Olives) splitting open. In Isa 5:25; Joel 2:10; and Ps 18:8 (Eng. 7) it is also mountains which shake/tremble.

statement of the small unit Matt 27:51b-53: "the earth 'shook'" (pass. of σείω). In contrast to Mark 15:39, the Evangelist Matthew then adds that the centurion and those with him at Jesus' Crucifixion saw this "earthquake" (σεισμός – v 54).

Most important for Matt 27:51b-53 is not Moses as accompanying Samuel when the medium of Endor raised him from the dead, as noted above, but another view. The printed edition of *Lev. Rab.* 'Emor 26/7 has on 1 Sam 28:13: "And some [authorities] say, 'And many righteous persons [הרבה צדקים] ascended with him in that hour/at that time.'"[62] This is repeated in many of the parallel accounts, showing it was a dominant tradition.[63] Most probably related to it is the remark regarding Samuel and 1 Sam 28:15 by R. Ḥanina (b. Isaac), a fourth generation Palestinian Amora,[64] that even "the righteous" (הצדיקים) fear the Day of Judgment.[65]

In light of the Mount of Olives setting (Zechariah 14) for the rising from the dead at Jesus' Crucifixion, the "many righteous" who arose with Samuel was changed by the Palestinian Jewish Christian author of Matt 27:51b-53 to "many saints." He borrowed the latter term from Zech 14:5.[66]

Matt 27:52 states that "many (πολλά) bodies of the saints who had fallen asleep (κεκοιμημένων) were raised (ἠγέρθησαν)." Dan 12:2 relates regarding the general resurrection: "many (רבים) of those sleeping (ישׁנ) in the earth's dust will awaken (יקיצו), some to eternal life, and some to shame and eternal contempt." Both the Septuagint and Theodotion have here πολλοί for "many," as in Matthew. They also both employ καθεύδω for "sleeping," a synonym of Matthew's κοιμάομαι.

The Palestinian Jewish Christian author of Matt 27:51b-53 probably borrowed the term "those sleeping" (in death) from Dan 12:2. Yet he thought of this imagery from Daniel because he was first of all aware of

---

[62]Margulies, *Leviticus Rabbah* 601, apparatus, translated in Soncino 4.332. Margulies strangely prefers "many elders," based on the זקן of 28:14. It is singular, however, in the textual tradition. See n. 63.

[63]Cf. *Midrash Haggadol*, Leviticus p. 590; *Pirq. R. El.* 33 (Eshkol 116; Friedlander 244); and *Midrash Samuel* 24/4 (Buber 119; Wünsche 133). In his Homily 5:7 on 1 Sam 28:3-25, Origen speaks out against the "holy souls of other prophets" or "angels" rising with Samuel (1 Sam 28:13). This appears to be directed against rabbinic tradition known to him. For the text, see Origène, *Homélies sur Samuel,* 192.

[64]Strack and Stemberger, *Einleitung* 98; he is forgotten in *Introduction* 103.

[65]Cf. the German of Bietenhard 2.120 on *Tanhuma B* 'Emor 4. It is not in the main text of Buber, who follows the Oxford MS. See also *Midrash Aggadah* (Buber 51).

[66]It should be noted, however, that the Sinaitic Syriac and Tatian have "the righteous" in Matt 27:52. See A. M'Neile, *The Gospel According to Matthew* (New York: St. Martin's, 1965) 424.

the fact that *"many* righteous persons *arose* with him (Samuel") in Judaic interpretation of 1 Sam 28:13 and 15. There are two main reasons for this assertion.

First, Dan 12:2 names no specific group at the general resurrection of the dead, only "many" persons, including the good and the evil. Judaic comment on 1 Sam 28:13 and 15, however, specifies the participants by designating them as "the righteous," a synonym of "the saints" in Matt 27:52.[67]

Secondly, in Dan 12:2 many of the dead who have been sleeping awaken, yet this is associated with no specific person's resurrection. This is the case, however, in Judaic comment on 1 Sam 28:13 and 15, where many righteous people arise at the rising from the dead of the individual Samuel. Only in Judaic comment on 1 Sam 28:13 and 15 does a phenomenon occur similar to that of Matt 27:51-53. The many righteous who accompany Samuel err, thinking the resurrection of the dead and the Day of Judgment have arrived. It is not stated what they do after rising with Samuel. The same is true in Matthew for the many saints who, when the individual Jesus dies, rise from their tombs near Jerusalem and enter the holy city, Jerusalem, appearing to many people. They, too, err, thinking that at Jesus' death, he immediately rises, and that the general resurrection, the turn of the ages before the Final Judgment, has thus arrived. After they enter Jerusalem, they, too, are never heard of again.

Excursus on 1 Samuel 28 and Psalm 22

Psalm 22 was interpreted at a very early stage by Palestinian Jewish Christians to apply to Jesus' Crucifixion. Two clear examples are the dividing of Jesus' garments among the Roman soldiers by the casting of lots (Ps 22:19 [Eng. 18] and Mark 15:24 par.; John 19:24), and the words "My God, my God, why hast Thou forsaken me?" spoken by Jesus before his expiring (Ps 22:2 [Eng. 1], and Mark 15:34 with Matt 27:46).[68]

Two Palestinian traditions associate Psalm 22 and Judaic interpretation of 1 Samuel 28.

---

[67]Cf. Mark 6:20; Acts 3:14; Rom 7:12, and the statement by K.G. Kuhn, art. *hagios* in *TDNT* 1.100: "The righteous of the OT are also called holy...." See also p. 110 and n. 72. One rabbinic example is *Sifre* Wezot habberakah § 344 on Deut 33:3 (Hammer 357), where "All his 'holy ones'" is interpreted as "the souls of 'the righteous,' who are kept in His treasury," as in 1 Sam 25:29.

[68]For other uses of this psalm at Jesus' Crucifixion, cf. my study "The Release of Barabbas (Mark 15:6-15 par.; John 18:39-40), and Judaic Traditions on the Book of Esther" in *Barabbas and Esther and Other Studies in the Judaic Illumination of Earliest Christianity* 11-14.

1) Justin Martyr.

Born at Flavia Neapolis (Nablus) near Jacob's Well at Sychar/Shechem[69] ca. 100 C.E. and martyred ca. 163-67 C.E.,[70] Justin in his "First Apology" 18 deals with proofs for immortality and the resurrection. He adduces pagan forms of "necromancy" and the "evoking of departed human souls" from the time of Homer on to persuade his readers that "even after death souls are in a state of sensation," "sensation remains to all who have ever lived...."[71]

In Justin's "Dialogue with Trypho the Jew," the converted neo-Platonic philosopher deals in chapters 98-106 with the various verses of Psalm 22 as fulfilled in Jesus' Crucifixion and Resurrection. In chap. 105 Justin interprets LXX Ps 21:20 (Heb 22:21) on "deliver my soul" of the suffering involved in Jesus' death on the Cross, including Jesus' prayer "that no one should take possession of his soul." At the end of life, the Christian "may ask the same petition of God." Justin continues:

> And that the souls survive, I have shown[72] to you from the fact that the soul (ψυχή) of Samuel was called up by the witch, as Saul demanded. And it appears also, that all the souls of similar righteous men (δίκαιοι) and prophets fell under the dominion of such powers, as is indeed to be inferred from the very facts in the case of that witch.[73]

God, says Justin, teaches us that at death we should pray that our souls may not be taken by a power such as a shameless evil angel. Precedence for such behavior is given by Jesus himself, who when dying on the Cross said: "Father, into Thy hands I commend my spirit" (Luke 23:46). [74]

Here Justin betrays knowledge of Palestinian Judaic interpretation of 1 Sam 28:13 and 15, where "many righteous people" "arose" with

---

[69]Cf. the art. "Sychar" by D.C. Pellett in *IDB* 4.471.

[70]Cf. L.W. Barnard, *Justin Martyr. His Life and Thought* (Cambridge: Cambridge University, 1967) 5 and 13.

[71]English in A. Roberts, J. Donaldson and A. Coxe, *The Ante-Nicene Fathers* 1.169. For the Greek, cf. J. Otto, *Iustini Philosophi et Martyris Opera* 1.56-60, with the relevant notes.

[72]No reference to 1 Samuel 28 is found earlier in the Dialogue. Either Justin refers to a lost section of his treatise on the resurrection (fragments are translated in *The Ante-Nicene Fathers* 1.294-99); the First Apology 18, noted above, where he may have thought he also mentioned 1 Samuel 28; or the text is corrupt and should read: "I (will now) show you...."

[73]English in *The Ante-Nicene Fathers* 1.252. The Greek is in Otto 2.376-378. See n. 9 on p. 377 in regard to 1 Samuel 28.

[74]*Ibid.*

Samuel.[75] He also connects the incident with the resurrection of the dead (before the Day of Judgment), Psalm 22, and Jesus' final words on the Cross in Luke 23 (see section D below).

That Justin's combination of 1 Samuel 28 and Psalm 22 most probably ultimately derived from an early Jewish exegetical tradition may also be echoed in targumic and other Judaic interpretation of an incident in the Scroll of Esther.

2) The Second Targum of Esther.

Because King Saul refused to kill King Agag of the Amalekites as the prophet Samuel had instructed him (1 Samuel 15), an Amalekite killed him at his battle with the Philistines (2 Sam 1:8-10).   In addition, however, Judaic tradition relates that just before Samuel killed Agag (1 Sam 15:33), the latter sired an ancestor of wicked Haman.[76]

In order to avert evil Haman's edict of annihilation of all the Jews in the Persian empire (Esth 3:9, 13; 4:7-8), Queen Esther first fasts for three days before going to her husband, King Ahasuerus, to ask for his intervention. She will do so even if she "perishes," for this action is against the Persian law (4:16). In 5:1 Esther then goes to the king on the third day with her petition.

This scene is greatly enlarged in Judaic tradition. Elsewhere I have pointed out that the third day, on which Esther proceeds to the king, is the fifteenth of Nisan, the first day of Passover. It is also the day on which Israel was often redeemed in the past, the day on which the Messiah is to come for redemption in the future, and the day of Jesus' Crucifixion.

Standing unsummoned before the king, Esther is seized "in the agony of death" and utters Ps 22:2 (Eng. 1): "My God, my God, why hast Thou forsaken me?" Other verses from the psalm are also applied to her by the rabbis in this terrible situation.[77]

The Second Targum on Esther, for all practical purposes a midrash, at 4:16 has Esther state that if she now perishes in this world, "I will have a 'portion' (חולקא) in the world to come."[78] Twelve thousand young

---

[75]For an analysis of Justin's knowledge of Judaic materials, cf. chapter IV of Barnard's *Justin Martyr* (39-52).

[76]Cf. 2 Targ Esth 4:13 (Grossfeld 156-157), and Ginzberg, *Legends* 4.422-23 and 6.470-71, n. 140, also referring to 4.68 and the relevant notes. Here in 2 Targ Esth 4:13 Mordecai also states that Esther is a descendant of King Saul. As such she should carry out the work of destroying all the descendants of evil Amalek, including wicked Haman.

[77]See the sources noted in *Barabbas and Esther* 8-10 and 12-14.

[78]The Aramaic is found in P. Cassel's *Aus Literatur und Geschichte. Zweites Targum zum Buche Esther* 54. English by B. Grossfeld, *The Two Targums of Esther*

priests at this point maintain that if Israel is annihilated, the sun and moon will be dark and not give their light.[79] They blow their trumpets, and the assembled Shushanite Jews cry so loudly that the hosts of heaven weep, "and the Patriarchs moved (נגו)[80] from their graves," that is, they left them.[81] L. Ginzberg paraphrases here by stating: "the Fathers came forth from their graves."[82]

The association of the motifs of the sun's darkening and the Patriarchs' rising from their graves, within the context of Esther's "agony of death" on the first day of Passover, is strikingly similar to two of the prodigia at Jesus' Crucifixion in Matthew, also described in terms of Psalm 22.

The Second Targum now comments on Esth 5:1 by having Esther pray to the God of Abraham, Isaac and Jacob before entering the palace, unsummoned and thus in danger of death, to speak to the king. She addresses Him by stating that "The inhabitants of Jerusalem have 'burst forth' (נעי)[83] from their graves because You have delivered their children to be slaughtered."[84] Dependent on a different text, L. Ginzberg notes here: "The nobles of Jerusalem came forth from their graves...."[85]

It is understandable that the three Patriarchs rise from their graves (in the cave of Machpelah in Hebron),[86] for Esther calls upon them to intercede with God for her people. Yet the rising of Jerusalem's dead (on the western slope of the Mount of Olives) is strange in the mouth of the Jewish queen of Persia. Perhaps Jerusalem is meant as the mother of all diaspora Jews, therefore she should mourn for her exiled children abroad (cf. Esth 2:6). The important thing to note here, however, is that this rising of the dead from their graves also takes place at the moment of Esther's agony of death on the first day of Passover, the fifteenth of Nisan, elsewhere described in terms of Psalm 22, as was Jesus'

158, with n. 32 on the "portion" in *Midrash Panim Aherim* 2. See also Cassel's *An Explanatory Commentary on Esther* 321.

[79]Aramaic in Cassel 55; English in Grossfeld 158 and Cassel 321.

[80]On this verb, cf. Jastrow 883.

[81]The Aramaic (Cassel 55) has מן, "from." Nevertheless, the English translator of Cassel, A. Bernstein, has "in" (p. 322), as does Grossfeld (p. 158).

[82]*Legends* 4.424. Ginzberg almost always employs the terminology of his original source. In his German translation, A. Sulzbach has the term "rise" ("auferstehen") here. Cf. his *Targum Scheni zum Buch Esther* 72.

[83]Jastrow 919 on this verb says see עוי, p. 583: burst forth, bloom, sprout. Grossfeld (160) has "have moved in."

[84]Cassel Aramaic 56, with מן, "from."

[85]*Legends* 4.425, perhaps employing the Rabbinic Bible. Sulzbach, *Targum Scheni* 73-74, has "the dead of Jerusalem." Neither variant is noted by Grossfeld (160, "j").

[86]Cf. *Legends* 1.288-290, 308, 416-17 and the relevant notes.

Crucifixion on the same day. A very early exegetical block of tradition regarding Esth 4:16-5:2, which included the rising of the dead and employment of Psalm 22, appears to lie behind both the accounts of Esther's dreaded appearance before King Ahasuerus and Jesus' Crucifixion in Matthew.

Elements from Esther's encounter with Ahasuerus in the Septuagint addition at Esth 5:2 may also point to the influence of Judaic tradition regarding 1 Samuel 28 here. She tells the king: "I saw you, lord, like 'an angel [ἄγγελος] of God,' and my heart was 'agitated/disturbed' [pass. of ταράσσω][87] from 'fear' [φόβος] of your glory" (5:2a). Then the king is also "agitated/disturbed" (pass. of ταράσσω; 5:2b). Esther's seeing Ahasuerus like an angel of God recalls the medium of Endor's seeing Samuel as a god in 1 Sam 28:13, in the Targum as an angel. Saul in the same verse tells her not to "fear." Only two verses later Samuel is "disturbed" by Saul (v 15).

This Septuagint addition at Esth 5:2 definitely had a Semitic "Vorlage" and may go back to the second century B.C.E.[88] It is part of Judaic comment on the events of Esth 4:16 – 5:2, including the Second Targum's reports of groups of people rising from their graves on this occasion, one resurrection taking place near Jerusalem. If it also betrays influence from Judaic interpretation of 1 Samuel 28, this is one more indication that this chapter was associated at a very early time[89] with the resurrection from the dead of definite groups of people, as in Matt 27:51b-53. More, unfortunately, cannot be stated.

---

[87]LSJ 1758, I.2. The Greek "A" text, which has a Semitic "Vorlage" here and which may go back to a Hebrew text older than that behind the present MT, also stresses Esther's great anguish and Ahasuerus' fierce anger. See D. Clines, *The Esther Scroll: The Story of the Story* (JSOTSup 30; Sheffield: JSOT, 1984) 233, and for the dating 93.

[88]Cf. C.A. Moore, *Daniel, Esther and Jeremiah. The Additions* (AB 44; Garden City, New· York: Doubleday, 1977) 155 on Addition "C," and 166 on this dating. See also *Esth. Rab.* 8/6 and 9/1 (Soncino 9.108-109) on this scene, as well as Josephus, *Ant.* 11.234-241, who was already acquainted with the addition.

[89]The *present* text of the Second Targum is very late. Grossfeld in *The Two Targums of Esther* 20 mentions 800 C.E. as an early dating. Nevertheless, each individual tradition incorporated in it must be considered on its own merits. One example is the second part of Esther's prayer, which L. Ginzberg thinks may be "the oldest specimen of an' Akedah" (*Legends* 6.472, n. 143), Judaic interpretation of the "binding" of Isaac by Abraham in Genesis 22.

4.   The Origin, Historicity, Date and Original Language of Matt 27:51b-53.

1)   The Origin.

The special material in Matt 27:51b-53 does not derive from the Evangelist himself, as I noted in section 1. above.[90]   Although incorporating elements from Zechariah 14, Ezekiel 37 and Daniel 12, it basically derives from Judaic tradition on 1 Samuel 28. There, too, (and only there), many of the righteous arise with a particular person, falsely thinking the Day of Judgment has arrived. Neither P. Billerbeck,[91] S. Lachs,[92] nor modern studies such as that of M. Riebl[93] have noted this OT and Judaic background.

It is very tempting to view Matthew's special material here as connected to the complex of 1 Samuel 28, Psalm 22 and Esth 4:16 – 5:2, discussed above in the Excursus. If an eclipse of the sun and the rising of a group of dead persons near Jerusalem were part of the scene of Esther's "agony of death" before going in to King Ahasuerus in pre-Christian Judaic sources, the Palestinian Jewish Christian author of Matt 27:51b-53 was most probably inspired by this complex. It also employed Psalm 22 to describe Esther's state of being forsaken in this hour, as the same psalm was used by Palestinian Jewish Christians to describe Jesus' own darkest hour, his Crucifixion. The author of the Matthean pericope then transferred the rising of certain dead persons in the Esther account, known to him, to Jesus' own agony of death.

If, as I maintain, Matt 27:51b-53 has its major origin in Judaic traditions on 1 Samuel 28, a number of statements made by early and modern authors must also be corrected (including the assertion that the pericope was composed by Matthew himself).

a)   It is not at all concerned with Jesus' "descent to Hades."[94]

b)   It is not of Hellenistic origin.[95]

---

[90]Against D. Senior, "The Death of Jesus and the Resurrection of the Holy Ones (Mt 27:51-53)" in *CBQ* 38 (1976) 321.

[91]Str-B 1.1046 only refers here to his excursus on the general or partial resurrection of the righteous in the messianic age.

[92]Cf. his *A Rabbinic Commentary on the New Testament. The Gospels of Matthew, Mark and Luke* (Hoboken: KTAV, 1987) 435.

[93]*Auferstehung Jesu in der Stunde seines Todes?* She nowhere mentions 1 Samuel 28, nor does she cite any rabbinic texts (27).

[94]Cf. Origen and other early writers cited by E. Fascher, *Das Weib des Pilatus (Matthäus 27, 19). Die Auferweckung der Heiligen (Matthäus 27, 51-53)* (Hallische Monographien 20; Halle: Niemeyer, 1951) 22-51.

[95]Cf. E. Klostermann, *Das Matthäusevangelium* 225. In his *Novum Testamentum Graecum* of 1752, 1.51, J. Wettstein had already called attention to Ovid, "Metamorphoses" 7. In 205-209 Medea speaks to the forces of nature, who help

c)   It is not a Jewish apocalyptic hymn describing the resurrection of the dead in the final age.[96]

d)   It is not a transposed resurrection account.[97]

e)   It is not a dramatization of John 5:25-29.[98]

f)   It is not due to someone's experiencing an earthquake and the removal of the closing stones of tombs, interpreted by that person with "a very bad conscience of his behavior toward Jesus," he considering "such buried saints as warning appearances."[99]

g)   It is not a "tradition gone wild," which originally only spoke of miraculous signs at Jesus' death (the Temple curtain tears, an earthquake)."[100]

h)   It does not indicate that at Jesus' "second coming, when all the dead are raised, he will be accompanied by the departed saints (I Thess. 4:16)."[101]

Other negative statements could be added to these.[102] All of them fail to recognize the major background of Matt 27:51b-53 in the rising of many righteous persons who thought the Day of Judgment had arrived, but who erred, in Judaic tradition on 1 Samuel 28.

---

her perform certain acts: the mountains shake, the earth rumbles, spirits go forth from their tombs, and the moon and sun become pale. Ovid finished this work in 7 c.e. (F.J. Miller in LCL I.xi). Klostermann also calls attention to Dio Cassius' "Roman History" 51.17, 5, where, before the taking of Alexandria in 30 B.C.E. by the Romans (not by Vespasian, as Klostermann maintains), "dead men's ghosts appeared" (E. Cary in the LCL edition). Neither passage is related directly to the death of a famous person.

[96]Cf. W. Schenk, *Der Passionsbericht nach Markus* (Gütersloh: Mohn, 1974) 77. He posits a possible Hebrew original, taken over by Matthew from a Jewish Christian tradition.

[97]D. Hutton, *The Resurrection of the Holy Ones (Mt 27:51b-53)*. A Study of the Theology of the Matthean Passion Narrative (unpublished 1970 Harvard Ph.D. dissertation), according to Senior, "The Death of Jesus" 314.

[98]Cf. W.F. Albright and C.S. Mann, *Matthew* (AB 26; Garden City, New York: Doubleday, 1971) 351, relying on W.G. Essame. Somewhat similar is R. Schnackenburg, *Matthäusevangelium* 16, 21–28, 20 (pp. 281-282): the text should be understood as "a dramatized theological thought." See also Schmauch, *Das Evangelium des Matthäus* 397.

[99]P. Gaechter, *Das Matthäusevangelium* (Innsbruck: Tyrol, 1963) 933.

[100]Haenchen, *Der Weg Jesu* 531.

[101]S. Johnson, "The Gospel According to St. Matthew" in *IB* 7.610.

[102]Riebl, *Auferstehung Jesu* 9-13, surveys additional opinions.

2) The Historicity.

Matt 27:51b-53 is the third of the prodigia which the First Evangelist relates regarding Jesus' Crucifixion and death, after an eclipse of the sun and the tearing of the Temple curtain (vv 45 and 51). Like similar prodigia at the deaths of famous non-Jewish and Jewish persons (see section B below), it was not meant by the original Palestinian Jewish Christian author to be taken literally. Rather, it primarily underscored the importance of Jesus' person. Using metaphorical language, it stated theologically that already at Jesus' death the turn of the ages had arrived. Jesus ascended to God, he was elevated/exalted from the Cross now (see below, section IV), not three days later. Therefore many of the pious dead were raised/arose with him, thinking the general resurrection had arrived. They erred, like the earliest Christians, who in spite of their original eschatological fervor had to come to the realization that first the gospel must be preached to all the nations (Mark 13:10 par.), allowing others also to partake in the salvation God offers in the Messiah Jesus. Only then would God cause all the dead to rise and the Final Judgment to take place.

One example of an aspect of Matt 27:51b-53 at the death of a rabbi shows that such prodigia should not be interpreted literally. The Jerusalem Talmud at '*Abod. Zar.* 3:1, 42c states that when R. Ḥanina of Beth Hauran died, Lake Tiberias "split open" (איתבזע).[103] The verb בזע is not found in biblical Hebrew.[104] It should be compared to בקע in Zech 14:4, where the Mount of Olives is "split" (in two) in the final time. This Aramaic verb may stand behind the original account of the rocks' being "split" in Matt 27:51 (pass. of σχίζω), as well as the Temple curtain's being "torn/rent" in the same verse, at Jesus' death.

No Palestinian Jewish contemporary of R. Ḥanina would have asked whether at his death Lake Tiberias in fact did split open, that is, part from side to side. This was simply an accepted haggadic manner of describing the importance of a noted person at his death. The same is true for an eclipse of the sun, to be discussed below, as well as other natural phenomena such as thunder, lightning, hail, comets, a star at noon, and a hurricane.[105]

---

[103]English in Neusner 33.112. The passage was noted by P. Billerbeck as one of many miraculous happenings at the death of rabbis, but not related by him to Matt 27:51 (Str-B 1.1040). The dates of this Palestinian rabbi are unknown (*ibid.,* 5/6.137).

[104]Cf. Jastrow 154: split, perforate, rend. One example given is *Lam. Rab.* 2:17 § 21 (Soncino 7.183), where God "rends" His purple (the Temple curtain), to be discussed below in section C.

[105]See the whole passage *y.'Abod. Zar.* 3:1, 42c (Neusner 33.112-113); *b. MoCed Qaṭ.* 25b on "rending" one's garments at a person's death in m. 3:7 (Soncino 163); and

In spite of the fact that Matt 27:51b-53 is not "historical,"[106] it is "true" in a religious sense. J. Schniewind correctly stated regarding this pericope that "'legend' can also speak of realities which were constantly proclaimed in Jesus' speech and in the preaching of the first Christian community."[107] The importance of Jesus' death, which signified for his followers the real turn of the ages, is such a reality, such a religious truth. It was clothed in the typically haggadic material of the time, prodigia at the death of important persons, today unfortunately often called "legendary" with a negative connotation.[108]

3) *The Date.*

E. Haenchen speaks of Matt 27:51b-53 as a "more recent legend."[109] In contrast to this, as noted above, K. Stendahl considers the pericope to be "a piece of a primitive Christology," and for J. Jeremias it is "a piece of the tradition's bedrock." Already in 1927 the Jewish scholar C.G. Montefiore had maintained that "this miracle" had become incompatible with later doctrine in the early church.[110]

In 1 Cor 15:3 Paul relates that he had received something as tradition from earlier Christians: Christ "was raised on the third day in accordance with the Scriptures." The influence of OT passages such as Hos 6:2 was so strong, unfortunately, that it all but extinguished a different interpretation of Jesus' death as the time of his ascension/exaltation/resurrection, at which others also rose from the dead, thinking the general resurrection and the Day of Judgment had arrived.

In section IV below, I will treat Jesus' ascension/exaltation/ resurrection from the Cross more extensively, especially in connection with Isaiah 53 and Hos 6:2. Before that I shall point out that the other

---

b. B. Meṣ. 86a (Soncino 496). Many other extraordinary phenomena are described here.

[106]Cf. now even the Roman Catholic exegete Schnackenburg, *Matthäusevangelium 16, 21-28, 20* 282, who compares Matthew 1-2 for this genre of style, which should not be interpreted historically.

[107]*Das Evangelium nach Matthäus* (NTD 2; Göttingen: Vandenhoeck & Ruprecht, 1956[8]) 273.

[108]Typical of a positive usage of the term is the title of L. Ginzberg's monumental work, *The Legends of the Jews*. To treat such material as fantastic, as belonging only to the realm of fairy tales and myth, is to completely misunderstand half of Judaic interpretation of Scripture (the other being "halakha," the legal material). On haggadah, see Strack and Stemberger, *Introduction* 259-260, as well as the art. "Aggadah" from the *Encyclopaedia Hebraica* in *EncJud* (1971) 2.354-64.

[109]*Der Weg Jesu* 531.

[110]Cf. his *The Synoptic Gospels* 2.349. He blames "Paul and his circle" for the later doctrine.

two prodigia at Jesus' Crucifixion, the eclipse of the sun and the tearing of the Temple curtain, are also dependent on early Palestinian Jewish Christian interpretation of 1 Samuel 28. If this is so, a good case can be made for Matt 27:51b-53 as a remnant of an extremely old tradition, one which was even earlier than, or at least as early as, the "after three days" tradition Paul notes in 1 Cor 15:3.

4)   The Original Language.

In section A1. above in regard to the vocabulary and grammar of Matt 27:51b-53, I maintained that the pericope was not from Matthew, who wrote in Greek. It betrays knowledge of Zechariah 14 and of the dead being buried on the Mount of Olives just east of Jerusalem. After the mountain splits open, the dead enter the "holy city." The author is a Palestinian, acquainted with the local Jerusalem conditions.

Each of the six clauses in the short episode also begins with καί, a translation of the Semitic *waw*. In addition, the many passive verb forms are a typical circumlocution for God's name, especially in Aramaic.[111] All the Judaic traditions on 1 Samuel 28, the background of the narrative, are in Hebrew, which was also the language of early scholarly debates and prayer. Yet Aramaic is more probable for the original because it was the language of the people. The early Jewish Christian who was the author of the short narrative in Matt 27:51b-53 intended it for use in the early Palestinian congregations, when they pondered the meaning of Jesus' Crucifixion and Resurrection. He therefore most probably composed it in his native Aramaic, which was immediately understood by all and did not first have to be translated, as Hebrew did.[112]

Matthew, whom I consider bilingual, probably composed his gospel in Syria in an environment in which both Aramaic and Greek were known.[113] While he himself could have translated the pericope into Greek, it is more probable that he already found it translated and appropriated it from there.

---

[111]J. Jeremias especially points this out in his various works. Cf. references in BDF § 130.1, p. 72; § 313, p. 164; § 342, p.176, as well as, for example, *The Parables of Jesus* (New York: Scribners, 1963) 16, n. 20.

[112]This is even more probable if he was acquainted with the tradition of the rising of Jerusalem's dead at the time of Esther's "agony of death," connected to Psalm 22, now only found in the Aramaic Second Targum to Esther analyzed above.

[113]Cf. Grundmann, *Das Evangelium nach Matthäus* 43-45. For probably Syria, perhaps Antioch, see U. Luz, *Das Evangelium nach Matthäus*. 1. Teilband, Mt 1-7 (EKKNT I/1; Zurich, Benziger; Neukirchen-Vluyn, Neukirchener, 1989²) 73-75; Luz does not exclude a Syrian's knowing Aramaic (63). For either Antioch or Damascus, see J. Gnilka, *Das Matthäusevangelium*. 2. Teil (Herder; Freiburg: Herder, 1988) 514-15.

B. The Sun's Eclipse.

Mark 15:25 states that Jesus was crucified at the third hour. According to Judaic time reckoning, the night was divided into twelve hours, as was the day.[114] That is, Jesus was attached to the Cross at ca. 9 A.M. Mark 15:33 par. continues by stating that "when the sixth hour had come, there was darkness (σκότος) over the whole land/earth until the ninth hour." Then Jesus breathed his last (vv 34-37). The sun's eclipse is described here as lasting three hours, from 12 o'clock noon until 3 P.M.[115] In Luke 23:45 this "darkness" is made explicit by the statement: "the sun's 'light failed'" (ἐκλείπω, root of the English "eclipse"), while other MSS read: "the sun 'was darkened' (σκοτίζομαι)."

Jesus was crucified on the first day of Passover, the 15th of Nisan.[116] A contemporary of Jesus, Philo of Alexandria, notes that the feast of Unleavened Bread begins on the 15th day (of Nisan) "when the moon is full" and "there is no darkness," "as the sun shines from morning to evening...."[117] Astronomically, a solar eclipse is completely impossible at this time. The solar eclipse closest to the year of Jesus' death took place in 29 C.E., yet not in the Passover season of March–April, but on November 24th. In addition, a total darkening of the sun lasts at the most seven minutes, a partial darkening at the most two hours.[118] No other eclipse, either complete or partial, has ever lasted three hours.

The origin of the three-hour long solar eclipse in Mark 15:33 par. must be sought elsewhere.

1. Solar Eclipses at the Death of Famous Non-Jews.

Jewish Christians in the earliest congregations lived partly within a Hellenistic culture, with which Palestinian Jews were forced to come to

---

[114]Cf. Str-B 2.442 and 543-44.

[115]John 19:14 only states that Pilate condemned Jesus to death at about the sixth hour; the time of his later death is not given. For secondary literature on the sun's eclipse in Mark 15:33 par., as well as on the tearing of the Temple curtain in v 38 par., cf. *The Gospel of Mark. A Cumulative Bibliography 1950–1990*, ed. F. Neirynck et al. 617. It may also be noted that at least during the century before the destruction of the Temple, the ninth hour was the usual time for the daily burnt offering of the evening, including an unblemished male lamb (Num 28:4,8). See Josephus, *Ant.* 14.65; 3.237; *m. Pesaḥ.* 5:1 (Danby 141); and Isa. 53:7.

[116]Mark 14:1-2 and 12, with Unleavened Bread; 14:26 and 15:6. See Lev 23:5-6. On these two festivals, cf. the art. "Passover and Feast of Unleavened Bread" by J.C. Rylaarsdam in *IBD* 3.663-68.

[117]*Spec. Leg.* 2.155 in the LCL translation of F.H. Colson.

[118]Cf. the art. "Finsternisse" by F. Boll in *PW* 6.2360 on Nov 24th, 29 C.E., and 2329-30. For his material, Boll is greatly dependent on F.K. Ginzel, *Spezieller Kanon der Sonnen- und Mond-Finsternisse für das Ländergebiet der klassischen Altertumswissenschaft* (Berlin, 1899), which treats the period 900 B.C.E. to 600 C.E.

terms ever since the dividing up of the Near East by the successors of
Alexander the Great at his death in 323 B.C.E. There were very many
Greek-speaking cities in first-century C.E. Palestine,[119] and the influence
of the occupational power Rome was everywhere present. The common
practice of both Hellenism and Rome of describing the death of famous
men in terms of miraculous natural phenomena, *prodigia,* including a
solar eclipse,[120] was certainly known to many Jews. Solar eclipses at
their death are known in regard to the following persons:

1) Romulus, 708 B.C.E.

2) Peisander, 394 B.C.E.

3) Gaius Julius Caesar, 44 B.C.E.

4) Nerva, 98 C.E.[121]

The Jewish historian Josephus, a native of Jerusalem but writing at
Rome at the end of the first century C.E., notes the contents of a letter
Mark Anthony sent ca. 41 B.C.E. or three years after Julius Caesar's death
to Hyrcanus, high priest and ethnarch in Jerusalem, and to the Jewish
nation. In it the Roman speaks of "unlawful acts against the gods, from
which we believe the very sun turned away, as if it, too, were loath to
look upon the foul deed against Caesar."[122] Many Palestinian Jews, not
only those who knew Greek or Latin, were thus probably aware of a
solar eclipse at the death of a famous non-Jew, here Caesar.

2. *Solar Eclipses at the Death of Famous Jews.*

Mark 14:50 states that when Jesus was arrested in the Garden of
Gethsemane the night before his death, "all [his disciples] forsook him
and fled." At the Crucifixion itself at Golgotha, the disciples, probably
afraid for their lives, were conspicuously absent. Only some female
followers are described as looking on from afar (15:40-41), and a stranger,
Joseph of Arimathea, supposedly buries Jesus (vv 43-46). Those who had
followed Jesus most closely could not or did not mourn him in the usual
fashion, for example by tearing part of their garment.[123] Yet his heavenly

---

[119]Cf. E. Schürer, *The history* 2.85-183.

[120]Boll, "Finsternisse" 2336, states that "the most common interpretation of an
eclipse was in regard to the death or fall of a great man, above all a ruler."

[121]For Peisander, cf. Plutarch, The Lives V, Agesilaus 17.2. For the others, see the
sources in Boll, "Finsternisse" 2353, 2359 and 2361 respectively.

[122]*Ant.* 14.309 in the LCL translation of R. Marcus.

[123]On Judaic mourning customs, cf. " 'Ebel Rabbati named Masseketh Semahoth,
Tractate Mourning," trans. J. Rabbinowitz in *The Minor Tractates of the Talmud*
1.325-400. See also the articles on "Mourning" by M. Gruber and A. Rothkoff in
EncJud (1971) 12.485-93; J. Eisenstein in *JE* (1905) 9.101-103; and E. Jacob in *IDB*
3.452-54.

Father mourned for him by causing a solar eclipse, as I shall elucidate below. This follows Judaic usage, whereby the sun is also darkened at the death of an important Israelite/Jew.

One example is found in *b. Sukk.* 29a, where "our rabbis taught" that the sun is eclipsed on account of four things, one of which is when the vice president of the Sanhedrin (the 'Ab Beth Din) dies and is not mourned fittingly.[124] Here darkness over the earth is a sign of mourning an important person, who is not mourned properly by his fellow Jewish citizens.

According to *Semahoth* 2:7 there is no (public) mourning allowed for one executed by a (Jewish) court of law.[125] This was also true of Jesus. Although sentenced to death by the Roman Pilate, it was with the encouragement of a small number of the self-serving Temple hierarchy. None of the customary mourning rites took place at his death, so the sun's darkness also played a substitutionary role here.

A key OT passage for a solar eclipse at the death of a famous Jew is Amos 8:9, employed in *b. Mo'ed Qat.* 25b:

> When the soul of R. Pedath went into repose, R. Isaac b. Eleazar opened his funeral address thus: This day is as hard for Israel as the day when the sun set at noon-tide, as it is written: "And it shall come to pass in that day...that I will cause the sun to go down at noon, and I will darken the earth in the clear day. And I will turn your feasts into mourning and all your songs into lamentation...as the mourning of an only son" (Amos 8:9-10). And, said R. Yohanan, that was the day of King Josiah's death.[126]

R. Isaac b. Eleazar and R. Yohanan (bar Nappaha) were second generation Palestinian Amoraim.[127] Here a solar eclipse is adduced at the death of a rabbi, a distinguished person. It is also described as taking place at that of a Judean king, just as in the cases of famous Hellenistic and Roman personages, but also of Jesus.

This scripture text, Amos 8:9-10, is very important in three respects. 1) Just before it, Amos 8:8 asks whether the land/earth (הארץ) should not "tremble/quake" (רגז) and everyone who dwells on it "mourn" (אבל). The Hebrew verb for "tremble/quake" (qal) is the same as in 1 Sam 28:15, where Samuel asks Saul why he has "disturbed" (hiphil) him by bringing him up. By argument of analogy, the second of the "seven

---

[124]Soncino 130.

[125]Soncino, *Minor Tractates* 1.331. The stipulation in 2:11 (p. 333) would not apply to Jesus.

[126]Soncino 162, which I have slightly altered. N. 4 correctly states that the Munich MS should be preferred here.

[127]Strack and Stemberger, *Introduction* 95 and 94. Str-B 5/6.215-16 has R. Pedath as Palestinian, ca. 300 C.E., connected with R. Yohanan.

exegetical rules of Hillel,"[128] an early Palestinian Jewish Christian could easily have associated the two passages. His goal was to describe God's "mourning" over the death of Jesus, at which the earth also trembled/quaked (Matt 27:51).

2) The gospels note that Jesus expired after hanging on the Cross for six hours, from approximately 9 A.M. to 3 P.M. In *y. 'Abod. Zar.* 3:1, 42c it is related that when R. Samuel b. R. Isaac died,[129] there were fire from heaven, peals of thunder, and flashes of lightning "for three hours."[130] If this length of time was traditional, as appears to be the case, it may explain why there was also an eclipse of the sun at Jesus' Crucifixion for three hours, from 12 o'clock noon until 3 P.M.

In all other Judaic accounts, prodigia of nature occur at the time of the famous/important person's actual death. Nature joins in mourning with humans. Yet at Jesus' Crucifixion the darkness over the whole land/earth takes place *before* his death. This has three reasons. First, if the number of three hours was traditional, this prodigium would have begun at Jesus' death at the ninth hour, 3 P.M., and ceased at the twelfth hour, i.e., 6 P.M. The taking down of Jesus' corpse from the Cross and burying it before evening, the beginning of a new day, in this case the Sabbath (Deut 21:23; Mark 15:42), would hardly have been possible timewise in regard to the impending sundown. Secondly, at least the latter part of the burial would have occurred during darkness. This would have been very difficult to describe literarily.

Thirdly, according to Amos 8:9 God's mourning for an only son (v 10) was to be accompanied by the sun's going down "at noon" (בצהרים). He would darken the earth/land in broad daylight. The fulfillment of Scripture was so important for the Palestinian Jewish Christian author of this prodigium that he intentionally changed God's mourning for His only Son, Jesus, from the moment of his death to three hours before. The "noon" of Amos is exactly the sixth hour, as in Mark 15:33. In the Synoptics God proleptically causes a solar eclipse three hours in advance so that Scripture can be fulfilled, something extremely important to the earliest Palestinian Jewish Christians.

---

[128]Strack and Stemberger, *Introduction* 21.

[129]He was a third generation Palestinian Amora (*ibid.* 99).

[130]Cf. Neusner 33.113. A parallel tradition is found in *y. Pe'a* 1:1, 15d (Neusner 2.58). On the three hours, see P. Kuhn, *Gottes Trauer und Klage in der rabbinischen Überlieferung (Talmud und Midrasch)* (AGJU 13; Leiden: Brill, 1978) 339, n. 7.

3)   Amos 8:10 states that God will make the occasion "like the mourning for an only son" (כאבל יחיד).[131] As noted above, the Palestinian Jewish Christian author of the solar eclipse at Jesus' Crucifixion was certainly attracted to this Amos passage also because it spoke of mourning for an "only son." The Septuagint has here ἀγαπητός, the same term employed by "a voice from heaven" (a קול בת, the Shekinah or indwelling of God) of Jesus at his baptism (Mark 1:11 par.) and his transfiguration (9:7 par.). Here Jesus is not only "beloved"; in the original Semitic he is the "only Son" of God.

In Genesis 22, the narrative of Abraham's "binding" his son Isaac as an offering, Isaac is described three times as Abraham's "only son" (vv 2, 12 and 16). The rabbis note that the ʿAqedah took place at Mount Moriah, Jerusalem. *Gen. Rab.* Vayera 56/3 on Gen 22:6 ("And Abraham took the wood of the burnt offering and laid it on Isaac his son") states that this is "like one who carries his own cross on his shoulder."[132] Early Palestinian Jewish Christians also described Jesus, for them God's only Son, in imagery from the ʿAqedah.[133] He, too, bore his own wooden Cross to the site of execution, Golgotha, just outside Jerusalem.

Mourning for an only son is also found in Jer 6:28 and Zech 12:10.[134] The latter passage is interpreted of King Josiah in Judaic sources, and it is very important in regard to the remark made by R. Yoḥanan above on Amos 8:9-10. He maintains that the solar eclipse mentioned by Amos took place on the day that King Josiah died. To this I shall now turn.

3.   *The Solar Eclipse at the Death of King Josiah, the Pierced One.*

In *b. Moʿed Qaṭ.* 25b, R. Yoḥanan maintains that the solar eclipse at noon in Amos 8:9 occurred on the day of King Josiah's death. The following material on this Judean king is important in regard to the noontime solar eclipse at Jesus' Crucifixion.

When the "book of the law" (2 Kgs 22:8) was rediscovered at the end of the seventh century B.C.E. in the Jerusalem Temple, King Josiah instigated a major reform program. J. Bright says that it was "by far the

---

[131]The continuation of the verse, "and the end of it like a bitter day," was also applied to mourning at an early date. Cf. *b. Ber.* 16b (Soncino 96-97) with Rabban Simeon b. Gamaliel, either a first or third generation Tanna (Strack and Stemberger, *Introduction* 74 and 85); *b. Sukk.* 25b (Soncino 109); *b. Moʿed Qaṭ.* 20a (Soncino 127); and *b. Zeb.* 100b (Soncino 483).

[132]English in Neusner, *Genesis Rabbah* 2.280; cf. Soncino 1.493. The Hebrew is found in Theodor and Albeck, 598.

[133]For a masterful treatment of this subject, see S. Spiegel, *The Last Trial* (New York: Behrman, 1979). See also the art. "Akedah" by L. Jacobs in *EncJud* (1971) 2.481, with references to Tertullian and Clement of Alexandria.

[134]Mourning for an only child, Jephthah's daughter, is also found in Judg 11:34-40. Cf. also Luke 7:12; 8:42; and John 3:16.

most thoroughgoing in Judah's history...."[135] For this reason Josiah was revered in later Judaic tradition, frequently being called "righteous," even one of the four righteous men to descend from King David.[136]

Like Saul, Josiah put away the mediums and wizards.[137] In addition, he commanded that the Passover be kept as it is prescribed in the book of the covenant. No such Passover had been kept since the time of the early judges, or since the days of Samuel the prophet. The Passover lamb was slaughtered in Jerusalem on the 14th day of the first month, i.e., Nisan.[138] It was eaten in the evening, that is, on the 15th of Nisan, the same day as that on which Jesus celebrated the Passover with his disciples, and on which he was crucified. The reintroduction of the Passover feast and its proper procedure was so important in Judaic tradition that in Babylonia, as noted above, when two days of Passover were later kept, the Josiah account in 2 Kgs 23:21-23 was used as the haftarah or prophetic reading for the second day.[139]

Directly after this account of Passover, the death of King Josiah is related in 2 Chr 35:20-27. When Pharaoh Neco II of Egypt proceeds north to help his ally Assyria, Josiah intercepts him, but is killed in battle by the Egyptian at Megiddo in 609 B.C.E.[140] Archers shoot him, causing him to ask his servants to take him away, "for I am 'badly wounded'" (החליתי מאד; v 23). Then they take him to Jerusalem, where he is buried, and all Judah and Jerusalem mourn for him (v 24). Even the prophet Jeremiah utters a lament for the king.[141] The targum on v 25 states that an ordinance was made to the effect that Israel should mourn "annually" for Josiah in their lamentations.[142]

---

[135]*A History of Israel* (Philadelphia: Westminster, 1959) 295. The section 294-303 deals with Josiah, showing his great importance.

[136]Cf. *t. Ta 'an.* 2:10 (Neusner 2.271); *Gen. Rab.* Vayechi 97, New Version, on Gen 49:8 (Soncino 2.900); *Lev. Rab.* Aḥare Moth 20/1 on Lev 16:1 (Soncino 4.250-51 on Eccl 9:2); and *Pirq. R. El.* 17 (interpreting Isa 57:1, Friedlander 121). In *Pesiq. Rav Kah.* 27/3 on Ps 102:18 (Braude and Kapstein 414) he is one of four righteous men to descend from David.

[137]2 Kgs 23:24 and LXX 2 Chr 35:19.

[138]Cf. 2 Kgs 23:21-23, greatly expanded in 2 Chr 35:1-19. Verse one of the latter passage gives the date. The targum on 2 Chr 35:1 has "Nisan." Cf. R. Le Déaut and J. Robert, *Targum des Chroniques* 1.174 French, 2.163 Aramaic. See also the art. "Passover" by L. Jacobs in *EncJud* (1971) 13.163, as well as the remarks by E. Kutsch in 13.170-71.

[139]Cf. *b. Meg.* 31a (Soncino 187).

[140]2 Kgs 23:29 states that [the troops of] Pharaoh Neco slew him. For the date, cf. Bright, *A History* 303.

[141]Josephus in *Ant.* 10.77 notes that Josiah was "magnificently buried."

[142]Aramaic in Déaut and Robert 2.166, French 1.177.

Judaic tradition interprets the Book of Lamentations as having been composed by Jeremiah. In 4:20 "the Lord's anointed" (משיח יהוה; LXX χριστὸς κυρίου) is considered to be King Josiah.[143] He was "seized in the Egyptians' slaughtering pit," i.e., killed by them at Megiddo.[144] This episode is thought to be the content of Jeremiah's lament mentioned in 2 Chr 35:25. Since Josiah is the Lord's "Anointed," early Palestinian Jewish Christians felt justified in transferring imagery from his death to the death scene of their own "Anointed One," the Messiah Jesus.

The MT at 2 Chr 35:23 has Josiah "badly wounded" by the enemy's archers. Josephus is aware of an haggadic expansion of this death scene,[145] and R. Ishmael, a second generation Tanna,[146] taught in regard to it: "Three hundred arrows did they shoot into the anointed of the Lord."[147] In *b. Ta'an.* 22b Rab Judah states in the name of Rab, a first generation Babylonian/Palestinian Amora,[148] in regard to Josiah's being "badly wounded": "This teaches that they made his whole body [perforated with arrows] like a sieve."[149] The Soncino editor, I. Epstein, notes that החליתי is connected here with the verb חלל, "to pierce through." H. Lazarus makes the same observation on the parallel tradition in *b. Mo'ed Qaṭ.* 28b.[150] It is the same verb as that employed of the Suffering Servant in Isa 53:5, who is "pierced/wounded (מחלל) for our transgression." Early Palestinian Jewish Christians applied this verse, in

---

[143]Cf. Josephus, *Ant.* 10.77-78, who also stresses the people's great mourning; Targ. 2 Chr 35:25 (Aramaic in Déaut and Robert 2.166, French 1.177); Targ. Lam 4:20 in E. Levine, *The Aramaic Version of Lamentations* 55 Aramaic, 73 English (Levine's suspicion of the influence of Christian exegesis here is unwarranted – p. 174); and the Tannaitic *t. Ta'an.* 2:10, with Josiah as the Lord's anointed of Lam 4:20 (Neusner 2.271). See also *Pirq. R. El.* 53 (Friedlander 432, with n. 7).

[144]Targ. Lam 4:20, as in the preceding note.

[145]*Ant.* 10.77: Josiah is "in great pain from his wound" and orders "the call to be sounded for the army's retreat."

[146]Strack and Stemberger, *Introduction* 79.

[147]Cf. *y. Qidd.* 1:7, 61a (Neusner 26.99) on the expression "slain by the sword" in 2 Sam 3:29. In *Lam. Rab.* 1/53 on Lam 1:18 (Soncino 7.142-43) this is spoken by R. Mani (I), a second generation Palestinian Amora (Strack and Stemberger, *Introduction* 96). He notes that Jeremiah attended Josiah at this point. Cf. also the targum on this verse (Levine, Aramaic 33, English 65). See also *b. Ta'an.* 22b (Soncino 113), as well as *Lam. Rab.* 4/1 on Lam 4:1 (Soncino 7.215-16). Cf. also *Midr. Samuel* on 2 Sam 3:29 in Wünsche, *Aus Israels Lehrhallen* 5.141.

[148]Strack and Stemberger, *Introduction* 93.

[149]See Jastrow 609 under כברה, and Soncino 112-113. The same tradition is found in *b. Sanh.* 48b (Soncino 325), *b. Mo'ed Qaṭ.* 28b (Soncino 189), and *y. Qidd.* 1:7, 61a (Neusner 26.99, here spoken by R. Yoḥanan).

[150]Soncino 189, n. 10. See also L. Goldschmidt, *Der Babylonische Talmud* 3.487, n. 40.

turn, to Jesus' being "nailed" to the Cross. This led them to interpret the whole section in Isaiah 53 of the Crucifixion.

Because חלל is a synonym of דקר, "to pierce, pierce through,"[151] Tannaitic rabbis interpreted Zech 12:10-11 of the anointed one Josiah. Verse ten states that the house of David and the inhabitants of Jerusalem "shall look upon him[152] whom they have 'pierced' (דקר), and they shall mourn for him as one mourns for an only son (היחיד)." Verse eleven speaks of this mourning as being as great as for someone "in the plain of Megiddo." Since Josiah was "pierced through/sorely wounded" by archers in the plain of Megiddo (2 Chr 35:22; cf. 2 Kgs 23:29-30), Judaic tradition related the Zechariah passage to him.[153]

John 19:37 applies Zech 12:10 to Jesus at his Crucifixion, "so that Scripture might be fulfilled" (v 36).[154] In *y. Sukk.* 5:2, 55b[155] an Amora says Zech 12:12, referring also to mourning over the pierced one of v 10, is a lamentation for the Messiah. The parallel in *b. Sukk.* 52a (Soncino 246) has R. Dosa, a fourth generation Tanna,[156] interpret Zech 12:12 of the slaying of Messiah b. Joseph. The Talmud continues by stating that this agrees well with Zech 12:10.

Even if belief in a Messiah b. Joseph may only have arisen after the tragic events of 132-135 C.E.,[157] the fact that early rabbis interpreted Zech 12:10 of a Messiah at all, coupled with John 19:37, probably written at the end of the first century C.E.,[158] shows that another early Palestinian

---

[151]Cf. Jer 51:4, with an archer's bending his bow in v 3, as well as Lam 4:9.

[152]The MT has "over Me," but this was read as "over him" by the rabbis, as in *b. Sukk.* 52a. See Str-B 2.583, as well as the RSV.

[153]Cf. *b. Mo'ed Qaṭ.* 28b and *b. Meg.* 3a (Soncino 188-89), where R. Aqiba, a second generation Tanna (Strack and Stemberger *Introduction* 79-80), cites Zech 12:11 in regard to the great necessity of mourning for the sons of R. Ishmael. Aqiba contrasts this to mourning for King Ahab, who only did one good deed (remaining in battle in spite of his being severely wounded). Ahab, like Josiah, was "pierced" by an archer, dying of the wound (1 Kgs 22:34-35; 2 Chr 18:33-34). Ahab and Josiah are contrasted in Targ. Zech 12:11 (English in Cathcart and Gordon 219; Aramaic in Sperber 3.495). The targum is cited in *b. Mo'ed Qaṭ.* 28b and *b. Meg.* 3a (Soncino 10).

[154]While it directly refers to a soldier's piercing Jesus' corpse with his spear in v 34, it probably also includes the wider context of Jesus' being pieced through/bored/nailed to the Cross. Cf. also the allusion in Rev 1:7, where Jesus Christ will come with the clouds, "and every eye will see him, everyone who pieced him."

[155]Neusner 17.121.

[156]Strack and Stemberger, *Introduction* 87.

[157]Cf. Str-B 2.292-299.

[158]Cf. for example 90–100 C.E. in R. Brown, *The Gospel According to John I-XII* (AB 29; Garden City, New York: Doubleday, 1966) LXXXVI.

Jewish Christian could have interpreted the piercing or nailing of the Messiah Jesus to the Cross in terms of Zech 12:10-11. Since these verses were interpreted of the death of the "anointed of the Lord," Josiah, at a very early date, it is understandable that other imagery associated with Josiah's death (the sun's setting at noon and the earth's becoming dark, which is like the mourning for an "only son": Amos 8:9-10) could be applied by an early Palestinian Jewish Christian to Jesus' death on the Cross. Here, too, as in *b. Mo 'ed Qaṭ.* 25b, which deals with Josiah,[159] God mourns by means of a solar eclipse, at noon, for His only Son, the pierced or sorely wounded one.[160]

4.   *Other Solar Eclipses.*

Six other factors may have been influential in causing the Palestinian Jewish Christian author of the solar eclipse at Jesus' Crucifixion to compose such a narrative.

1)   *Saul and the Medium of Endor.*

According to the rabbis necromancy was only possible during the day.[161] For this reason, although 1 Sam 28:8, 20 and 25 expressly state

---

[159]Cf. also *Pirq. R. El.* 17 on "Loving Service to Mourners" (Friedlander 121), where the Sages made the rule that great mourning such as that done for Josiah should also be done for all the Sages of Israel and for their great men. For the early Palestinian Jewish Christian author of the solar eclipse at Jesus' death, the prophet from Nazareth was such a great man, and thus to be mourned as Josiah was. In the same section, the (belated) proper mourning for Saul is cited as a positive example, for him "who secured his portion with Samuel the prophet" (Friedlander 119-120).

[160]This expression, being "badly wounded," also occurs of the anointed one Saul when he dies in battle in 1 Sam 31:3 (ויחל מאד; the parallel in 1 Chr 10:3 omits "badly"). Since he was badly wounded "by the archers," he is also represented here as being pierced (by their arrows). If this verb derives from חול (BDB 296-97), it should be noted that it is parallel to רגז in Deut 2:25 and Ps 77:17 (Eng. 16), the same verb found in 1 Sam 28:15. The verb חלל, to bore, pierce (BDB 319), is employed of an archer in Prov 26:10; it is also used at Isa 53:5. This may also be the root in 1 Sam 31:3.

The Septuagint states at 1 Kgdms 31:3 that Saul was "wounded in the abdomen." Josephus in *Ant.* 6.370 has Saul receive on this occasion "many wounds," which he also describes as "the great number of his wounds" in 7.3. Saul's dying by many wounds/being pierced by arrows is the fulfillment of 1 Sam 28:19, Samuel's prophecy that he will be with him tomorrow. The catchword of Saul's being "pierced/sorely wounded" may thus also have aided in the Palestinian Jewish Christian's application of the solar eclipse at the death of King Josiah, the pierced one, to Jesus, the one pierced at the Cross.

[161]Cf. Ginzberg, *Legends* 6.236, n. 75. In addition, Samuel rose from the dead, thinking it was the Day of Judgment. Since for the rabbis judgment was only allowed by day, this, too, may have contributed to the scene's being considered to

that Saul consulted the medium of Endor at night, Judaic tradition on v 8 asks whether it was really night. The answer is no. The hour in which Samuel and many righteous rose from their graves was only "as dark/gloomy (אפלה) for them [Saul and his servants] as night."[162]

This darkness during the day, which took place when many righteous people rose from their graves, may also have influenced the Palestinian Jewish Christian author of the prodigia at Jesus' Crucifixion, which included the rising of many saints, to think of a solar eclipse.

2) Zech 14:6-7.

As noted above in A.2, the Septuagint interprets the unclear Hebrew of Zech 14:6 as: "In that day there shall be no light...." The next verse continues by stating that "at evening time there shall [again] be light." Since the splitting open of the Mount of Olives east of Jerusalem provides part of the background for Matt 27:51b-53, it is possible that the tradition of darkness during the day, still found in LXX Zech 14:6-7, may also have encouraged the Palestinian Jewish Christian author of the prodigia at Jesus' Crucifixion to narrate a solar eclipse.

3) 2 Targ. Esth 4:16-5:1.

In the Excursus on 1 Samuel 28 and Psalm 22 in section A, I noted that at the time of Esther's agony of death, when the rabbis applied Ps 22:1 to her, and the Patriarchs moved out of their graves, as did the inhabitants of Jerusalem, the "sun and moon will eclipse their light and not illuminate...."[163]

This complex may form a partial background to Jesus' own agony of death, described by a Palestinian Jewish Christian also in terms of Ps 22:1 in Mark 15:34 par. If so, the solar eclipse mentioned in the Esther haggadah, also associated with people rising from their graves near Jerusalem, may also have influenced the choice of a solar eclipse at Jesus' Crucifixion.

4) God's Complete Mourning for His Only Son.

The rabbis assumed that when God mourned in heaven, He followed human mourning customs. These are treated most extensively in a midrash which is now available in greatly varying rescensions. Perhaps the oldest is now found in *Pesiq. Rav Kah.* 15/3 on Lam 1:1, "How lonely

---

have taken place in the daytime. See, for example, *b. Meg.* 21a (Soncino 126) and *b. Sanh.* 34b (Soncino 217-18).

[162]Cf. *Lev. Rab.* Emor 26/7 on Lev 20:27. English in Neusner, *Judaism and Scripture* 457, and Soncino 4.332 with n. 1. The Hebrew is in Margulies, *Leviticus Rabbah* 600. Parallel traditions are noted by Ginzberg, *Legends* 6.236, n. 75. See also Jastrow 105 on אפל.

[163]English in Grossfeld, *The Two Targums of Esther* 158 on 4:16.

sits the city...." God here mourns the fall of the city of Jerusalem, including the destruction of the Temple, through the Babylonian, King Nebuchadnezzar, in the seventh century B.C.E.[164]

The author of this rescension is Bar Qappara, a fifth generation Tanna.[165] The fact that seven different mourning customs are enumerated points to completeness. It also may recall the usual seven days of mourning (cf. this, for example, at the death of Saul in 1 Sam 31:13). Two of the seven mourning customs are relevant to the prodigia at Jesus' Crucifixion. The sixth is God's rending His purple garment, i.e., the curtain of the Temple. I will return to this in section C below. In regard to the second custom, Bar Qappara relates that God asks His angels what a mortal king does in mourning. They answer: "He extinguishes the lamps." Thereupon God decides to do likewise. For this Joel 2:10 = 4:15 (Eng. 3:15) is adduced: "The sun and the moon are darkened (קדר), and the stars withdraw their shining." Before this in 2:10 the earth "quakes" (רגז), the same verb as employed in 1 Sam 28:15.

The verb קדר is frequently employed in the MT of mourning,[166] which certainly encouraged the rabbis to associate this Joel verse with God's mourning.

In the rescension of this midrash now found in *Lam. Rab.* 1:1 § 1,[167] it is related in the name of R. Joshua b. Levi, a first generation Palestinian Amora,[168] that God asks the ministering angels what is customary for a human king to do in mourning if he had a son who died. Their second reply causes the citation of Joel 2:10 = 4:15, as above.

P. Kuhn has analyzed this midrash extensively, pointing out that the son is Israel and the king God, as in a number of similar texts.[169] Here God causes a solar eclipse when His (only) son dies, just as God mourns over the death of His (only) Son Jesus on the Cross by also causing a solar eclipse.

---

[164]Cf. the English in Braude and Kapstein 276-277, with n. 1 on p. 275. The Hebrew is found in Mandelbaum 1.250-251.

[165]Strack and Stemberger, *Introduction* 90-91.

[166]Cf. the examples cited in BDB 871.

[167]English in Soncino 7.67.

[168]Strack and Stemberger, *Introduction* 92-93. Since he was a pupil of Bar Qappara, he may have this from his teacher, who is cited in *Pesiq. Rav Kah.* 15/3 on Lam 1:1.

[169]*Gottes Trauer* 181-198; God and Israel, king and son, are discussed on p. 187. He also notes Amos 8:10 and Zech 12:10. Strangely, he considers the solar eclipse at Matt 27:45 par. not to be a sign of God's mourning, but one of threatening final judgment (191,n. 43).

Finally, it should be noted that this midrash is also cited in *Lam. Rab.* 3:28 § 9.[170] Directly after this, on 3:29, Rabbi (Judah the Prince) weeps over various scriptural verses dealing with the Final Judgment, as noted above in section A.3 with n. 59. The first passage cited here is 1 Sam 28:15, where Samuel asks why Saul has "disturbed" (רגז) him by having him raised from the dead.[171]

If Joel 2:10 = 4:15 was associated in very early Jewish tradition with 1 Sam 28:15 via the verb רגז, this would be one more reason for the Palestinian Jewish Christian author of the prodigia at Jesus' Crucifixion to include not only an earthquake and the rising of many saints, but also a solar eclipse.

5) A Solar Eclipse at Adam's Death.

The pseudepigraphical writing "The Life of Adam and Eve" was probably written originally in Hebrew in Palestine, sometime at the end of the first century C.E.[172] In 43:2 the statement is made that "great wonders in heaven and on the earth and in the lights of heaven" will be seen when the soul of Adam leaves his body. This is fulfilled in 46:1, when "for seven days [of mourning] were the sun, moon and stars darkened."[173]

In the parallel from the Apocalypse of Moses, Eve asks her son Seth who the "two dark-skinned persons" are who aid in heaven praying for Adam. He answers in 36:1, "These are the sun and the moon, and they themselves fall down and pray for my father Adam." Eve then asks where their light is, "and why they have become dark?" Seth replies in 36:3, "They are not able to shine before the light of all, and this is why the light is hid from them."[174]

Here at the death of Adam, sun and moon mourn by being in eclipse. They cannot shine before Adam, "the light of all." In Rom 5:12-21 Paul compares the one man Adam with the one man Jesus Christ. Adam "was a type of the one who was to come" (v 14). In 1 Cor 15:21-22 the Apostle contrasts the two in regard to death and the resurrection of the dead. If the source of Paul's Adam/Christ comparisons and contrasts was ultimately Palestinian Jewish Christianity, the tradition of the sun's

---

[170]Soncino 7.203-204. J. Wettstein had already noted its relevance to Matt 27:45 in 1752. Cf. his *Novum Testamentum Graecum* 1.539.

[171]Another passage is Amos 4:13 with "who makes the morning darkness." The Septuagint interprets this messianically: "Therefore, behold, I [the Lord] am He who strengthens the thunder and creates the wind, and proclaims to men His Anointed One, making the dawn and cloud-like darkness."

[172]Cf. M.D. Johnson in *OTP* 2.251-52.

[173]*OTP* 2.274 and 288, respectively.

[174]*OTP* 2.289.

being in eclipse in mourning at the death of Adam may also have influenced the sun's being in eclipse in mourning at the death of the last Adam/man, the Messiah, whom the Evangelist John calls the "true light that enlightens every man..." (1:9); he is the "light of the world" (8:12).

6) Darkness at the Taking Away of Enoch.

Gen 5:24 states that "Enoch walked with God; and he was not, for God 'took' him." This "taking away" of Enoch is described in Second or Slavonic Enoch in chapter 67.

The Lord sends darkness/gloom onto the earth. It becomes dark, and the darkness covers the men standing with Enoch. The angels hurry, grasp Enoch, and carry him to the highest heaven. There the Lord receives him, making him stand before Him forever. Then the darkness departs from the earth, and it again becomes light. The people look, but cannot figure out how Enoch "had been taken away."[175]

The place where Enoch was taken up is called "Akhuzan" in 68:5.[176] A Melchizedek fragment makes it certain that this is Jerusalem.[177] The term most probably derives from אחזה, "possession/property," employed of Jerusalem in Ezek 45:5-8 and 48:20-22.[178] According to L. Ginzberg, this site may be connected with the place of Jesus' Crucifixion just outside Jerusalem, Golgotha.[179]

While R.H. Charles considered the author of 2 Enoch to be an Egyptian Jew writing in the first half of the first century C.E.,[180] modern scholarship is very reticent about the date and provenance of the writing.[181] Nevertheless, it is significant that when Enoch is taken up to heaven, God produces darkness, which departs again after Enoch's "ascension." To be sure, Enoch remains alive, while Jesus dies at the Crucifixion. Yet if Jesus' soul is thought of in one form of early Palestinian Christianity as ascending to God directly from the Cross, as I propose below, the darkness at Enoch's ascension – if early – may also have encouraged the Palestinian Jewish Christian author of the prodigia to have a "darkening" or solar eclipse at this point.

---

[175]Cf. the two major rescensions translated by F. Andersen in *OTP* 1.194-195, as well as R.H. Charles in *APOT* 2.469. They agree at all essential points here.

[176]Cf. *OTP* 1.196-197; *APOT* 2.469. See also 64:3.

[177]Cf. the text in Ginzberg, *Legends* 5.162, n. 60. See also *APOT* 2.469, note on 68:5-7.

[178]On this, cf. Ginzberg, *Legends* 5.117, n. 109. He omits, however, the reference to Ezek 45:5-8.

[179]*Ibid.*, and 5.126, n. 137.

[180]*APOT* 2.429.

[181]Cf. F. Andersen in *OTP* 1.94-97. Andersen himself inclines to place it "early" and "in a Jewish community" (97).

* * *

In light of the materials surveyed in sections 1.–4. above, it would have been very difficult for a Palestinian Jewish Christian who sought to describe prodigia at Jesus' Crucifixion *not* to have included a solar eclipse. The main scriptural text he employed as background material was Amos 8:9-10, connected by the verb רגז in v 8 to 1 Sam 28:15. The earthquake and rising of many saints in Matt 27:51b-53, based in part on Judaic tradition on the latter passage, and the solar eclipse at Jesus' Crucifixion, are part of a larger, interrelated complex. The third and final prodigium, the tearing/rending of the Temple curtain, remains to be discussed.

C. The Tearing/Rending of the Temple Curtain

While Samuel is still living, he prophesies to Saul that because of his negative behavior the Lord has "torn" (קרע) the kingdom of Israel from him, to give it to his successor David (1 Sam 15:28). This Samuel repeats when the medium of Endor raises him from the dead at Saul's request (28:17). Samuel's further prediction, that Saul would be with him the next day when he dies in battle with the Philistines (v 19), is fulfilled in chapter 31. Three days after this battle a man comes to David with his clothes "rent" (קרע: 2 Sam 1:2), and he relates the king's demise. David's reaction is to take hold of his clothes, "rend" (קרע) them, and mourn for the slain king (vv 11-12), the Lord's "Anointed One" (vv 14 and 16). He even composes a lament for the king and his son Jonathan (vv 17-27).

This emphasis on mourning for the slain Anointed One Saul by "rending/tearing" one's garments, connected with 1 Sam 28:17, provided the Palestinian Jewish Christian describing the death of the Anointed One Jesus at his Crucifixion with the background for his final prodigium, the "tearing/rending" of the Temple curtain, which is frequently also called a "veil."

Mark 15:38 states that directly after Jesus breathed his last, "the curtain of the Temple was torn/rent in two, from top to bottom" (τὸ καταπέτασμα τοῦ ναοῦ ἐσχίσθη εἰς δύο ἀπ' ἄνωθεν ἕως κάτω). In 27:51, Matthew reproduces this Markan sentence literally, merely placing "in two" at the end. In the same verse he notes that the rocks were "split," employing the same verb as before, σχίζω. Luke places the curtain of the Temple being torn in two (μέσον)[182] together with the solar eclipse in 23:45, that is, before Jesus expires in v 46. It is quite unlikely that Luke was not acquainted with the Jewish custom of tearing/rending

---

[182]For this expression, cf. Theodotion Sus 55: σχίσει σε μέσον.

one's garment(-s) *after* someone's death. More probably, he simply felt the need to group the two prodigia together.[183]

It should be noted that as in the numerous verbs employed in Matt 27:51b-52, the passive is also used in Mark 15:38 and Matt 27:51a: ἐσχίσθη. Again, this is the *passivum divinum*. It is God Himself who tears/rends the curtain of His dwelling, the Temple, in mourning over the death of His only Son.

The following observations help to explain this statement.

1. *Tearing/Rending a Garment in Mourning.*

Ever since Gen 37:29 and 34, Reuben's and Jacob's mourning over the (ostensible) death of Joseph, it was customary for Israelites and later Jews to tear or rend their garments at the death of a relative or friend.

Chapter 9 of *Semaḥoth*, one of the Minor Tractates of the Babylonian Talmud, is concerned with when and how to tear/rend properly while mourning.[184] It is based for the most part on statements from *b. Mo'ed Qaṭan* 22b and 26a-b. For other people who have died, one rends a handbreadth [in depth]. The biblical proof text for this is David's rending his garments at the news of Saul's death in 2 Sam 1:11. For one's father or mother, however, [one rends] until one bares one's heart [chest].[185] This was a rent which was not to be sewn up again,[186] after the seven days of mourning, as in 1 Sam 31:13 for Saul.

The direction should be noted here. One rends, starting from the top of the garment (the human shoulder,),[187] down to the heart/chest.[188] This is the reason for the seemingly redundant "torn in two, from top to bottom" in Mark 15:38. Beyond the connection of mourning and rending "in two," mentioned below, it is important that God in mourning rends His purple garment/curtain (see section 2.) completely, starting from the top, as was usual. Yet because of His intense mourning for His Son, He rends not only down to the heart/chest or navel, but to the very bottom of the garment/curtain.

---

[183]He thereby overlooked the fact that no one could observe the rent Temple curtain because of the solar eclipse.

[184]Soncino 374-79.

[185]See *b. Mo'ed Qaṭ* 22b in Soncino 142.

[186]See *b. Mo'ed Qaṭ.* 26a (Soncino 164).

[187]Rending one's garments leads to baring the shoulder. Cf. *m. Mo'ed Qaṭ.* 3:7 (Danby 210). This does not seem to be a separate act. Cf., however, *Semaḥoth* 9:2 (Soncino, *The Minor Tractates* 1.374).

[188]In *b. Mo'ed Qaṭ.* 26b (Soncino 170) the navel is mentioned along with the heart. The latter is based on Joel 2:13. See also *Semaḥoth* 9:6 in Soncino, *The Minor Tractates* 1.375: "One only rends 'as far down as' the region of the navel."

Although not explicitly stated in regard to a son or daughter, the same procedures of rending described above were assumed to apply to them. Jesus' relatives and friends, when learning of his death through crucifixion, would have rent their garments, either a handbreadth deep, or at the most to the chest. At his Crucifixion, Jesus' heavenly Father, God, however, rent His garment not only from top to bottom, but also completely, "in two." The Temple curtain was torn "in two."[189]

The latter imagery also derives from the same mourning custom. In *b. Mo 'ed Qaṭ.* 25a on the "rending" of *m.* 3:7, the solar eclipse of Amos 8:9-10 is applied to a rabbi's death, as well as to the day of King Josiah's death, commented upon above. Then in 26a the rule that a rent for one's father, mother, or master who taught one wisdom is not to be sewed up again, is derived from 2 Kgs 2:12. At Elijah's ascension into heaven, his disciple Elisha "took hold of his own clothes and rent them into 'two rent pieces' (לשנים קרעים; LXX εἰς δύο ῥήγματα). This means that "the severed parts ever remain rent [apart] in two."[190] In 22b[191] this tradition is given with the interpretation that the garments "appeared as if torn into two [separate] pieces" (שנראין קרועים כשנים).[192]

God's rending of the Temple curtain at Jesus' Crucifixion not only makes it "appear" to be torn in two. As at Elijah's ascension into heaven, the rent is complete, much more than the usual extent of torn material noted above. The curtain's being torn into two pieces (εἰς δύο in Mark 15:38 and Matt 27:51) demonstrates the great intensity of God's mourning for His only Son.

---

[189]For God as thought of not only as enthroned in heaven, but also as dwelling in the Jerusalem sanctuary directly below, cf. for example the Tannaitic midrash *Mek. R. Ish.* Shirata 10 on Exod 15:17 (Lauterbach 2.78) with Ps 11:4 and 1 Kgs 8:13. See also the Shekinah or indwelling of God as descending to the Jerusalem Temple in *'Abot R. Nat.* A 34 (Goldin 140-41) with Ezek 44:2. The final descent of God will be to the Mount of Olives, as in Zech 14:4 (cf. also *b. Sukk.* 5a in Soncino 15). It should also be noted that on the third day of mourning, a person was expected not to go to the right around the Temple Mount (and make an offering), but to the left. Upon thus being recognized as a mourner, he was told: "May He who dwells in this House comfort you." See *Semaḥoth* 6:11 (Soncino, *The Minor Tractates* 1.353). Other benedictions with "May He who dwells in this House" follow. This appears to be derived from *m. Mid.* 2:2 (Danby 591). Cf. also Matt 23:21.

[190]Soncino 164.

[191]Soncino 143.

[192]When R. Joshua, a second generation Tanna (Strack and Stemberger, *Introduction* 77), died, R. Aqiba began his funeral oration before the mourners with the same verse, 2 Kgs 2:12. This also shows its importance in a context of mourning. See *b. Sanh.* 68a (Soncino 463-64).

2 Kgs 2:12 is the only OT passage in which a tearing "into two pieces" occurs. While Judaic tradition associated it with mourning for a close relative, it is just as important to note that Elisha's behavior takes place at Elijah's ascension into heaven. This is relevant to the discussion below of Jesus' ascension into heaven after dying on the Cross, at which time God rends His "garment," the Temple curtain, completely, into two pieces.

Finally, 2 Kgs 2:12 is also a proof text for not sewing up a rent upon hearing God's name blasphemed.[193] If this was a very early tradition, as seems probable, it is part of the background for the Jewish high priest Caiaphas' rending/tearing his garments when he accuses Jesus of blaspheming in Mark 14:63-64 and Matt 26:65.[194] This took place at night, according to Judaic time reckoning part of the day on which Jesus died, at which time God also tore His garment. The descriptions of these two episodes, both connected to 2 Kgs 2:12, may have influenced each other.

2. *God's Complete Mourning by Rending His Purple Garment.*

In section B above I called attention to *Pesiq. Rav Kah.* 15/3, where Bar Qappara has God ask the ministering angels how a human king mourns. He follows the seven human customs, including "extinguishing the lamps" by causing a solar eclipse (Joel 2:10 = 4:15).

The sixth manner of mourning is for a mortal king to "rend his purple garment (מבזע פירפרין שלו)." The midrash then has God state: "I will do likewise." Lam 2:17 is now cited as "The Lord has done what He purposed, He has 'rent His state garment' (בצע אמרתו)." Here בצע is not understood as to "accomplish," but as to "cut."[195] The noun אמרתו is also not considered to be from אמרה, "utterance, speech, word,"[196] but from אימרה, which Jastrow defines as "fringe, border, skirt; trnsf. the bordered garment, (toga praetexta), state garment."[197]

The midrash continues by asking: "What does this mean, 'He rent His state garment'"? R. Jacob of Kefar Ḥanan[198] said: "He rent His purple garment" (מבזע פירפיריה). Here the verb בזע is employed in the sense of "rend."[199]

---

[193]Cf. *b. Moʿed Qaṭ.* 26a (Soncino 164, and 166 with n. 4). See also *b. Sanh.* 60a (Soncino 408).

[194]Luke omits this at 22:71.

[195]Cf. BDB 130 and Jastrow 184.

[196]BDB 57, only here.

[197]*Dictionary* 51.

[198]He was a Palestinian, active ca. 280 C.E. See Str-B 5/6.167.

[199]Jastrow 154. The Hebrew is in Mandelbaum 1.251. Braude and Kapstein (*Pesikta de-Rab Kahana* 277, n. 5) incorrectly derive אמרה from עמר, "wool" (Jastrow

This midrash deals with God's mourning over the fall of Jerusalem, including the destruction of the Temple on the Ninth of Ab under Nebuchadnezzar in the sixth century B.C.E.[200] A purple garment was reserved for an earthly king.[201] God, the King of kings, is presented here as also wearing purple. He rends His purple garment in grief over the great destruction of city and Temple. In a major variant of the midrash, He does so, however, because of the death of His only son.

Since the curtains of both the tabernacle and the Second Temple were also made of purple,[202] it was natural for the rabbis to think that God in mourning rent His royal purple garment in heaven when His dwelling on earth, the Temple, was destroyed by the Babylonians. This was made easier by the fact that the term פְּרָגוֹד/פַּרְגּוֹדָא, used for the heavenly curtain separating God on His throne from the angels and the souls of the righteous, also means "garment, tunic."[203]

The Palestinian Jewish Christian author of the prodigia at Jesus' Crucifixion borrowed from this motif complex, altering it for his own purposes.[204] In the midrash, God only rends His purple garment

---

1091). A parallel is found in *Lam. Rab.* 1:1 § 1 (Soncino 7.67-68). See also *Pesiq. R.* 27-28/2 (Braude 2.549 with n. 12). R. Jacob's statement is also found in *Lam. Rab.* 2:17 § 21 (Soncino 7.183), and *Lev. Rab.* Vayyikra 6/5 on Lev 5:1 (Soncino 4.84). See also the references in Mandelbaum's notes (1.250-51), as well as Kuhn, *Gottes Trauer* 184.

[200]Cf. *Pesiq. Rav Kah.* 15 in Braude and Kapstein 275,n. 1, and *Pesiq. R.* 27-28 in Braude 545.

[201]Cf. for example Herod the Great's lying in state in a crown of gold and a purple robe in 4 B.C.E. in *Bell.* 1.671, as well as *Ant.* 14.173. For God presented as a king with a purple garment in numerous rabbinic parables, see the sources cited in Kuhn, *Gottes Trauer* 196. In *Midr. Ps.* 9/13 on Ps 9:13 (Braude 1.145-46), God notes upon His purple robe the name of every righteous person killed as a martyr, using it at the Judgment as evidence against the persecutor. See Jastrow 1148 for a related statement from Yelamdenu.

[202]The curtains of Moses' tabernacle are described in Josephus, *Ant.* 3.124-29 and 183, as well as in 8.72. See also Philo, *Cong.* 117, and *Mos.* 2.86. For the Herodian Temple, see Josephus, *Bell.* 5.212 with καταπέτασμα, 6.390, as well as the plural in 7.162.

[203]Cf. *b. Hag.* 15a (Soncino 95, with n. 10, referring to the Latin *paraganda*, "a garment ornamented with a border"), and other references cited by Jastrow in 1214. See also the discussion of *b. Hag.* 12b and Targ. Job 26:9 in Str-B 1.976. Other sources are noted by H. Bietenhard in *Die himmlische Welt im Urchristentum und Spätjudentum* (WUNT 2; Tübingen: Mohr, 1951) 73-74. See also 3 Enoch 45:1 (*OTP* 1.296, with a note a, and 240, note 56).

[204]A later Christian author also combined the rending of garments and the Temple's mourning. In the "Protevangelium of James" 24:3 (Hennecke and Schneemelcher 1.388), at the slaying of John the Baptist's father Zacharias in the Temple, "the panel – work of the ceiling of the temple wailed, and they rent their

(curtain) in heaven according to rabbinic custom, at the most to the chest or navel. At Jesus' Crucifixion, however, God rends His garment, the purple curtain of the Jerusalem Herodian or Second Temple, His earthly dwelling, in two, from top to bottom, because of intense grief over the death of His only Son. The derivation of "in two" from 2 Kgs 2:12 was pointed out above. It is assumed that as God acts in heaven (rending His purple garment/curtain), so He acts in His earthly dwelling, the Temple.

M. Jastrow is wrong in interpreting the above midrash on Lam 2:17 as God's allowing "the Temple curtain to be cut through by Titus" at the fall of Jerusalem in 70 C.E.[205] In *b. Giṭ.* 56b Titus is described as entering the Holy of Holies, spreading out a scroll of the Torah, and having intercourse with a harlot upon it. Then he is supposed to have slashed the curtain, maintaining that he has thereby killed God. Yet this haggadah strangely continues by relating that Titus then took the (slashed!) curtain, put all the holy vessels into it, and sent them by ship to Rome for his triumph.[206]

Nowhere else is it reported that a curtain of the Temple was slashed. Josephus, for example, states that some time after Titus and his generals in 70 C.E. entered and beheld the contents of the Holy of Holies, without touching anything, a priest voluntarily handed over to him the curtains.[207] Josephus also describes Vespasian's and Titus' triumphal procession in Rome. He expressly mentions "the purple hangings of the sanctuary" which were afterwards not placed with other booty in the Temple of Peace, but in the palace.[208] Rabbinic tradition also reports Sages' later seeing (the inner) Temple curtain in Rome, bespattered with blood from the Day of Atonement,[209] but not slashed.

The haggadah of Titus' slashing the Jerusalem Temple curtain in 70 C.E. is unhistorical. Like the description of his having intercourse with a

---

clothes from the top to the bottom." This is obviously dependent on Mark 15:38 par. and Matt 23:35.

[205]*Dictionary* 154 on בֶּגֶד. He is followed, for example, by A. Cohen in *Midrash Rabbah*, Soncino 7.68.

[206]Soncino 259. In *'Abot R. Nat.* B 7, it is Vespasian who slashes the curtain. See Saldarini 68, with the many variant traditions cited in his n. 14 on pp. 67-68. If it earlier took 300 priests to immerse the curtain in order to restore its ritual purity (*m. Šeqal.* 8:5 in Danby 161), Titus alone could hardly have cut through it.

[207]Cf. *Bell.* 6.260 and 389-90. In Syr Bar 6:7 the veil of the Holy of Holies is also preserved at the destruction of Jerusalem by Nebuchadnezzar (*OTP* 1.623). Actually, the destruction of 70 C.E. is meant (1.615). The writing appears to have been originally in Hebrew, from Palestine, in "the first or second decade of the second century" C.E. (1.617).

[208]Cf. *Bell.* 7.162. They were certainly carried in the procession and are most probably included in the tapestries "of the rarest purple" in 134.

[209]Cf., for example, *t. Yoma* 2:16 in regard to *m.* 5:4, in Neusner 2.199.

harlot on a scroll of the Torah in the Holy of Holies, it seeks by imaginative exaggeration to portray his grossly evil character. The destroyer of God's holy dwelling on earth could not be described in terms which were evil enough for the later Sages.[210]

When God in heaven rent His purple garment at the destruction of the Temple in the midrash on Lam 2:17, it was due to the action of Nebuchadnezzar in the sixth century B.C.E., not to Titus' slashing the Second Temple curtain in 70 C.E. This means that the later rabbinic tradition regarding Titus exerted no influence on the Palestinian Jewish Christian author of the Temple curtain's being torn/rent, now found in Mark 15:38. He formed his narrative *before* the destruction of Jerusalem in 70 C.E. and the writing of Mark at about that time, basing it in part on Judaic traditions regarding God's mourning over the destruction of the Temple in the sixth century B.C.E.

3. *Which of the Two Temple Curtains is Rent in Mark 15:38?*

Mark 15:38 par. speaks of *the* curtain of the Temple as being rent. Yet the Herodian or Second Temple definitely had two curtains. Josephus, a native of Jerusalem who was personally acquainted with the Temple, states that the outer and larger one before the first building of the sanctuary, which "alone stood exposed to view, from top to bottom,"[211] was 55 x 16 cubits (some 82 by 23 feet, or 24.4 by 7.1 meters)[212] large and "of Babylonian tapestry, with embroidery of blue and fine linen, of scarlet also and purple (πορφύρα), wrought with marvelous skill."[213] During the day, when the front gate was open, it was visible to everyone in the forecourt.[214]

Before the inner building, the Holy of Holies, there was also a curtain. Josephus does not describe its appearance.[215] It could only be viewed by the few priests on duty in that section.

---

[210]Contrast Josephus' description of how even to the very end of the war, Titus sought to spare the city and the Temple. See *Bell.* 5.456 and 6.95, 128, 216, 254, 262 and 266. Even if Josephus exaggerates this motif and favors the Romans, the general tendency will have been correct.

[211]Cf. *Bell.* 5.209. The latter phrase is διηνεκὲς εἰς τὸ ὕψος, literally "continually to the top."

[212]Cf. the art. "Weights and Measures" by O.R. Sellers in *IDB* 4.838; there a common cubit is 17.49 inches.

[213]Cf. *Bell.* 5.212.

[214]Cf. also W. Lane, *The Gospel According to Mark* (NICNT 2; Grand Rapids, Michigan: Eerdmans, 1974) 575.

[215]Cf. *Bell.* 5.219. This may be to avoid Gentile ridicule of animal worship, for the two cherubim were portrayed on it (see *Ant.* 3.137 and Thackeray's note on 126).

The question must therefore be raised as to which of these two curtains is meant in the Synoptics. To decide this, four factors should be considered.

1)   The origin of the Temple curt5ains' being rent, as shown above, is in God's rending His purple garment in heaven when He mourns, whether over the Temple destroyed by Nebuchadnezzar, or in a major variant, over His only son (Israel). Since the same Aramaic and Hebrew word for "garment" also means "curtain," and the Temple curtains were also purple, the Palestinian Jewish Christian author of this prodigium at Jesus' Crucifixion could easily maintain that God now mourned for His only Son Jesus by rending His purple garment/curtain also on earth, at the site of His indwelling presence, the Temple. God in heaven has only *one* purple garment/curtain, which He rends. Therefore only one of the Temple curtains is rent, corresponding to it. The Palestinian Jewish Christian author of this prodigium, certainly aware of there being two curtains in the Jerusalem Second Temple, remains faithful to his background material, however, and has God rend only *one* Temple curtain in mourning.

2)   The rending of one of the Jerusalem Temple curtains never took place historically.   While Luke's statement in 24:53, that the first Christians were "continually in the Temple blessing God" (cf. Acts 2:46 and 3:1), is certainly an exaggeration, it cannot be denied that a Christian community soon established itself there under the leadership of Peter, James and John, considered to be the three "pillars" of the "new" Israel, the Christian church.[216] Their fidelity to the Jerusalem Temple is never questioned, and Paul himself later in the fifties participated in a Nazirite vow there, which led to his imprisonment (Acts 21:26).

Nowhere else in Christian or Judaic sources is it noted that a Temple curtain at roughly the time of Jesus' Crucifixion was rent in two, from top to bottom. Just as the story of Titus' slashing the curtain before the Holy of Holies is a haggadah, so is this Christian prodigium. The earliest Christians in Jerusalem before the fall of the Temple in 70 C.E. did not have to decide which of the two Temple curtains God tore or rent in mourning over His Son Jesus' death because they knew that this mourning was meant symbolically. They appreciated the fact that Judaic haggadah, with which they were well acquainted, was not meant literally, just as no one actually believed that at the death of R. Yose (all)

---

[216]Cf. my art. "Three Pillars and Three Patriarchs: A Proposal Concerning Gal 2:9" in *ZNW* 70 (1979) 252-61.

"the roof gutters at Sepphoris ran with blood."[217] The meaning was rather symbolic or figurative.

3) When Mark incorporated this Palestinian Jewish Christian prodigium into his gospel, the earliest available to us, he did so somewhat clumsily. In chapter 15, v 39 could easily follow after v 37. The Temple curtain's being torn in v 38 interrupts the sequence. Yet "Mark" correctly inserted it at this point, in contrast to Luke, because it belonged to the moment of Jesus' death.

The question then arises which of the two Temple curtains Mark himself meant. The nature of a prodigium is that it is visible or audible to all. It is meant to impress by its size, intensity or unusual character. The other Markan prodigium at Jesus' Crucifixion relates, for example, that for three whole hours there was a solar eclipse "over the whole earth/ land" (15:33 par.).

This is the main reason the outer, larger[218] curtain of the Temple should be favored for Mark. As noted above, it "alone stood exposed to view, from top to bottom" (Josephus). In contrast to the curtain before the Holy of Holies, seen at the most by a small number of priests on duty at the time, the outer curtain was visible to all.

In addition, its composition favors its choice as a prodigium. Josephus relates that its four colors signified the four elements of nature: fire, earth, air and water. It is an "image/pattern of the universe" (εἰκὼν τῶν ὅλων), portraying a "panorama of the heavens."[219] If this is the case, God's mourning for His crucified Son by rending the outer curtain has cosmic overtones. The whole universe is portrayed as mourning with God, just as the solar eclipse covered the whole earth/land.

4) Finally, when the centurion facing Jesus, after the tearing of the Temple curtain, sees that Jesus "thus" (οὕτως) breathes his last, he states: "Truly this man was the Son of God" (Mark 15:39). In the present context the "thus" also applies to the tearing of the Temple curtain. We have no idea of "Mark's" knowledge of the geography of Jerusalem. If

---

[217]Cf. *b. Mo'ed Qaṭ.* 25b (Soncino 163).

[218]In the Gospel of the Nazarenes, Fragment 21, cited by Jerome, the curtain of the Temple is not rent. Rather, "the lintel of the temple 'of wondrous size' collapsed" (Hennecke and Schneemelcher 1.150). The medieval Fragment 36 also speaks of the lintel's "immense size" (1.153). It supported the outer curtain, which thereby collapsed. Although this gospel is probably from the middle of the second century C.E. (1.146), the notice about the lintel's immense size appears to be correct.

[219]See *Bell.* 5.212-13. Cf. *Ant.* 3.183 of the Mosaic tabernacle, as well as Philo, *Cong.* 117. In *Bell.* 4.324, Josephus speaks of the Temple priests who recently began "cosmic" services.

he considered Golgotha to be located on the western slope of the Mount of Olives, however, as one modern writer maintains,[220] then the centurion in looking down or west into the Temple area could have seen the outer curtain being rent. The inner one would have remained invisible to him.[221]

4. What the Tearing/Rending of the Temple Curtain Does Not Mean.

The rending of the Temple curtain had the meaning sketched above for the Palestinian Jewish Christian describing the great significance of Jesus' death by means of prodigia. When it was appropriated by Mark, however, its meaning changed greatly. For him, who perhaps wrote his gospel shortly after the destruction of the Temple and Jerusalem in 70 C.E.,[222] it was a sign *ex eventu*, proleptically announcing the later happening. It takes up the testimony falsely attributed to Jesus in 14:58 and 15:29b, as well as 12:9 and 13:2. To this extent the Jewish commentator C.G. Montefiore correctly noted that "The rending of the veil means the mourning of the Temple; it bewails, not the death of Jesus, but its own imminent destruction."[223] To my knowledge, he alone mentions the motif of mourning which I emphasize above. No one else was acquainted with the Judaic background of this motif.[224]

It is also true that Mark himself may have thought not of the outer curtain, but of the inner one before the Holy of Holies. If so, its tearing signified direct access to God through belief in Jesus as the Son of God (15:39), both for Jewish non-priests and for Gentiles, like the centurion at the Cross.

Nevertheless, certain things are also not true of the tearing of the Temple curtain.

---

[220]Cf. E.L. Martin, *Secrets of Golgotha* (Alhambra, CAL: ASK, 1988), 12-16 and the quotation from *m. Mid.* 2:4 (Danby 592) on p.34. See also H. Jackson, "The Death of Jesus in Mark and the Miracle from the Cross" in *NTS* 33 (1987) 23-24.

[221]The sanctuary of the Temple faced the East, i.e., the Mount of Olives. In Matt 27:54 the centurion and those with him see the earthquake "and what took place." Then they are filled with awe and make their confession. In the context, "and what took place" includes the curtain's being torn in v 51a and the saints rising in vv 52-53. In section A above, I proposed that they did so from tombs located on the west slope of the Mount of Olives.

[222]J. Gnilka, *Das Evangelium nach Markus, (Mk 1-8,26)* 34-35: perhaps in the first three years after 70 C.E.

[223]Cf. his *The Synoptic Gospels*, 388.

[224]According to H. Chronis, "The Torn Veil: Cultus and Christology in Mark 15:37-39" in *JBL* 101 (1982) 109, n.64, R. King in an article not available to me, "The Torn Veil: A Sign of Sonship" in *Christianity Today* 18:13 (1974) 7, understands 15:38 as "the Father's rending of his garments in mourning for his beloved Son."

1) H. Jackson maintained that the "tearing of the Temple curtain need originally have had no connection whatsoever with Jesus' death...."[225] The opposite is the case. God mourns over His only Son by tearing His garment/curtain.

2) E. Haenchen thought that it was perhaps a "local legend from the Roman [Christian] congregation which entered the Roman gospel of Mark."[226] Many scholars today do not view Mark as originating in Rome. More importantly, the origin of the motif is Palestinian, not Roman, as pointed out above.

3) S. Motyer believes that the tearing of the Temple curtain is a "Markan Pentecost," "a proleptic bestowal of the Spirit analogous to the proleptic destruction of the Temple."[227] While the tearing is semantically connected to that in Mark 1:10, where at Jesus' baptism the Spirit descends on him, to see in 15:38 a "proleptic bestowal of the Spirit" is very far-fetched. There is no other evidence for this proposal.

4) Finally, a favorite interpretation of the tearing of the Temple curtain says that at Jesus' death the Temple and its cult have lost their significance for Christians.[228] This may have been the view of Mark and other Christians *after* the destruction of the Temple in 70 C.E. Yet as shown above in regard to the earliest Christian community in Jerusalem under the leadership of the three pillars, as well as Paul's association with the Temple, this was simply not true before that date. For these Jewish Christians who believed in Jesus as the Messiah, their new faith did not entail giving up worshiping God in the Jerusalem Temple. Jesus' death had redemptive significance for them, yet it did not exclude continued active participation in the Jewish cult. Indeed, at the annual Passover meal, for which the lamb was slaughtered in the Temple, they would have been especially close to him who was their own Passover Lamb, who gave his life on the Cross for all.

---

[225]"The Death of Jesus" 32.

[226]*Der Weg Jesu* 534.

[227]Cf. his "The Rending of the Veil: A Markan Pentecost?" in *NTS* 33 (1987) 155-57.

[228]Cf. this as one of the two main lines of interpretation sketched by Gnilka, *Das Evangelium nach Markus (Mk 8, 27-16, 20)* EKK II/2; Zurich: Benziger, 1979) 323.

D. Jesus' Promise to the Repentant Criminal of Participation in Paradise Today (Luke 23:39-43).

Just before the two prodigia of a solar eclipse and the curtain of the Temple being torn in two in Luke's passion narrative, he inserts a special tradition dealing with Jesus' encounter with the two persons "hanged" (on a tree = crucified) with him (23:39-43). In Mark 15:32, followed by Matt 27:44, those crucified with Jesus both "revile" (ὀνειδίζω) him. The author of Luke's special material creates a separate scene at this point in which one of the "criminals/ evil-doers" (κακοῦργος) first "blasphemes" (imperfect: several times) Jesus. If he is indeed the Christ, he should save himself and the other two as well. The second criminal thereupon rebukes the first, among other things stating that they now are justly (δικαίως) receiving what they are worthy of/deserve (ἄξιος). In contrast, Jesus has done nothing "evil/wrong/improper" (ἄτοπος). This criminal continues by asking Jesus to remember him when he comes in his kingdom.[229] Jesus' reply is: "Truly, I say to you, today[230] you will be with me in Paradise" (v 43). Three verses later he breathes his last, dying on the Cross.

Just as the three prodigia of an earthquake with many saints rising from the dead, the solar eclipse, and the tearing of the Temple curtain are connected to Judaic interpretation of 1 Samuel 28, so this special scene, directly before the latter two signs in Luke, also is.

1. Saul to Be with Samuel.

When Saul has Samuel raised from the dead via the medium of Endor in order to find out what the outcome of his battle with the Philistines will be the next day, the great Israelite prophet tells him a number of things. The last is: "And tomorrow you and your sons [shall be] with me" (ומחר אתה ובניך עמי – 28:19). Samuel's prophecy after death is fulfilled the next day when Saul and three of his sons die in battle on Mount Gilboa (chapter 31).

When Josephus in the first century C.E. retells this incident in *Ant.* 6.336, he has Samuel tell Saul: "Know...that you yourself, with your sons [lit. children – τέκνα], will fall tomorrow in the battle, and you [sing.] shall be with me." Here Josephus betrays knowledge of a Judaic tradition primarily emphasizing that Saul will be with Samuel the next

---

[229]This is preferable in v 42 to "into your kingdom." See the apparatus of *The Greek New Testament*, ed. K. Aland et al. 312.

[230]For reasons why "today" cannot belong to "I say," but to "you will be," cf. T. Zahn, *Das Evangelium des Lucas* (Leipzig: Deichert, 1920[4]) 702. He also notes the emphasis on "today" by its being placed at the very beginning (704, n. 22).

day.[231] This made it easier for a Palestinian Jewish Christian author describing Jesus' Crucifixion to portray one criminal as being with Jesus soon in Paradise. The Septuagint at 1 Kgdms 28:19 has, "and tomorrow you and your sons with you shall fall" (3rd per. pl.). It changes the Hebrew "with me" (Samuel) into "with you" (Saul), showing that although Josephus knew of the Septuagint at this point ("fall"), he nevertheless relied on Judaic tradition for Samuel's going to be with Samuel the next day.

The early rabbis wanted to know the exact meaning of עִמִּי, "with me," in 1 Sam 28:19. They pondered what Samuel could have meant by this, since he was buried in his native city of Ramah (v 3; cf. 25:1), which was located in the hill country of Ephraim, some 25 miles or 37 km northwest of Jerusalem, roughly at the middle of a line between Joppa and Shiloh.[232] Endor, where the medium raised him, however, was some 48 miles or 80 km north-northeast of Ramah.

Rabbinic tradition pictured the deceased Samuel as already being in heaven. In *Lev. Rab.* 'Emor 26/7, for example, he tells Saul that if he accepts (God's) judgment upon him as just, "by tomorrow you and your sons [shall be] with me." What does "with me" mean? R. Yoḥanan, a second generation Palestinian Amora,[233] said: "'With me': 'in my division' (מְחִיצָה)."[234] M. Jastrow notes this passage *ad verbum*, adding in parentheses: "in heaven."[235] Other midrashim dealing with the same verse repeat the statement.[236]

Philo of Alexandria, writing in the first half of the first century C.E., speaks in *Ebr.* 143 of Samuel as "the greatest of kings and prophets." Indeed, "his place has been ordered in the ranks of the divine army...."

---

[231]The so-called "Lucianic" text of the Septuagint has: "You [Saul] and Jonathan your son [will be] with me." This is also a reduction from the plural "your sons" of the MT and the LXX. I also understand the Targum as: "And tomorrow you and your son [will be] with me." Cf. Sperber 2.153, including the variant in MS "f 5": Saul and his son will be "with me in the treasury of eternal life."

[232]Cf. the art. "Ramah," 4., by W.R. Morton in *IDB* 4.8.

[233]Strack and Stemberger, *Introduction* 94-95.

[234]Margulies, *Leviticus Rabbah* 605-06.

[235]Cf. his *Dictionary* 760-61. J. Slotki in Soncino 4. 335 translates: "in my heavenly division." L. Ginzberg in *Legends* 4.71 relates this as: "by to-morrow thou wilt be united with me in Paradise."

[236]Cf. *Tanḥuma* 'Emor 2 (Eshkol 2.600); *Midr. Aggadah on the Pentateuch* 'Emor 4, ed. S. Buber 52; *Midr. Samuel* 24/6 (Wünsche, *Aus Israels Lehrhallen* 5.135; Buber 120: "in the midst of my division"); *Pirq. R. El.* 33 (Eshkol 117; Friedlander 246, where the Epstein MS adds: "in heaven"); *b. Ber.* 12b (Soncino 71, with "Heaven"; the English translator M. Simon adds to "in my compartment": "in Paradise"); and *b. 'Erub.* 53b (Soncino 371), where the English translator I. Slotki adds: "in my [celestial] division."

Although Philo here raises the question of whether Samuel ever really existed as a human being, his description of the prophet as now in the divine army indicates that Alexandrian Judaism probably also considered Samuel now, after death, to be in heaven with God.

Finally, it should be noted that in *Lev. Rab.* 'Emor 26/7, Samuel tells Saul he will be with him in his division (of heaven) "by tomorrow" (למחר).[237] This "by" is one step away from the "tomorrow" of the MT, and towards the "today" of Jesus' promise on the Cross to the repentant criminal: "'Today' you will be with me in Paradise."

2. *Samuel's Division Under the Throne of God, Paradise, and Luke 23:43.*

Early Judaism pictured God as sitting on His throne of glory in heaven, surrounded by the ministering angels, yet separated from them by a curtain. Underneath this throne there are various "divisions" or "compartments."[238]

In *b. Šabb.* 152b, for example, a certain heretic asks R. Abbahu[239] how it was possible for the medium of Endor to raise Samuel by necromancy if, as maintained by the Jews, "the souls of the righteous are hidden under the Throne of Glory."[240] Directly before this a baraitha or non-Mishnaic Tannaitic tradition has R. Eliezer (ben Hyrcanus), a second generation Tanna,[241] state that "the souls of the righteous are hidden under the Throne of Glory," which he derives from 1 Sam 25:29. This area preserved for the righteous can also be called God's "treasury."[242]

Samuel was not the only prominent righteous or saintly person in his division, all awaiting the resurrection of the dead and the Day of Judgment. Judaic tradition relates that at Moses' death, God Himself took his soul and placed it in safekeeping under the throne of glory, "next to the Cherubim, Seraphim, and other troops of angels."[243]

---

[237]For this translation, cf. Jastrow 685 on -ל: "within," that is, before or by a certain time.
[238]On this, cf. the many sources cited in Str-B 2.265-269.
[239]A third generation Palestinian Amora, in part a pupil of R. Yoḥanan and in controversy with "minim" – heretics. Cf. Strack and Stemberger, *Introduction* 98.
[240]Soncino 780.
[241]Strack and Stemberger, *Introduction* 77.
[242]Cf. *Sifre Deut.* Ve'zot ha'Brachah 344 on Deut 33:3 (Hammer 357, with 1 Sam 25:29), as well as 3 Enoch 43:2-3 (*OTP* 1.294, with "storehouse"). See also *b. Ḥag.* 12b (Soncino 71). The targum of 1 Sam 25:29 also reads: "the soul of my master will be hidden in the treasury of eternal life before the Lord our God." See Harrington and Saldarini, *Targum Jonathan of the Former Prophets* 150.
[243]*Deut. Rab.* Ve'zot ha'Brachah 11/10 (Soncino 7.187); Ha'azinu 10/4 on Deut 32:1 (Soncino 7.169, with 1 Sam 25:29); 'Abot R. Nat. A 12 (Goldin 65) and B 25 (Saldarini 150). In *b. Tem.* 16a (Soncino 109), Moses at his death is spoken of as departing for the Garden of Eden.

This explains how Samuel, when raised by the medium of Endor in 1 Samuel 28, according to very early Judaic tradition thought it was the Day of Judgment.[244] He therefore took Moses, from the same division, along with him to testify that he, Samuel, had fulfilled all that Moses had written down in the Torah.[245] The "many righteous" who arise with Samuel also think it is the Day of Judgment. As pointed out in section A above, they as the "many saints who had fallen asleep" form a major part of the background for Matt 27:51b-53.

The division of the righteous under God's heavenly throne of glory could also be considered (the preliminary) "Paradise," the realm in which the righteous dead await the resurrection and the Day of Judgment.[246] When Samuel tells Saul he will be with him by tomorrow in his division (in heaven, under the throne of glory), he thus means in (the preliminary) "Paradise." For this reason it was not difficult for the Palestinian Jewish Christian author of Luke 23:39-43 to rephrase Samuel's words to Saul into Jesus' statement to the repentant criminal on the cross next to him: "Today you will be with me in Paradise" (v 43).[247]

In this rephrasing, the original "with me" remained. "In my (heavenly) division" was changed to "in Paradise." Since Jesus was thought by his earliest followers to have been elevated to God's right hand (Ps 110:1), the repentant criminal could not share that highly exalted position reserved for the Son. He could not enter Jesus' special "division" just next to the Father. Therefore a more general term was needed, "Paradise." If the Palestinian Jewish Christian who created the episode of Luke 23:39-43 was bilingual or had at least a working knowledge of Greek, the term παραδώσει from the key verse, 1 Kgdms (1 Sam) 28:19, may also have influenced his choice here of פרדיסא, פרדים/παραδείσος.

As noted above, 1 Sam 28:19 has Samuel tell Saul: "'Tomorrow' (מחר) you and your sons [will be] with me." This refers to the death of Saul

---

[244]Cf. *Pseudo-Philo* 64:7 (OTP 2.377, with n. "j"), as well as *Lev. Rab.* 'Emor 26/7 (Soncino 4.334; Neusner 459).

[245]Cf. *b. Ḥag.* 4b (Soncino 16-17).

[246]See J. Jeremias, art. παράδεισος in *TDNT* 5.767–769. However, he has nothing in regard to 1 Samuel 28. Cf. also Str-B 2.265; 3.533-34; and 4.1119, 1130-44. The first Paradise is the Garden of Eden, the third is final union with God in heaven after the resurrection of the dead and the final judgment. Plummer in *The Gospel According to S. Luke* 536 notes that the Curetonian Syriac substitutes "in the garden of Eden" for "paradise" in Luke 23:43.

[247]It is interesting to note in the late midrashic work *Pesiq. R.* 36/1 (Braude 677), that even before creation God placed the Messiah under His throne of glory to await the time of his appearance in the world. See also 1 Enoch 39:7 and 70 (*OTP* 1.31 with "C" in n. "h," and 1.49), and 4 Ezra 14:9 (*OTP* 1.553, where "Son" was probably originally "servant").

and his sons on the battlefield the next day (1 Samuel 31). In his retelling
of this narrative, also as shown above, Josephus in the first century C.E.
betrays knowledge of Judaic tradition, which primarily emphasized
Saul's being with Samuel the next day. Finally, the midrashim, such as
Lev. Rab. 26/7, modify "tomorrow" to "by tomorrow" (למחר). This also
made it easier for the Palestinian Jewish Christian author of Luke 23:39-
43 to have Jesus say to the repentant criminal, "today."

The term מחר, as found in 1 Sam 28:19, can at times mean not
"tomorrow," but "some time in the future," as in the RSV of Exod 13:14
and Josh 22:24. Yet in rabbinic Hebrew it can also be interpreted as עכשיו:
"presently, now."[248] This also may have aided the Palestinian Jewish
Christian author of Luke 23:39-43 in changing the "tomorrow" of 1 Sam
28:19 to "today" in v 43. "Presently/now" is not only possibly
tomorrow, but also "now/today."

In the Palestinian Jewish-Christian traditions on the prodigia and
here, Jesus' soul is conceived to have ascended to God at the moment of
his death on the Cross. The later majority view, that God raised him
physically from the grave after three days, would have forced the author
of Luke 23:39-43 to have Jesus say: *"After three days* you will be with me
in Paradise." Yet he remained faithful to his tradition and had Jesus
instead say, "today." I shall comment more extensively on the ascension
of Jesus' soul from the Cross below in section IV. Several other motifs
from Samuel's final encounter with Saul in 1 Samuel 28 in Judaic
tradition, however, are also of relevance to Luke 23:43 and should be
noted here.

3.   *Saul's Kingdom, and Jesus' Kingdom.*

At Jesus' Crucifixion, the Roman soldiers mock him, saying: "If you
are the King of the Jews, save yourself!" (Luke 23:37). Then the
inscription above him is quoted: "This is the King of the Jews" (v 38). In
the Greek, Jesus' kingship is emphasized by its being located at the
beginning of the phrase.[249]

In the special Lukan material of vv 39-43 the motif of Jesus' kingship
is further developed. In v 42 the repentant criminal crucified with Jesus
voices the request: "Remember me when you come in your kingdom
(βασιλεία)."[250] As J. Jeremias notes, this means when Jesus comes (again)

---

[248]Cf. Jastrow 1080 and *Mek. R. Ish.* Pisha 18 on Exod 13:14 (Lauterbach 1.166,
who has "the next day," which is too definite).
[249]In the Gospel of Luke, Jesus' reign as king is connected to his exaltation in
1:32-33, as well as to his death predicted at the Lord's Supper the evening before
his Crucifixion (22:29-30).
[250]Cf. n. 229.

as king, i.e., on the Day of Judgment.[251] This is an indirect acknowledgment on the part of the repentant criminal that Jesus is the Messiah since the usual designation of the Messiah at the time was "the messianic king" (Hebrew מלך המשיח, Aramaic מלכא משיחא).[252] The Messiah is literally "the Anointed One." At the beginning of Israel's history he was also the king, and in the first century C.E. the combined expression prevailed.

The first king and thus anointed one of Israel was Saul (1 Sam 9:16; 10:1). Because of his misdeeds, however, the prophet Samuel must tell him that the Lord "tore"[253] the kingdom from him (15:28). When Saul has Samuel raised from the dead, the prophet repeats this statement (28:17).

Judaic sources emphasize the motif of the kingdom here. In 1 Sam 28:8 Saul "disguises himself" (חפש), putting on other garments before having the medium of Endor raise Samuel. The midrashim remark on this, the Hebrew verb should not be read with a *sin,* but with a *shin:* Saul "divested himself" (חפשׁי) of the kingdom.[254]

Pseudo-Philo at this point has Saul state that when he was "king" in Israel, non-Jews knew that he was Saul even if they hadn't seen him before. When the medium of Endor acknowledges that she has seen Saul often, but doesn't recognize him now, Saul "went outside and wept and said, 'Behold, now I know that my appearance has been changed, and the glory of my kingdom has passed from me.'"[255] This is also an haggadic interpretation of חפש in 28:8.

Finally, when the risen Samuel states 28:17 to Saul, this is followed very shortly by Saul's being with him by tomorrow in his (heavenly) division (v 19).[256] This close association of the kingdom and Saul's being with Samuel in his heavenly division certainly contributed to the emphasis on Jesus' kingdom in Luke 23:42, directly followed by a rephrasing of Samuel's statement to Saul in v 43.

4. *Saul's Acknowledgment of His Sins, and Expiation Through Death,*
   and the Repentant Criminal's Acknowledgment of His Sins, and Expiation
   Through Death.

In Luke 23:39-43 one of the two criminals crucified with Jesus rebukes the other for blaspheming Jesus. He asks him whether he

---

[251]Cf. his art. *paradeisos* in *TDNT* 5.770.

[252]Cf. Str-B 1.6-7.

[253]The same verb, קרע, is employed here as in tearing/rending a garment.

[254]Cf. for example *Lev. Rab.* 26/7 (Neusner 457, Soncino 4.331), and Jastrow 493 *ad verbum.*

[255]Cf. 64:4 (*OTP* 2.376-77).

[256]Cf. *Lev. Rab.* 26/7 (Neusner 460, Soncino 4.335).

doesn't reverence/fear God since he is under the same (verdict of) condemnation (v 40).[257] Then he states: "And we justly so (δικαίως), for we are receiving that which is comparable to (ἄξιος) what we have done. Yet this man (Jesus) has done nothing wrong (ἄτοπος – v 11)." This confession of guilt on the part of a criminal condemned to death is accepted by Jesus. The criminal voices the request that the Galilean prophet remember him when he comes (again) as the (messianic) king. Jesus then goes much beyond this by promising that the criminal will be with him the very same day in Paradise (v 43).

These motifs of condemnation for murder, acknowledgment of the just nature of one's sentence, and forgiveness all derive from Judaic interpretation of Saul's final hours. Connected to them is the Judaic principle of atoning for all one's sins through death.

1)   The Murderer Saul's Sins, and the Crucified Criminal's Sin.

If the repentant criminal in Luke 23:39-43 acknowledges that by being crucified he is receiving a punishment corresponding to what he has done, he is a murderer. His life is now taken because he earlier took someone else's life.

Saul, too, was a murderer. Because the priest of Nob, Ahimelech, provided Saul's enemy David with provisions and the sword of Goliath, the king suspected all the priests of conspiring with David. He therefore had 85 of them killed, in addition to their wives, children and animals (1 Samuel 21-22).

Lev. Rab. 26/7 states that this was one of the five sins for which Saul died.[258] According to R. Levi, a third generation Palestinian Amora,[259] when Moses asks God why the first king of Israel is falling by the sword on the battlefield, He tells him to speak to the priests whom Saul slew, "for they are drawing up the indictment (מקטרגין) against him."[260]

Like the criminals crucified with Jesus, Saul had committed murder.

2)   Acknowledgment of the Just Nature of One's Condemnation.

As pointed out above, the repentant criminal crucified with Jesus acknowledged his punishment as just (δικαίως); he was now receiving

---

[257]On this meaning of κρίμα, cf. BAGD 450-51.
[258]Cf. Neusner 460-61, Soncino 4.336, where the other four are enumerated. They elucidate 1 Sam 28:18.
[259]Strack and Stemberger, *Introduction* 98; he was a pupil of R. Yoḥanan.
[260]Margulies 608; Neusner 461; Soncino 4.336. I prefer the reading "whom he slew," as in Soncino. See Jastrow 1353 on קטרג, bring charges, accuse; as well as κατηγορέω (LSJ 926). On this, cf. also *Tanḥuma B* Meṣor'a 4 on Lev 14:1-2 (Bietenhard 2.73, with n. 12).

what he deserved (ἄξιος). The same is true for the murderer Saul in Judaic tradition.

When Samuel, for example, in *Lev. Rab.* 26/7 informs Saul that "the Lord will give Israel also with you into the hand of the Philistines" (1 Sam 28:19a), Saul asks if he should flee. Samuel replies that if he does so, he will be saved. Considering himself encouraged, Saul asks if he then shouldn't make battle preparations. Samuel informs him that if he does, he will be victorious. However, "if you acknowledge the divine judgment upon you as just (אם צדקת עליך את הדין), by 'tomorrow you and your sons [will be] with me'" (v 19b).[261] R. Yo'anan then interprets "with me" as meaning in Samuel's (heavenly) division. Saul, according to R. Simeon b. Laqish, a second generation Palestinian Amora,[262] then took his three sons to battle, knowing that all four of them would be slain. Indeed, he "rejoiced over the divine attribute of justice which would strike him."[263]

Here Saul, like the repentant criminal on the cross next to Jesus, acknowledges his punishment as just. He goes off to certain death, however, with the promise that by the next day he will be with Samuel in his (heavenly) division. Acknowledgment of the justice of one's punishment, connected with the promise of being in a heavenly compartment very soon, was a very early motif in Judaism.[264] When Jesus expires on the Cross in Luke 23:46, citing Ps 31:6 (Eng. 5: "Into Thy hand[s] I commit my spirit"), this was probably also due to the early association of this phrase with accepting the divine attribute of justice in regard to one's fate.[265]

---

[261]Margulies 605-606; Neusner 460; Soncino 4.335.

[262]Strack and Stemberger, *Introduction* 95; he was a brother-in-law of R. Yo'anan.

[263]Margulies 606; Neusner 460; Soncino 4.336.

[264]Cf. *b. 'Abod. Zar.* 18a (Soncino 91-93), and in abbreviated form *Sifre Deut.* Ha-'azinu 307 on Deut 32:4 (Hammer 312). For other references to martyrs suffering for their sins, see U. Kellermann, *Auferstanden in den Himmel. 2. Makkabäer 7 und die Auferstehung der Märtyrer* (SBS 95; Stuttgart: Katholisches Bibelwerk, 1979) 32 and 38, n. 29. For the souls of the martyrs as found in the division closest to God's throne, see the texts cited by him on p. 108.

[265]Cf. *Mek. R. Ish.* Shirata 9 on Exod 15:12 (Lauterbach 2.67), referring to the pursuing Egyptian soldiers, who acknowledged God's righteousness. This procured for them a place of burial. See *Sifre Num.* Pin'as 139 on Num 27:16 (Kuhn 569), where Ps 31:6 is employed for entrusting one's spirit to God during one's lifetime, after which it is placed in the Treasury, where only the righteous reside. While Ps 31:6 was later used as a prayer before retiring at night (see the sources cited in Str-B 2.269), its early association with acknowledging God's justice is primary in Luke 23:46. In contrast to his asking why God abandons him (Ps 22:1) in Mark 15:34 and Matt 27:46, Jesus submits here to the divine plan.

That God ("Heaven") pardons Saul for murdering the priests of Nob is shown by reference to the key passage 1 Sam 28:19b in *b. Ber.* 12b, with a parallel in *b. 'Erub.* 53b.[266]

3) Samuel's Intercession for Saul, Jesus' Intercession for the Crucified Criminal, and the Servant's Intercession in Isa 53:12.

In the MS Vaticanus Ebr. 34 of *Tanḥuma B*,[267] Emor 4 on Lev 20:27, Samuel tells Saul: If you enter battle, do not flee. You will be killed, but "I will ask for your pardon in the future (ואני מפייס עליך לעתיד). 'And tomorrow you and your sons [will be] with me'" (1 Sam 28:19b).[268] A parallel is found in *Midrash Aggadah*.[269]

The verb פיס in the pael form פַּיֵּיס can mean "ask for (someone's) pardon."[270] Here Samuel promises Saul that if he is willing to die in battle, (his death will atone for his sins – see the following section), and the prophet in his division under God's heavenly throne will ask God to pardon his sins. The term "in the future" is immediately explained by the "tomorrow" of 1 Sam 28:19b.

In Luke 23:39-43 one of the criminals crucified with Jesus acknowledges his sins and that his punishment is just. When he asks Jesus to remember him when he comes (again) as (the messianic) king (on the Day of Judgment), Jesus far exceeds his request by telling him he will be with him that very day in Paradise. Since the earliest Palestinian

---

Luke's source, already translated into Greek, employs the pl. "hands" of LXX Ps 30:5.

[266]Soncino 70-71 and 371, respectively. The *Berakoth* passage begins with 1 Sam 28:15, quoted as an example of all one's sins being forgiven a person if one is ashamed of them. Saul's silence in v 15 in regard to consulting the Urim and Thummim "shows that he was conscience-stricken" (71, n. 2). In *Exod. Rab.* Mishpatim 30/16 (Soncino 3.365-66) it is stated that the (other Israelite) priests had pardoned Saul for killing the priests of Nob, yet the Gibeonites refused to do so. *Tanḥuma B* 'Emor 4 on Lev 20:27 with 1 Sam 28:15 (Buber 3.83) has R. Isaac (II), a third generation Palestinian Amora and pupil of R. Yoḥanan (Strack and Stemberger, *Introduction* 98), quote Prov 14:10 ("The heart knows its own bitterness"). This is followed by: "because he (Saul) slew Nob the city of priests." Here Saul is pictured as full of remorse because of his slaying the priests.

[267]H. Bietenhard employs it as the basis of his German translation in *Midrasch Tanḥuma B*. Buber followed the MS Oxford Opp. 20. The Vaticanus MS at times varies considerably.

[268]Cf. Bietenhard 2.120. I thank him for sending me a photocopy of this Hebrew passage from the Vaticanus MS.

[269]See *Midrash Aggadah on the Pentateuch*, ed. S. Buber, 52. It lacks "in the future," but adds: "for you will be with me in my division, and your sons."

[270]Cf. Jastrow 1166-67. It can also mean to pray for someone. For Samuel as a great intercessor, second only to Moses, see Ps 99:6 and Jer 15:1.

Jewish Christians believed that Jesus now sat at the Lord's right hand in heaven (Ps 110:1), it was not difficult for one of them to picture Jesus as promising a repentant criminal a place within one of the divisions under God's throne. Then exalted and sitting on the place of honor next to God, Jesus could intercede with his Father to pardon a repentant person. The authority to do so is already hinted at in the phrase of Luke 23:43, "Truly I say to you." Samuel's very similar intercession for Saul probably helped the author to compose his episode as he did.

Another scriptural text very important to the earliest Jewish Christians probably also played a major role here. The fourth Servant Song in Second Isaiah is found in 52:12 – 53:12. In 53:5 the Servant is "pierced" for our transgressions, which was thought to apply to Jesus' being nailed to the Cross.[271] The final verse, twelve, states that the Servant "poured out his soul to death and was numbered with the transgressors; yet he bore the sin of many, and 'made intercession' for the transgressors."

The "transgressors" here are פשעים, from פשע, to rebel, transgress.[272] The Targum has מרודיא for them, from מרד, to rebel, to incite to rebellion.[273] For the earliest Palestinian Jewish Christians, it would have been hard not to think here of the two "robbers" or "insurrectionists" (λῃστής),[274] i.e., political rebels who had murdered to achieve their goals,[275] crucified with Jesus (Mark 15:27; Matt 27:38). Indeed, the *textus receptus* quotes Isa 53:12 in the next verse, Mark 15:28: "And the Scripture was fulfilled which says, 'He was reckoned with transgressors.'"[276]

The Hebrew of Isa 53:12 says the Servant "made intercession" (יַפְגִּיעַ) for the rebels. The hiphil of פגע with ל means to interpose on behalf of someone,[277] i.e., to intercede for, to make intercession for, as in the RSV. The Targum states here regarding the Servant: "he shall make intercession (בעי) for many debts/sins, and the rebellious shall be

---

[271]The term "sword" in Luke 22:36, associated with "piercing," probably led to the quotation of Isa 53:12 in the next verse. Verse 38 also has "swords."

[272]BDB 833.

[273]Cf. Jastrow 836. The text and an English translation are found in Stenning 180-81. The Targum translates the other occurrence of "transgressors" with the same Aramaic term.

[274]BAGD 473.

[275]See the description of Barabbas in Mark 15:7.

[276]I cannot address the question here of whether Isa 53:12 even led Palestinian Jewish Christians to create the entire scene of Jesus' being crucified between two rebels. Cf. in this respect E. Klostermann, *Das Lukasevangelium* 226, referring to Feigel and Loisy.

[277]BDB 803.

forgiven for his sake."[278] "Shall be forgiven" is the ithpe. of שבק: to be remitted, forgiven, pardoned.[279]

While rabbinic application of this Isaiah verse to the first redeemer of Israel, Moses, at his death may have been made to counteract Christians' applying it to the final redeemer of Israel, the Messiah Jesus,[280] the Targum only reinforces the direction of the Hebrew text itself. The Servant's intercession with God for rebels leads to their being forgiven for his sake. Coupled with Samuel's asking (God) for the pardon of Saul in the Judaic interpretation of 1 Sam 28:19, Isa 53:12 as understood by early Palestinian Jewish Christians probably provided the conceptual background for Luke 23:43.

4) Saul's Death and the Crucified Criminal's Death as Atonement for Their Sins.

In Pseudo-Philo, as stated above probably a Palestinian work originally in Hebrew and roughly from the time of Jesus,[281] Samuel, raised from the dead by the medium of Endor, tells Saul that tomorrow he and his sons will be with him (1 Sam 28:19). Saul then replies in 64:9, "Behold, I am going to die with my sons; perhaps my destruction will be an 'atonement' *(exoratio)* for my iniquities."[282]

The same thing is probably meant by Sir 46:20, which is from the first quarter of the second century B.C.E. and was written in Jerusalem in Hebrew, also as stated above.[283] It reads in the RSV: "Even after he (Samuel) had fallen asleep he prophesied and revealed to the king his death, and lifted up his voice out of the earth in prophecy, to blot out the wickedness of the people." As L. Ginzberg points out, the final phrase, "the wickedness of the people" (ἀνομίαν λαοῦ), "is not represented in the Syriac, and is based on a misunderstanding," actually referring to Saul's

---

[278]Cf. Stenning 180-81, whose English I slightly modify.

[279]Jastrow 1516-17.

[280]Cf. *b. Soṭ.* 14a (Soncino 73-74 and the reference to Moore in n. 2 of p. 74). However, the Tannaitic midrash *Sifre Deut. Ve' zot ha' Brachah* 355 on Deut 33:21 (Hammer 373) also applies it to Moses. See also S. Schechter, *Aspects of Rabbinic Theology. Major Concepts of the Talmud* (New York: Schocken, 1961; original 1909) 310.

[281]Cf. D.J. Harrington in *OTP* 2.298-300.

[282]Cf. Harrington in *OTP* 2.377, who has "my wickedness" for the plural *iniquitatum mearum (Les Antiquités Bibliques,* 1.384). J. Cazeaux on p. 385 has the plural, "mes iniquités," agreeing with 1 Sam 28:18 and the five sins of Saul cited above from *Lev. Rab.* 26/7. The final verse of the Biblical Antiquities, 65:5, deals with the dying Saul's asking David not to be "mindful of my hatred or injustice" *(OTP* 2.377). Here too, Saul seeks forgiveness at the moment of his death.

[283]Cf. Nickelsburg, *Jewish Literature* 55 and 64.

death in battle "to atone thereby for his sins...."[284] I suggest that a scribe who venerated Saul, or thought it unfair to emphasize only his wickedness, later changed either αὐτοῦ (his = Saul's) or Σαυλοῦ (Saul's) into the similar-sounding λαοῦ (the people's). If this is basically correct, Saul's death was thought to atone for his sins in Judaic tradition not only in the first half of the first century C.E., but already at the beginning of the second century B.C.E.

In *Pirqe de Rabbi Eliezer*, generally thought to be a very late midrash, this atonement motif has been retained. In chapter 33, R. Yoḥanan[285] says that in contrast to all other prophets, Samuel prophesied both during his lifetime and after his death. This is true because "Samuel said to Saul: 'If thou wilt hearken to my advice to fall by the sword, then shall thy death be an atonement (כפרה) for thee, and thy lot shall be with me in the place where I abide.'"[286] Like Pseudo-Philo and probably Sirach, this midrash views Saul's death as atoning for his iniquities. It leads to his being with Samuel in his heavenly division (under the throne of God).[287]

Tannaitic Judaic texts support the idea of a condemned criminal's death atoning for all his sins. After such a person is led out to the site of execution, if he does not know how to confess, according to *m. Sanh.* 6:2 he should say: "May my death be an atonement (כפרה) for all my sins."[288] Before this the general statement is made that "everyone that makes his confession has a share in the world to come."[289] In *m. Yoma* 8:8 it is stated that "death and the Day of Atonement effect atonement if there is repentance."[290] The same thought is probably meant in 1 Cor 5:5, where Paul suggests that an immoral person be delivered "to Satan for the destruction of the flesh, that his spirit may be saved in the day of the Lord Jesus."[291]

* * *

The above sources, especially the very early ones on repentant Saul's death in battle as an atonement for his iniquities, in connection with

---

[284]*Legends* 6.237, n. 77, referring also to Pseudo-Philo and the rabbis.

[285]The first editions have R. Nathan, a fourth generation Tanna (Strack and Stemberger, *Introduction* 88).

[286]Friedlander 246, based on MS Epstein. The Hebrew is found in Eshkol 116. This shows that even a rather late midrash can at times retain a very old motif.

[287]Cf. Friedlander 246: "With me in my division in heaven."

[288]Danby 390; Hebrew in Albeck 4.186. Josh 7:19 and 25 serve as the proof texts, the latter verse also being applied to the world to come.

[289]Danby, *ibid.*

[290]Danby 172; Hebrew in Albeck 2.246.

[291]For many other references, cf. chapter 17, "Forgiveness and Reconciliation with God," in Schechter, *Aspects* 293-312.

Samuel's then promising that he will be with him the next day in his heavenly division, under the throne of God, make it very probable that this whole complex formed the background for the Palestinian Jewish Christian author who composed Luke 23:39-43. Like the repentant murderer Saul, the repentant criminal on the cross next to Jesus is granted life with him in Paradise. The confession/acknowledgment of his guilt, as well as his death, atoned for all his sins. As a special reward, Jesus promises to intercede with his heavenly Father for him so that the repentant criminal, after expiring, can be with him even today, in Paradise.[292]

5.   Corrections of Previous Interpretations of Luke 23:39-43.

In light of the results obtained in section 1-4 above, many previous views of Luke 23:39-43 must be modified or even radically changed.

1)   None of the commentators has recognized the major significance of Judaic interpretation of 1 Samuel 28, especially v 19, in this pericope.[293] The secondary literature nowhere alludes to it.[294]

2)   While it has been recognized that Luke 23:39-43 does not derive from Luke, up to now the episode has been attributed to "special Luke," i.e., the source ("L") at least informing the material in his passion narrative which differs from that in Mark and Matthew.[295] The analysis above, however, connects it very closely to the two prodigia which immediately follow it in Luke 23:44-45. They, too, are dependent on Judaic interpretation of 1 Samuel 28. The Palestinian Jewish Christian author of Luke 23:39-43 therefore may very well be the same as for the prodigia. He cannot, however, be shown to be responsible for any other material in "L."

---

[292]The possibility of "last minute repentance" certainly became a popular parenetic motif at an early time in the Christian congregations. Cf. R. Bultmann, *The History of the Synoptic Tradition* 283. See also W. Wiefel, *Das Evangelium des Lukas* 398. To my knowledge only A. Plummer in *The Gospel According to S. Luke* 535 calls attention to death as expiation for one's sins. However, he only cites the modern "Confession on a Death Bed" from the *Authorized Prayer Book* for this. He is followed here by L. Sabourin, *L'Evangile de Luc* (Rome: Pontifical Gregorian University, 1985) 369.

[293]Only P. Billerbeck in Str-B 2.264-65 had noted *Pirq. R. El.* 33. He did not describe it in its history of tradition, however.

[294]Cf. relevant bibliography in J. Fitzmyer, *The Gospel According to Luke, X-XXIV* (AB 28A; Garden City, New York: Doubleday, 1985) 1511; G. Wagner, *An Exegetical Bibliography of the New Testament. Luke and Acts* 303-305; W. Wiefel, *Das Evangelium des Lukas* 396; and F. van Segbroeck, *The Gospel of Luke. A Cumulative Bibliography, 1973-1988* (Leuven: University Press, 1989).

[295]Cf. Fitzmyer, *The Gospel According to Luke* 1507, who states here, referring to J. Jeremias: "Lucan redaction in this episode is at a minimum...."

3)   R. Bultmann maintained that Luke 23:39-43, in contrast to Mark 15:32 and Matt 27:44, began to differentiate between the criminals crucified with Jesus, which is "a sign of secondary [and thus later] formulation."[296] While this is generally true, here it is not. The differentiation of the criminals took place in Palestinian Jewish Christian circles already *before* the writing of Mark, with which Luke is otherwise acquainted and from which he borrows. In this respect it is similar to the extensive narrative of the beheading of John the Baptist in Mark 6:17-29, which is a typical Palestinian Jewish Christian haggadic development to explain exactly how Herod Antipas had John beheaded (v 16). It was then also translated into Greek and so became available to Mark *before* the writing of his gospel.[297]

E. Haenchen maintained that Luke 23:43 was "a lateral shoot, which does not belong to the oldest tradition."[298] Yet K.H. Rengstorf is more probably correct in asking whether behind this verse there is a "very old view, later suppressed, according to which Jesus ascended to heaven immediately after his death."[299] In section IV below I will discuss the ascension of Jesus' soul (not body) from the Cross and maintain that Rengstorf's hunch is probably correct. The pericope Luke 23:39-43 does differentiate between the criminals at Jesus' Crucifixion. This is, to be sure, a further development of the earliest tradition. Yet it is a development which was pre-Markan, and which allowed a very early Christology to be expressed (v 43). In this respect it is similar to Matt 27:51b-53, also in part dependent on Judaic tradition regarding 1 Samuel 28.

4)   G. Schneider maintains in regard to Luke 23:43 that the criminal's request is granted immediately after death and not just at the parousia. Jesus' answer emphasizes the aspect of "where," and develops the christological idea of "exaltation." He states: "This correction is a component of Luke's overcoming the eschatological problem of the delay of the parousia...."[300]

---

[296]Cf. his *The History* 309.

[297]See my study *Water into Wine and the Beheading of John the Baptist*. Early Jewish-Christian Interpretation of Esther 1 in John 2:1-11 and Mark 6:17-29, 39-74.

[298]Cf. his *Der Weg Jesu* 530.

[299]*Das Evangelium nach Lukas* 273.

[300]*Das Evangelium des Lukas, Kapitel 11-24* (ÖTKNT 3/2; Gütersloh: Mohn; Würzburg: Echter, 1977) 485. He refers to his own work, *Parousiegleichnisse im Lukas-Evangelium* (SBS 74; Stuttgart: Katholisches Bibelwerk, 1975) 83-84. Schneider even speaks of Jesus' answer as an "astonishing correction of the parousia expectation of the petitioner" (485).

The problem for Schneider is that Luke himself did not compose the scene. The change from the "tomorrow" of 1 Sam 28:19 into "today" already took place in his source, narrated by a Palestinian Jewish Christian who believed Jesus' soul ascended to heaven directly from the Cross. In this respect the narrative resembles Lazarus' being carried immediately at death by angels to Abraham's bosom in 16:22. This, too, does not derive from the Evangelist, but from a special Palestinian Jewish Christian source. Luke himself does no "correcting" in the formulation of 23:43. The passage should therefore not be adduced in regard to his own theology.

5) J. Fitzmyer asks in regard to Luke 23:39-43, "who can say for sure that it did not take place?"[301] He and others like him would like to rescue the historicity of the episode. All attempts to do so are unsuccessful, however, because in light of the analysis above, it was composed by a Palestinian Jewish Christian on the basis of Judaic traditions on 1 Samuel 28. It emphasizes the ascension of Jesus' soul to heaven from the Cross; the possibility of forgiveness as leading to new life, even at the last moment before the death of a base criminal; and the authority of Jesus as the Messiah, very soon to be exalted to heaven next to his Father, to grant such a privilege. These are the religious truths the narrative conveys in spite of the fact that it never took place historically.

6) According to A. Loisy, the impenitent crucified criminal who blasphemes Jesus is unbelieving Judaism. The faith of the repentant criminal indicates the conversion of the world.[302] For the reader of the Gospel of Luke, the first criminal indeed was a Jew and could be thought to represent post-70 C.E. Judaism, which for the most part rejected Jesus as the Messiah. Yet to make the second, repentant Jewish criminal into a Gentile is no longer exegesis, but theological eisegesis.[303]

* * *

The above corrections of viewpoints held by various scholars concerning Luke 23:39-43 should not be seen primarily as negative. Rather, they help to emphasize the positive aspects of the narrative by pointing out what is not true of it. Shadows help the observer to perceive the true lines and extent of an object, here the masterful little incident of a repentant criminal who, to his own surprise, is already

---

[301] *The Gospel* 1508, in dialogue with E. Lohse.

[302] Cf. his *L'Evangile selon Luc* 560.

[303] Cf. Plummer, *The Gospel According to S. Luke* 535: "It is all but certain that the robber was a Jew," and "to a heathen the word 'paradise' would hardly have been understandable."

today granted the privilege of being together with Jesus, the messianic King, in Paradise.

IV
The Ascension of Jesus' Soul from the Cross

Introduction.

In the special Matthean material analyzed in section III.A above, related to Judaic interpretation of the medium of Endor's raising Samuel from the dead in 1 Samuel 28, at Jesus' death many bodies of deceased saints were raised/arose and entered Jerusalem, appearing to many (27:51b-53).[304] These, like the "many righteous" who rose with Samuel, thinking the Day of Judgment had arrived, believed that at Jesus' death the general resurrection had begun. They therefore arose with him. This only makes sense if they are pictured as thinking Jesus' soul ascended to God from the Cross.

In Luke 23:43, also dependent on Judaic interpretation of 1 Samuel 28, Jesus promises the repentant criminal crucified with him: "Today you will be with me in Paradise." No mention is made of "after three days," i.e., only later on Easter Sunday. These words of Jesus also presuppose that his soul ascends to heaven at the time of his death. He promises the repentant criminal crucified with him the same fate, "today."

This is buttressed by Jesus' quotation of Ps 31:6 (Eng. 5) directly before he expires in Luke 23:46: "Into Thy hands I commit my spirit." The Sages, as well as most Jews and Jewish Christians acquainted with Scripture, knew the continuation of this verse: "Thou hast redeemed me, O Lord, faithful God." Here Jesus is described as being confident that God will redeem him from death at the moment he expires on the Cross, and not just after three days.

It thus appears that at least one section of early Palestinian Jewish Christianity, which was well acquainted with and further developed Judaic interpretation of 1 Samuel 28, pictured Jesus' soul as ascending to heaven directly from the Cross. This idea must originally have been widespread, otherwise it could not have survived and entered two of the four canonical gospels, Matthew and Luke, which do not make use of each other.

---

[304]For the reasons mentioned there, "after his [Jesus'] resurrection" should be read as "their," or deleted as a later gloss.

In the Gospel of Peter, composed around the middle of the second century C.E., probably in Syria,[305] between the prodigia of a solar eclipse and the rending of the Temple curtain, 5:19 states: "And the Lord called out and cried, 'My power, my power, thou hast forsaken me!' And having said this 'he was taken up.'"[306]

To my knowledge this is the only remnant of the ascension of Jesus' soul from the Cross in a later gospel. It is significant that it survived in a gospel which was favored by Docetists,[307] who thought Jesus only "appeared" to have suffered and died. The mainstream of Christian tradition had accepted Jesus' resurrection from the dead as occurring after three days, and a non-conformist view could only survive in what later became heretical Christianity.

In the following section I shall first indicate how early Palestinian Jewish Christians came to believe Jesus was exalted already from the Cross, that is, his soul (not his body) ascended to God from there. Then I shall discuss the main reasons for the suppression of this belief in mainstream Christianity. Finally, I shall propose that this belief is at least as old as, if not older than, the view that Jesus was resurrected with both soul and body, three days after his death on the Cross.

1.   *The Origin of the View of Jesus' Soul Ascending from the Cross.*

No text from the Hebrew Bible was more important to the earliest Palestinian Jewish Christians for understanding the Crucifixion than Isa 52:13-53:12, the fourth Servant Song.[308] I pointed out the relevance of the servant's "making intercession for the transgressors/rebels" (53:12) to Jesus' words to the repentant criminal in Luke 23:43 above. The same Isaianic verse states before this that the servant "was numbered with the transgressors/rebels," which was applied by early Christians to Jesus' being crucified with two other persons. His followers also interpreted v 5, "But he was wounded/pierced for our transgressions," as Jesus' being nailed to the Cross. Verse 9, "And they made his grave with...a rich man in his death," was also thought to apply to Joseph of Arimathea, whom Matthew expressly labels "rich" (27:57).

Two other verses from this Servant Song are responsible for the idea of the ascension of Jesus' soul to heaven at his death. First, Isa 52:13 has God state: "Behold, My servant shall prosper, he shall be exalted and lifted up, and shall be very high." The Targum, certainly not anti-

---

[305]Cf. C. Maurer, "The Gospel of Peter," in *New Testament Apocrypha,* ed. E. Hennecke and W. Schneemelcher, 1.180.

[306]*Ibid.* 1.184.

[307]*Ibid.* 1.180. The expression "he was taken up" is not simply another way of expressing death, as Maurer maintains (181). It indeed means ascension.

[308]Cf. the similar statement of J. Jeremias in *Die Abendmahlsworte Jesu* 83.

Christian at this point, speaks here of "My servant, the Messiah."[309] The Septuagint has the servant's being "exalted" (ὑψωθήσεται) and "glorified exceedingly" (δοξασθήσεται σφόδρα),[310] which is almost Johannine. This "exaltation" in the Servant Song can only be thought of as taking place at the time of the servant's death (53:8-9).

Rabbinic tradition relates this Isaiah verse of the King, the Messiah. In *Midr. Ps.* 2/9 on Ps 2:7 ("He said to me, 'You are My son'"), Isa 52:13 is one of three proof texts for the Israelites as God's sons. This is certainly stated against Jesus as God's Son, for the midrash continues by citing Isa 42:1 of an individual, and then Ps 110:1 and Dan 7:13-14, standard texts employed of the Messiah and the son of man.[311] in *Tanhuma* B Toledoth 20 and *Tanhuma* Toledoth 14, the "great mountain" of Zech 4:7 is interpreted as the messianic King, who is called so because he is greater than the three Patriarchs, whereby Isa 52:13 is cited. He is also "exalted," "lifted up" and "very high," more than Abraham, Moses and the ministering angels. The Messiah descends from Zerubbabel and from David, and as the cloud man of 1 Chr 3:24 he is the same figure as in Dan 7:13.[312]

While parts of these two rabbinic comments employing Isa 52:13 are probably quite late, the basic messianic tendency is certainly early, as in the targum, which is not anti-Christian. These traditions show that early Palestinian Jewish Christians could also have interpreted the same verse messianically, applying the servant's being exalted, lifted up and very high, in the context of his death, to God's exaltation of Jesus at the moment of his death on the Cross.

Secondly, directly before it is stated of the servant that "they made his grave...with a rich man in his death" (Isa 53:9), v 8 has: "By oppression and judgment he was 'taken away' (לֻקָּח)"; he was "cut off" out of the land of the living, "stricken" for the transgressions of God's people. For the second phrase the Septuagint has: "For his life is 'taken away' (αἴρεται) from the earth. Because of the iniquities of My people he was led [off] to death." Although I know of no Judaic interpretation of this verse, I suggest that early Palestinian Jewish Christians also

---

[309]Cf. Stenning, *The Targum of Isaiah* 178.

[310]There may be an allusion to this Septuagint verse in Acts 3:13, where Peter in a portico of the Jerusalem Temple says God "glorified his servant Jesus" when he was delivered up and killed. Here, however, the resurrection is mentioned (v 15).

[311]Cf. Braude 1.40-41. In two other interpretations of the same psalm verse, one speaks of God the King and the lord Messiah, and the other states that God does not have a son. Rather, Israel is like a son to Him. The latter is also clearly against Christian appropriation of this passage for Jesus.

[312]Cf. Bietenhard 2.149-150 and Singermann 178-179, respectively.

considered it not to apply to Jesus' being "taken off" to be crucified. Rather, for them it meant his soul was "taken away" to heaven at the moment of his death, before his body was placed in the grave of a rich man, Joseph of Arimathea.[313]

While other texts from the Hebrew Bible may have influenced early Palestinian Jewish Christians' thinking that Jesus' soul was taken up or ascended to heaven at his death on the Cross,[314] Isa 52:13 and 53:9 appear to have been the first and most important passages in this regard.

This is attested by one of the oldest pieces in the NT, the "Christ Hymn" in Phil 2:6-11. Appropriated by Paul from elsewhere (see below), it must have arisen within the first decades after Jesus' death.

In Phil 2:7 the hymn states that Jesus "'emptied himself' (ἑαυτὸν ἐκένωσεν), taking the form of a servant." The verb κενόω primarily means "to empty," but also "to empty out, pour away."[315] I suggest that this "emptying oneself" derives from the passage concerning the servant of Isa 52:13 – 53:12, who is rewarded in the final verse "because he 'poured out' (הערה) his soul to death and was numbered with transgressors/rebels."[316] The verb ערה in the piel can mean "to empty," as a water jar in Gen 24:20, or a chest in 2 Chr 24:11. The hiphil here in Isa 53:12 means to "pour out."[317] The Targum says the servant (himself) "delivered" his soul to death,[318] and the Septuagint turns this into the divine passive: "because his soul 'was delivered' (παρεδόθη) to death." The "emptying" or "pouring out" of one's soul from the body (= sacrificial dying) is thus only found in the Hebrew and Aramaic. The "himself" (ἑαυτὸν) of Jesus' "emptying himself" was necessary in Greek to express the servant's pouring out "his soul."

Phil 2:7 continues by stating that Jesus was "born in the likeness of men." This would indicate that the previous clause regarding the servant's "emptying himself" refers to his leaving his heavenly Father

---

[313]Isa 53:7-8 are quoted in Acts 8:32-33, where the evangelist Philip interprets them of Jesus to the Ethiopian eunuch. It is interesting to note that Philip is presented as converting the man, beginning with this Septuagint passage of Jesus' "humiliation" (on the Cross), parallel to his being "taken up from the earth." Nothing is said here of a resurrection three days later.

[314]Cf., for example, Ps 110:1.

[315]LSJ 938.

[316]After finishing this study, I was able to consult the significant work by R.P. Martin, *Carmen Christi. Philippians ii 5-11 in Recent Interpretation and in the Setting of Early Christian Worship* (SNTSMS; Cambridge: Cambridge University, 1967), who traces this idea back to 1911 (p. 183, n. 3).

[317]Cf. BDB 788. See Ps 141:8, "Do not pour out my soul" = slay me, and the hithpael ptc. in Ps 37:35, "pouring himself." On the verb in the sense of pouring, see also Jastrow 1116.

[318]Stenning 180-81.

and becoming man, as in John 1:14. Yet the origin of the phrase is nevertheless found in Isa 53:12.[319]

This is corroborated in the following, where Phil 2:9 states that Jesus "humbled himself" (ἐταπείνωσεν ἑαυτὸν) and became obedient unto death, even death on a Cross. This "humbling" or "humiliating" (ταπεινόω) probably derives from LXX Isa 53:8, where the Hebrew states: "By 'oppression' (עֹצֶר) and judgment he was taken away." The Septuagint translates "oppression" by "humiliation" (ταπείνωσις). This is also the catch word root which appealed to Paul in inserting the Christ Hymn at this point, for in Phil 2:3 he appeals to his addressees to count others better than themselves "in humility" (τῇ ταπεινοφροσύνῃ). This mind-set is then elaborated in vv 5-11.

Phil 2:9 continues by saying that because Jesus humbled himself through death on the Cross, God has "highly exalted" (ὑπερύψωσεν) him, bestowing on him the name ("Lord"). The verb ὑπερυψόω, found only here in the NT, translates the Hebrew רוּם in Dan Theod. 4:34 and 11:12A. The original author of the Christ Hymn probably employed רוּם also in his Semitic original, deriving it from the very beginning of the Servant Song, Isa 52:13: "Behold, My servant shall prosper, he shall be 'exalted' (יָרוּם) and lifted up, and shall be very high." This רוּם was then translated into Greek in a Hellenistic Jewish Christian setting as ὑπερυψόω, as in Daniel. The מְאֹד, "very," of being "high, exalted" in the same verse may have encouraged the choice of this Greek verb with ὑπερ-. The messianic interpretation of this verse in Judaic sources was noted above.

Finally, if E. Lohmeyer is correct in his assertion that the ὡς ἄνθρωπος at the end of Phil 2:7 derives from the Aramaic "kᵉbarnash," "like a/the son of man," in Judaic apocalypses and Revelation the title for the divine redeemer,[320] the Semitic, probably Aramaic background of the Christ Hymn is made more probable.[321] Since it certainly took some time for it to be translated into Greek, in which form it became available to Paul, it is indeed one of the earliest testimonies as to how the first

---

[319]Cf. the similar thought by J. Jeremias, cited in Martin, *Carmen Christi* 186.

[320]Cf. his *Die Briefe an die Philipper, Kolosser und an Philemon* (Meyer 9; Göttingen: Vandenhoeck & Ruprecht, 1964[13]) 95. See also other allusions to the Servant Song noted by Lohmeyer, for example Isa 52:14 in Phil 2:6's "form" (p. 91, n. 5).

[321]On a possible Aramaic original for the Christ Hymn, cf. Martin, *Carmen Christi* 40-41. On p. 60 he considers it to be possibly from Paul, who originally wrote it in Aramaic. The latter is highly improbable. Paul borrowed it from elsewhere precisely because of its *Greek* catchword root "humble," which fit his train of thought very well. O. Hofius in *Der Christushymnus Philipper 2, 6-11. Untersuchungen zu Gestalt und Aussage eines urchristlichen Psalms* (WUNT 17; Tübingen: Mohr, 1991[2]) has nothing about a possible Semitic original, although on pp. 70-74 he discusses Isa 52:13–53:12 as the background of the Hymn.

Palestinian Jewish Christians viewed Jesus' humiliation on the Cross and exaltation. To do so, they employed motifs and vocabulary from the Suffering Servant Song of Isa 52:13–53:12, including the servant's being "exalted" at the time of his death, when he was "taken away."

When God in Phil 2:8-9 highly exalts and bestows the name "Lord" upon Jesus because he humbles himself by becoming obedient to death on the Cross, Ps 110:1 ("The Lord said to my lord, 'Sit at My right hand...'") is also in the conceptual background. It cannot be emphasized enough that there is no mention of the resurrection here, especially not of "after three days" on Easter Sunday.[322] The Christ Hymn of Philippians, most probably originally in Aramaic, is thus a major support for the thesis that the idea of the ascent of Jesus' soul from the Cross, his "exaltation," basically derives from the Suffering Servant Song of Isa 52:13 – 53:12, especially verses 52:13 and 53:8. When the repentant crucified criminal is described in Luke 23:43 as being with Jesus in Paradise on the same day, and many of the deceased saints rise from their tombs already at Jesus' death in Matt 27:51b-53, these two passages from the Synoptics reflect the same early Christology found in the Christ Hymn of Philippians two: Jesus was exalted already at his death on the Cross, or expressed differently, his soul already then ascended to his heavenly Father.

2.   *The Ascension of Martyrs to Heaven Immediately After Their Death, and Judgment Directly After Death.*

A.

Many modern commentators on Luke's Passion Narrative note that Jesus is described here as a martyr.[323] Belief in a special resurrection to heaven directly after a martyr's death is already found in 2 Maccabees 7, from the middle of the second century B.C.E., a writing which deals with the severe persecution under Antiochus Epiphanes.[324] As G. Nickelsburg notes in regard to 2 Maccabees, the "theme of suffering and

---

[322]Cf. already G. Bertram, "Die Himmelfahrt Jesu vom Kreuz aus und der Glaube an seine Auferstehung" in *Festgabe für Adolf Deissmann zum 60. Geburtstag, 7. November 1926*, ed. K.L. Schmidt (Tübingen: Mohr, 1927) 197 and 206. On p. 209, n. 2, Bertram calls attention to Isa 53:8. See also Lohmeyer, *Die Briefe an die Philipper*...97, who notes that the idea of the Resurrection is constitutive for Paul, which is simply overlooked in the Christ Hymn. I thank C. Wolff of Berlin for calling my attention to Bertram's essay, as well as to several other works.

[323]Cf. for example W. Wiefel, *Das Evangelium nach Lukas* 397-98.

[324]Cf. U. Kellermann, *Auferstanden in den Himmel*. 2 Makkabäer 7 und die Auferstehung der Märtyrer, who connects this belief with Daniel 12, a work also dealing with Antiochus' persecution. He refers to Luke 23:39-43 on pp. 115-116.

vindication draws on a traditional interpretation of Isaiah 52-53."[325] This corroborates my proposal above that the ascension of Jesus' soul from the Cross is based on this Servant Song, primarily 52:13 and 53:8. The martyrs of 2 Maccabees are vindicated by being raised to heaven immediately; the martyr Jesus is also vindicated by being exalted (= raised) to heaven at his death. He enters Paradise "today," before the crucified criminal to whom he grants the same privilege in Luke 23:43.

Rabbinic sources maintain that there is a special division for the martyrs' souls under God's throne of glory. Indeed, their souls are closest to Him.[326] Regarding the well-known martyrdom under Hadrian of R. Ḥanina b. Teradion, a second generation Tanna,[327] Rabbi (Judah the Prince), a fourth generation Tanna,[328] states that he has obtained "eternal life in a single hour."[329] In another version of the story, a philosopher who objects to Ḥanina b. Teradion's being put to death with his wife and daughter is given the same sentence. He then rejoices in this "good news" that "tomorrow my portion will be with them in the world to come."[330]

This narrative, along with other passages from the pseudipigrapha and rabbinic writings,[331] shows that in many Judaic sources one's portion or lot is determined directly at death. This is especially true of the martyrs, who at their death are thought of as immediately entering the division of the righteous under God's throne.

---

[325]Cf. his *Jewish Literature* 121. For the dating, see p. 118.

[326]Cf. respectively *b. Pes.* 50a (Soncino 239, with n. 9; a parallel is found in *b. Bab. Bat.* 10b, Soncino 49-50), and *Eccl. Rab.* 9:10 § 1 (Soncino 8.239). See also 4 Macc 17:18.

[327]Strack and Stemberger, *Introduction* 81.

[328]*Ibid.*, 89-90.

[329]Cf. *b. 'Abod. Zar.* 18a (Soncino 93). Like Jesus and the repentant crucified criminal, Ḥanina b. Teradion caused his executioner, who jumped into the fire with him, to "enter into the life to come." See also *Midr. Ps.* 11/7 on Ps 11:7 (Braude 1.116-117), where in a time of religious persecution a man condemned to death bears the beam for his own gallows. His nephew first mocks him, but later repents and kills himself, thereby preceding his uncle into the Garden of Eden "by a brief hour." Section 11/6 deals with the seven different divisions near God for the righteous in the world to come, comparable to the seven habitations for the wicked in Gehenna (Braude 1.163-166, referring to Ginzberg, *Legends* 5.30).

[330]See *Sifre Deut. Haʾazinu* 307 on Deut 32:4 (Hammer 312).

[331]Cf. the sources cited by Volz, *Eschatologie* 256-65. For the larger context within early Judaism, see now G. Stemberger, "Auferstehung der Toten, I/2. Judentum" in *TRE* 4 (1979) 443-50, with secondary literature on pp. 449-50, and H. Cavallin, "Leben nach dem Tode im Spätjudentum und im frühen Christentum," "I. Spätjudentum," in *Aufstieg und Niedergang der römischen Welt* II 19/1 (1979) 240-345.

B.

A form of judgment directly after death and not just at the end of the ages, i.e., after the general resurrection of the dead, is also found in many Judaic sources. One rabbinic example is that of R. Yoḥanan b. Zakkai, a first generation Tanna,[332] who at his death says he has two roads (directly) before him, one to Paradise (lit. the "Garden of Eden"), and one to Gehenna. He weeps because he doesn't know whether God will sentence him to the latter, or allow him to enter Paradise.[333] Another is that found in *Lev. Rab.* 'Emor 26/7 on Lev 20:27, cited above in section A.3. There Samuel rises (from under the throne of God), thinking the Day of Judgment has arrived. In connection with this it is stated that even the smallest details are written down in a man's (heavenly) account book, which is read out to him at the moment of his death.[334] Other rabbinic examples, as well as some from Hellenistic Jewish sources, are given by P. Volz.[335]

* * *

The above Judaic sources show that when Jesus' soul is depicted in Luke 23:43 as ascending directly to God at his death, this was a common view in early Judaism especially in regard to the death of a martyr.

3. *Early Christian Suppression of the Belief in the Ascension of Jesus' Soul to Heaven from the Cross.*

It was extremely difficult for the early Palestinian Jewish Christian view that Jesus' soul already ascended to heaven from the Cross to maintain itself. This was basically due to two factors: Docetism, and the very strong influence of Hos 6:2.

Both the Apostles' Creed and the Nicene Creed state regarding Jesus after his Crucifixion: "On the third day he rose again." In the latter creed this is followed by "in accordance with the Scriptures." This phrase in turn is based on 1 Corinthians 15, where Paul states that he delivered/handed on to the addressees as of primary importance what he himself received from other, earlier Christians: "that Christ died for our sins in accordance with the Scriptures, that he was buried, that he was raised on the third day in accordance with the Scriptures" (vv 3-4). The first clause is based on the Servant Song of Isa 52:13 – 53:12,

---

[332]Strack and Stemberger, *Introduction* 74-75.
[333]Cf. *'Abot R. Nat.* A 25 (Goldin 106), with a parallel in *b. Ber.* 28b (Soncino 173).
[334]Cf. Soncino 4.333, in regard to Amos 4:13. See also *b. Ta'an.* 11a (Soncino 49), and *y. Ḥag.* 2:1, 77a (Neusner 20.42).
[335]See his *Eschatologie* 265-270, as well as *Midr. Prov.* 14 (Visotzky 73).

described above as also the origin of the idea that Jesus' soul was taken up to heaven from, he was exalted at, the Cross.[336]

The third clause refers primarily to Hos 6:2, "After two days He will revive us; on the third day He will raise us up, that we may live before Him." This verse played such a dominant role in Palestinian Judaism that it would have been almost impossible for early Palestinian Jewish Christians describing Jesus' being raised, his resurrection, not to employ it. Before elucidating this, I would like to propose a short possible reconstruction of Jesus' burial which helps to account for the later application of Hos 6:2 to the Nazarite prophet's being raised up.

Mark 15:42-47 par. with John 19:38-42 has Joseph of Arimathea, a "respected member of the council/Sanhedrin," receive permission from Pilate to take down Jesus' body from the Cross and to bury it.[337] It is extremely improbable that a respected member of the Sanhedrin, which had just demanded that Pilate have Jesus killed, would concern himself with a condemned and executed man's body. For this reason later (however, pre-Marcan) tradition justified Joseph of Arimathea's behavior by proposing that he, too, was looking for the kingdom of God (Mark 15:43 and Luke 23:51). Even later it was thought that he had not consented to the Sanhedrin's "purpose and deed" (Luke 23:51), or he was even secretly a disciple of Jesus (John 19:38). The only thing probably true of this strange account is that the Roman Pilate may have asked the Jewish Sanhedrin, which itself wanted to be rid of the very uncomfortable prophet Jesus, to take care of his burial. The Jews also wanted his death, they could then relieve the Roman soldiers of an unpleasant task, that of disposing of the corpse. Someone delegated by the Sanhedrin, (who was not a member of the council), would then have placed Jesus' body in one of the "two burying places (בתי קברות)...kept in readiness by the court, one for them that were beheaded or strangled, and one for them that were stoned or burned."[338] It should be recalled

---

[336]Cf., for example, C. Wolff, *Der erste Brief des Paulus an die Korinther* (THKNT 7/II; Berlin: Evangelische Verlagsanstalt, 1982) 160: only Isaiah 53 "deals with dying for others."

[337]Matt 27:57, as noted above, already makes Joseph rich, to fulfill Isa 53:9.

[338]Cf. *m. Sanh.* 6:5 (Albeck 4.189; Danby 391). The beginning of the statement is also found in *b. Yeb.* 47b (Soncino 313). There is nothing on these burial sites at *b. Sanh.* 47b (Soncino 314). Nor does *y. Sanh.* 6:10, 23d (Neusner 31. 193) describe them. It only notes that the victims were sinners and bloodthirsty men (Ps 26:9), to be buried off by themselves. The earliest Palestinian Jewish Christians could see in Jesus' body being placed in such a burial site the fulfillment of Isa 53:9 – "And they [the Sanhedrin] made his grave with the wicked." The question of whether the Sanhedrin at this time still had the power of execution (cf. John 18: 31) is immaterial here. Its two burial sites were certainly still available.

that when Jesus was taken captive in the Garden of Gethsemane, *all* his followers forsook him and fled (Mark 14:50 par., and v 27).[339] The earliest tradition has them return to Galilee, where Jesus appeared to them (Mark 16:7; 14:28; John 21). No one knew any longer exactly where Jesus was buried near Jerusalem because, out of fear, *all* his adherents had fled far north to escape the same fate as their master.

Another factor may have also played a role here. In early Palestinian Judaism Moses was considered Israel's first redeemer. The final (second or great) redeemer is the Messiah.[340] God himself buried His servant Moses on Mount Nebo/the top of Pisqah, in Moab, opposite Jericho, "but no man knows the place of his burial to this day" (Deut 34:6). As the exact place of the first redeemer Moses' grave was unknown, so the exact site of Israel's final Savior, the Messiah Jesus, was originally also unknown. In section D.2, n. 243 above I cited rabbinic sources which maintain that at Moses' death his soul was taken immediately to heaven to be close to God[340a] . The same was true for Jesus, whose soul was thought to have ascended to heaven already at his Crucifixion. He was in Paradise the same day (Luke 23:43).

Yet at a very early time, because Jesus' grave site was not known, non-Christians maintained that he did not really die on the Cross. He only appeared to die there, but in fact survived. They said, he himself, still alive, then appeared to his followers. For this reason the Gospel of Matthew, for example, already has guards placed at Jesus' tomb (27:62-66). In addition, "doubting Thomas" may see in Jesus' hands the nailprints, and place his finger in the mark of the nails, and his hand in Jesus' side (John 20:25, 27; see also Luke 24:39). The possibility of only an apparent death was now excluded. The entire narrative of the burial of Jesus by Joseph of Arimathea, in a specific tomb, the site observed by some female followers of Jesus, is a typically Jewish haggadic development to explain what actually happened to Jesus' body, whose burial site was simply unknown.[341] In some respects this development is similar to that regarding the originally unknown grave site of Jesus' mother Mary. Christian tradition later made it specific by locating it

---

[339]The citation of Zech 13:7 in Mark 14:7 was *later* selected to show that yet one more passage of Scripture was fulfilled in Jesus' passion.

[340]Cf. the sources cited in Str-B 1.68-70.

[340a] Cf. also Ginzberg, *Legends* 3. 471-473, and other earlier sources cited in 6. 161-164, as well as K. Haacker and P. Schäfer, "Nachbiblische Traditionen vom Tod des Mose" in *Josephus-Studien*. Festschrift Otto Michel (Göttingen: Vandenhoeck & Ruprecht, 1974) 147-174.

[341]Cf. the similar creation of the figure of Barabbas at Jesus' trial, in my *Barabbas and Esther* 1-27. On the legendary character of the story of the empty tomb, see also Bultmann, *The History* 284-91.

slightly north of the present Garden of Gethsemane at the bottom of the Mount of Olives,[342] as well as near Ephesus.[343]

In the narrative of Jesus' burial by Joseph of Arimathea, which arose at a very early time,[344] Hos 6:2, so popular in Palestinian Judaism, as I will shortly show, was to play a major role. It was first maintained that Jesus' soul ascended directly to God from the Cross. To counter early Docetic speculation, however, the (unknown) whereabouts of Jesus' body had to be explained. Here Hos 6:2 was very helpful. To resolve the question of the unknown burial site of Jesus' body, and to fulfill Scripture (important for gaining Jewish converts), the ascension or resurrection of his soul from the Cross was later modified to mean that God raised him, soul *and* body, "after two days," "on the third day," from a specific tomb into which Joseph of Arimathea had placed him.

According to Jewish calculation, the day began at sundown. If Jesus was crucified on Friday afternoon, this counted as one day, the ensuing Sabbath as the second, and Easter Sunday morning as the third. The problem of the unknown site of Jesus' grave, leading to Docetic reproaches, was solved via the Joseph of Arimathea narrative, and Scripture (Hos 6:2) was simultaneously fulfilled. For these reasons, already at a very early time there was little interest in retaining traditions such as Luke 23:43 and Matt 27:51b-53. They were suppressed by the great majority of Christians.

The main reason Hos 6:2 was applied to Jesus' resurrection from his tomb, however, was probably another. As I pointed out in the "Excursus on 1 Samuel 28 and Psalm 22" in section A above, at the threat of the total annihilation of Persian Jewry through the plans of evil Haman, Esther tells Mordecai to gather all the Jews in Susa and to hold a fast on her behalf, neither eating nor drinking for "three days, night or day." She and her female attendants will do the same. After this she will go to King Ahasuerus, although it is against the law. "And if I perish, I perish" (4:16). "On the third day" Esther then proceeded with her request to her husband (5:1).

---

[342]In the same subterranean Greek Orthodox church the tombs of Joseph, as well as of Mary's parents, Joachim and Anne, are shown today. See Vilnay, *Israel Guide* 155.

[343]This is based on John 19:25-27. On this, see for example S. Erdemgil, *Ephesos* (Istanbul: Net Turistik Yayinlar, 1989) 20-21. In 1950 Pope Pius XII made it into a dogma that Mary "was assumed body and soul into heavenly glory." Cf. the text in A. Dulles, "The Dogma of the Assumption," in *The One Mediator, the Saints, and Mary*. Lutherans and Catholics in Dialogue VIII, ed. H. Anderson, J. Stafford and J. Burgess (Minneapolis: Augsburg, 1992) 289.

[344]It should be noted that Paul never speaks of the empty tomb, although it certainly could have been employed by him to good advantage.

As noted, the Second Targum at this point relates that the sun and moon will be dark and not give their light, and the Patriarchs and inhabitants of Jerusalem leave their graves, similar to the solar eclipse at Jesus' death, and the bodies of many saints rising from their graves in Matt 27:51b-53.

Judaic tradition often labels Esther a "redeemer" of Israel because she saves her people from total destruction.[345] It also says she is seized in the "agony of death" and utters Ps 22:1 directly before encountering the king, which takes place on the third day of the fast, the 15th of Nisan. Motifs and terminology from this, her most terrible hour, were applied by Palestinian Jewish Christians to their Redeemer Jesus' own "agony of death," his Crucifixion, at which he, too, was depicted as uttering Ps 22:1 before expiring. Other verses from the psalm, such as dividing his garments by lot, were also applied to him.[346]

It is precisely in this terrible setting of Esth 5:1 ("Now it came to pass on the third day...") that *Esther Rabbah* relates: "Israel are never left in dire distress more than three days." "This miracle" (of Esther's not perishing, but rather finding grace in the eyes of Ahasuerus, who called off the annihilation of all the Persian Jews and ordered Haman to be hanged/crucified) "also was performed after three days of their fasting." Directly before this Gen 22:4; 42:17; Jonah 2:1 (Eng. 1:17) and Hos 6:2 are cited as examples of God's never leaving His children alone for more than three days when they are in a terrible situation.[347] Variants of this tradition are found in *Midr. Ps.* 22/5 on the "three days" of Esth 4:16, whereby Esther is considered the "hind of the dawn" of Ps 22:1, who "brought forth the morning out of darkness,"[348] and in *Gen. Rab.* Vayera 56/1 on Gen 22:4.[349]

Before Hos 6:2 is cited in this *Esther Rabbah* passage, it is stated: "The dead also will come to life only after three days."[350] *Gen. Rab.* 56/1 cites Hos 6:2 as "the third day of resurrection."[351] The Targum of Hos 6:2 corroborates this, interpreting the phrase "on the third day He will raise us up" as "on the day of the resurrection of the dead He will raise us

---

[345]Cf. the sources I cite in *Barabbas and Esther* 6-7, as well as *Gen. Rab.* Lech Lecha 39/13 on Gen 12:4 (Soncino 1.324), and *Esth. Rab.* 6/7 on Esth 2:7 (Soncino 9.77).

[346]*Ibid.*, pp. 11-14.

[347]Cf. *Esth. Rab.* 9/2 on Esth 5:1 (Soncino 9.112).

[348]Braude 1.301-302.

[349]Soncino 1.491, with the relevant notes. See also *Gen. Rab.* Mikketz 91/7 on Gen 42:17 in Soncino 2.843. I had already called attention to this motif in *Barabbas and Esther* 9.

[350]Soncino 9.112.

[351]Soncino 1.491.

up."[352] The Septuagint already changes the active of the expression "on the third day He will raise us up" to the middle, "on the third day we shall rise up" (ἀναστησόμεθα), indicating very early interpretation of the verse.

In many other rabbinic sources Hos 6:2 is applied to the resurrection.[353] I therefore suggest that early Palestinian Jewish Christians borrowed Hos 6:2 from the context of the "agony of death" of Israel's redeemer Esther, which included use of Psalm 22, and applied it to describe God's rescuing His only Son, the Redeemer Jesus, from the agony of his Crucifixion, also described in terms of Psalm 22, by raising him "after two days," "on the third day," i.e., on Easter Sunday from the grave. God remained "faithful" by redeeming His Son, who had committed his spirit into His hand when he expired on the Cross (Ps 31:6 in Luke 23:46). He did not "forsake" (Ps 22:1) His Son at the time of his greatest peril, but took him to Himself by raising him "on the third day" of Hos 6:2.

Two other examples of God's delivering imperiled Israelites on the third day aided in applying Hos 6:2 to God's raising Jesus "on the third day." In the Q tradition of Matt 12:40, Jesus says: "For as Jonah was three days and three nights in the belly of the whale, so will the Son of man be three days and three nights in the heart of the earth."[354] Matthew in his version of Q inserted the reference to the "three days and three nights" from Jonah 2:1 (Eng. 1:17) to express Jesus' being in the grave from Good Friday afternoon to Easter Sunday morning. Here early Palestinian Jewish Christians interpreted one more of the standard texts included with Hos 6:2 in the midrashic tradition cited above to indicate that God would not leave Jesus in dire straights in the grave longer than three days, just as He rescued Jonah from the belly of the large

---

[352]Cathcart and Gordon 41, with n. 4. The Aramaic is in Sperber, *The Bible in Aramaic* 3.395.

[353]Cf. *y. Ber.* 5:2 (Neusner 1.202); *y. Sanh.* 11:6, 30c (Neusner 31.388); *Sifre Deut.* Ha'azinu 329 on Deut 32:39 ("I kill and I make alive") in Hammer 340; *Deut. Rab.* Ki Thabo 7/6 on Deut 28:12 (Soncino 7.137); *Eliyyahu Rabbah* 5(6), p. 29 (Braude and Kapstein 107); and *Pirq. R. El.* 51 (Friedlander 411). The second petition of the "Eighteen Prayer," dealing with dew and the resurrection, probably also alludes to Hos 6:2-3. See *Deut. Rab.* Ki Thabo 7/6 above. The talmudic texts *b. Roš. Haš.* 31a (Soncino 147) and *b. Sanh.* 97a (Soncino 657), the latter in a context of when the Messiah is to come, may also refer to the time of the resurrection. Some of these passages are cited by Str-B in 1.647, 649, 747 and 760. M.K. McArthur in "On the Third Day," *NTS* 18 (1971-72) 81-86, also notes many of these rabbinic passages, yet he is not aware of the central importance of the Esther episode. The same is true for K. Lehmann, *Auferweckt am dritten Tage nach der Schrift* (QD 38; Freiburg: Herder, 1968) 266.

[354]The three days and nights are not found in Luke 11:30.

fish/whale after three days. Jonah 2:1 was given the same application as Hos 6:2 because it belonged to an already formed unit of tradition.

Another such text is Gen 22:4's "on the third day," mentioned above with Hos 6:2 and Jonah 2:1. Here, in Judaic tradition, Abraham undergoes his "last trial" by God, of the ten as weighty as all the others combined.[355] The following, derived from various midrashim, indicates points of relevance to Jesus' Crucifixion.

Abraham is to sacrifice his "only son" Isaac at the place he sees "on the third day," which for the rabbis is Mount Moriah at Jerusalem. There Isaac, considered to be thirty-seven years old, willingly accepts his father's "binding" ('Aqedah) him very firmly to the wood of the altar erected there. On the way Abraham had taken the wood of the burnt offering and laid it on his son (22:6). As noted before, rabbinic comment states here: "It is like one who carries his own cross on his shoulder."[356] In one tradition, when Abraham informs Isaac that he, and not a lamb, is to be offered, Isaac states: "May my blood be an atonement for all Israel."[357] Finally, when the blade of Abraham's knife touches Isaac's neck, his soul flees. He then hears God tell Abraham, "Do not lay your hand on the lad" (Gen 22:12). His soul then returns to his body, and Abraham releases him. Thus realizing that the dead would be so revived in the time to come, Isaac is thought to have stated the second benediction of the Eighteen Prayer mentioned above: "Blessed art Thou, O Lord, who quickeneth the dead."[358] As I noted above, Hos 6:2-3 probably lies behind this benediction. G. Friedlander states at this point: "The benediction is appropriately placed in Isaac's mouth, for he had also been bound unto death and then set free. The benediction speaks of the loosening of the bound, as well as of the resurrection."[359]

---

[355]For the phrase, cf. *Gen. Rab.* Vayera 66/11 on Gen 22:15-16 (Soncino 1.501). As I noted in section B.2.3) above on God's "only Son," the monograph by S. Spiegel, *The Last Trial*, is exemplary here. See also the many sources cited by Ginzberg in *Legends* 1.271-86, with the relevant notes.

[356]Cf. Neusner, *Genesis Rabbah* 2.280.

[357]Cf. the text from Midrash ha-Gadol cited by M. Kasher in *Encyclopedia of Biblical Interpretation (Torah Shelemah)*, ed. H. Freedman, 3.144. Isaac's willingness to be sacrificed is already found in *Pseudo-Philo* 32:3, from about the time of Jesus (OTP 2.345).

[358]*Pirq. R. El.* 31 (Friedlander 228). Cf. the parallels in Kasher, *Encyclopedia* 3.150. The tradition is given in the name of R. Judah (bar Ilai), a third generation Tanna (Strack and Stemberger, *Introduction* 84-85). While many of the rabbis' names cited in this midrash are pseudonymous, each statement must be considered by itself. See also Ginzberg, *Legends* 1.282 and 5.251, n. 243.

[359]*Pirke Rabbi Eliezer* 228, n. 7. See also the text of the first editions cited in n. 6. For a different treatment of the 'Aqedah narrative, see Lehmann, *Auferweckt* 267-72.

The many motifs in Judaic traditions concerning the "binding" of Isaac which are similar to Jesus' Crucifixion just outside Jerusalem made it very difficult for early Palestinian Jewish Christians not to apply them to him. One definitely early motif was the use of Hos 6:2 in the scene, indicating that as God caused Abraham's only son Isaac, bound to wood, to be released on the third day, thought of as exemplary of the resurrection, so He released His only Son Jesus from death on the wood of the Cross by raising him from the dead on the third day, Easter Sunday.

The above scriptural texts, Hos 6:2, Esth 5:1, Jonah 2:1 and Gen 22:4, all connected with God's delivering an Israelite from the greatest peril "on the third day," make it understandable that early Jewish Christians whom Paul cites in 1 Cor 15:4 could maintain: Christ "was raised on the third day in accordance with the Scriptures," plural.[360]

* * *

In light of the extremely great influence scriptural texts exerted which were associated in early Judaism with God's rescuing an Israelite from the greatest peril "after three days" and with resurrection, it is remarkable that the earlier view of Jesus' soul ascending to heaven already at his death on the Cross was not suppressed by the mainstream tradition even more. In retrospect, we must be grateful to the Palestinian Jewish Christian communities which dared, probably in spite of great opposition, to preserve traditions such as Luke 23:43, Matt 27:51b-53, and the Gospel of Peter 5:19. The ascension of Jesus' soul from the Cross at his death, to be with God today in Paradise, and the concomitant rising from the dead of many deceased saints, are indeed remnants of a very early Christology, part of bedrock tradition. The latter, as noted, was maintained by K. Stendahl and J. Jeremias on Matt 27:51b-53, and by K. Rengstorf on Luke 23:39-43. The above study corroborates their conclusions, and it shows the close affiliation of these gospel texts with Judaic interpretation of Saul's having Samuel raised from the dead in 1 Samuel 28.

---

[360]They also probably influenced the Son of man's rising "after three days" in the passion predictions of Mark 8:31; 9:31; and 10:34 par.

Sources and Reference Works

I. *The Bible*

Kittel, *Biblia Hebraica*, ed. R. Kittel et al. (Stuttgart: Privilegierte Württembergische Bibelanstalt, 1951[7]).

Lévi, *The Hebrew Text of the Book of Ecclesiasticus*, ed. I. Lévi (SSS 3; Leiden: Brill, 1951; original 1904).

F. Vattioni, *Ecclesiastico*. Testo ebraico con apparato critico e versioni greca, latina e siriaca (Naples: Istituto Orientale di Napoli, 1968).

Rahlfs, *Septuaginta*, ed. A. Rahlfs (Stuttgart: Württembergische Bibelanstalt, 1962[7]).

Ziegler, *Sapientia Iesu Filii Sirach*, Septuaginta, Vetus Testamentum Graecum 12:2, ed. J. Ziegler (Göttingen: Vandenhoeck & Ruprecht, 1980[2]).

Nestle/Aland, *Novum Testamentum Graece*, ed. E. Nestle, K. Aland, et al. (Stuttgart: Deutsche Bibelgesellschaft, 1990[26]).

The Greek New Testament, ed. K. Aland, M. Black, B. Metzger and A. Wikgren (London: United Bible Societes, 1966).

Hebrew New Testament, by F. Delitzsch (Berlin: Trowitzsch and Son, 1885).

Hebrew New Testament (Jerusalem: The United Bible Societies, 1979).

II. *The Targums*

Sperber, *The Bible in Aramaic*, ed. A. Sperber (Leiden: Brill, 1959), 4 volumes.

Aberbach and Grossfeld, *Targum Onkelos to Genesis*, ed. and trans. M. Aberbach and B. Grossfeld (New York, Ktav; Denver: University of Denver, Center for Judaic Studies, 1982).

Drazin, *Targum Onkelos to Exodus*, ed. and trans. I. Drazin (New York, Ktav; Denver: University of Denver, Center for Judaic Studies, 1990).

Rieder, *Targum Jonathan ben Uziel on the Pentateuch*, ed. with a Hebrew translation by D. Rieder (Jerusalem, 1984), 2 volumes.

Díez Macho, *Neophyti 1*, Tomo I, Génesis, ed. and trans. A. Díez Macho (Madrid/Barcelona: Consejo Superior de Investigaciones Cientificas, 1968). Tomo II, Éxodo, 1970.

Klein, *The Fragment-Targums of the Pentateuch*, ed. and trans. M. Klein (AnBib 76; Rome: Biblical Institute, 1980), 2 volumes.

Etheridge, *The Targums of Onkelos and Jonathan Ben Uzziel on the Pentateuch with the Fragments of the Jerusalem Targum*, trans. J. Etheridge (New York: KTAV, 1968; original 1862).

Harrington and Saldarini, *Targum Jonathan of the Former Prophets*, trans. D. Harrington and A. Saldarini (The Aramaic Bible 10; Edinburgh: Clark, 1987).

Stenning, *The Targum of Isaiah*, ed. and trans. J. Stenning (Oxford: Clarendon, 1949).

Cathcart and Gordon, *The Targum of the Minor Prophets*, trans. K. Cathcart and R. Gordon (The Aramaic Bible 14; Edinburgh: Clark, 1989).

Levine, *The Aramaic Version of Lamentations*, ed. and trans. E. Levine (New York: Hermon, 1981).

Grossfeld, *The First Targum to Esther*, ed. and trans. B. Grossfeld (New York: Sepher-Hermon, 1983).

Grossfeld, *The Two Targums of Esther*, trans. B. Grossfeld (The Aramaic Bible 18; Edinburgh: Clark, 1991).

Cassel, *Aus Literatur und Geschichte. Zweites Targum zum Buche Esther. Im vocalisirten Urtext*, ed. P. Cassel (Leipzig and Berlin: Friedrich, 1885).

Cassel, *An Explanatory Commentary on Esther* (with an English translation by P. Cassel of the Second Targum; Edinburgh: Clark, 1888).

Sulzbach, *Targum Scheni zum Buch Esther*, German by A. Sulzbach (Frankfurt am Main: Kauffmann, 1920).

Le Déaut/Robert, *Targum des Chroniques (Cod. Vat. Urb. Ebr. 1)*, ed. with a French translation by R. Le Déaut and J. Robert (AnBib 51; Rome: Biblical Institute, 1971).

III. The Mishnah and Tosefta

Albeck, *Shisha Sidre Mishna*, ed. Ch. Albeck (Jerusalem and Tel Aviv: Bialik Institute and Dvir, 1975), 6 volumes.

Danby, *The Mishnah*, trans. H. Danby (London: Oxford University, 1933).

Zuckermandel, *Tosephta*, ed. M. Zuckermandel, with a supplement by S. Liebermann (Jerusalem: Wahrmann, 1970).

Neusner, *The Tosefta*, trans. J. Neusner et al. (Hoboken, New Jersey: KTAV, 1977-1986), 6 volumes.

IV. The Talmuds

Soncino, *The Babylonian Talmud*, ed. I. Epstein, various translators (London: Soncino, 1952), 18 volumes and index.

Soncino, *The Minor Tractates of the Talmud*, ed. A. Cohen, various translators (London: Soncino, 1965), 2 volumes.

Goldschmidt, *Der Babylonische Talmud*, ed. with a German translation by L. Goldschmidt (Haag: Nijoff, 1933), 9 volumes.

Krotoshin, *Talmud Yerushalmi*, Krotoshin edition (Jerusalem: Shilah, 1969).

Neusner, *The Talmud of the Land of Israel*, trans. J. Neusner et al. (Chicago: University of Chicago, 1982-), 34 volumes.

Horowitz, *Berakhoth*, German of the Talmud Yerushalmi by C. Horowitz (Tübingen: Mohr, 1975).

Hüttenmeister, *Megilla*, German of the Talmud Yerushalmi by F. Hüttenmeister (Tübingen: Mohr, 1987).

Wewers, *Hagiga*, German of the Talmud Yerushalmi by G. Wewers (Tübingen: Mohr, 1983).

V. Halakhic Midrashim

Lauterbach, *Mekilta de-Rabbi Ishmael*, ed. and trans. J. Lauterbach (Philadelphia: The Jewish Publication Society of America, 1976), 3 volumes.

Horowitz, *Siphre ad Numeros adjecto Siphre zutta,* ed. H. Horowitz (Jerusalem: Wahrmann, 1976).

Neusner, *Sifré to Numbers,* trans. J. Neusner (BJS 118-119; Atlanta: Scholars, 1986), 2 volumes.

Kuhn, *Der tannaitische Midrasch Sifre zu Numeri,* German by K. Kuhn (Stuttgart: Kohlhammer, 1959).

Finkelstein, *Sifre on Deuteronomy,* ed. L. Finkelstein (New York: The Jewish Theological Seminary of America, 1969).

Hammer, *Sifre.* A Tannaitic Commentary on the Book of Deuteronomy, trans. R. Hammer (YJS 24; New Haven: Yale University, 1986).

Neusner, *Sifre to Deuteronomy.* An Analytical Translation, trans. J. Neusner (BJS 98 and 101; Atlanta: Scholars, 1987), 2 volumes.

VI. *Haggadic Midrashim*

Soncino, *Midrash Rabbah,* ed. H. Freedman and M. Simon (London: Soncino, 1939), 9 volumes and index.

Theodor and Albeck, *Midrash Bereshit Rabba,* ed. J. Theodor and Ch. Albeck (Jerusalem: Wahrmann, 1965), 3 volumes.

Neusner, *Genesis Rabbah,* trans. J. Neusner (BJS 104-106; Atlanta: Scholars, 1985), 3 volumes.

Margulies, *Leviticus Rabbah: Midrash Wayyikra Rabbah,* ed. M. Margulies (Jerusalem: Ministry of Education and Culture of Israel, American Academy for Jewish Research, 1953-1960).

Neusner, *Judaism and Scripture.* The Evidence of Leviticus Rabbah, trans. J. Neusner (Chicago Studies in the History of Judaism; Chicago: University of Chicago, 1986).

Midrash Tanḥuma, Eshkol edition (Jerusalem: Eshkol, no date).

Singermann, *Midrasch Tanchuma* (only Genesis), ed. with a German translation by F. Singermann (Berlin: Lamm, 1927).

Buber, *Midrasch Tanchuma:* Ein agadischer Commentar zum Pentateuch, ed. S. Buber (Vilna: Romm, 1985).

Bietenhard, *Midrasch Tanḥuma B,* German by H. Bietenhard (Judaica et Christiana 5-6; Bern: Peter Lang, 1980-1982), 2 volumes.

Buber, *Midrash Aggadah on the Pentateuch,* ed. S. Buber (Vienna: Fanto, 1894), 2 volumes.

Buber, *Aggadat Bereshit*, ed. S. Buber (Cracow: Fischer, 1902; reprint Vilna: Romm, 1925).

Midrash Haggadol on the Pentateuch, ed. M. Margulies. Leviticus, ed. A. Steinsalz (Jerusalem: Kook, 1976).

Schechter, *Aboth de Rabbi Nathan* (A and B), ed. S. Schechter (Vienna, 1887; reprinted New York: Feldheim, 1945).

Goldin, *The Fathers According to Rabbi Nathan (A)*, trans. J. Goldin (YJS 10; New Haven: Yale University, 1955).

Neusner, *The Fathers According to Rabbi Nathan. An Analytical Translation and Explanation*, trans. J. Neusner (BJS 114; Atlanta: Scholars, 1986).

Saldarini, *The Fathers According to Rabbi Nathan (B)*, trans. A. Saldarini (SJLA 11; Leiden: Brill, 1975).

Mandelbaum, *Pesikta de Rav Kahana*, ed. B. Mandelbaum (New York: The Jewish Theological Seminary of America, 1962), 2 volumes.

Braude and Kapstein, *Pesikta de-Rab Kahana*, trans. W. Braude and I. Kapstein (Philadelphia: Jewish Publication Society of America, 1975).

Neusner, *Pesiqta de Rab Kahana. An Analytical Translation*, trans. J. Neusner (BJS 122-123; Atlanta: Scholars, 1987).

Friedmann, *Pesikta Rabbati*, ed. M. Friedmann (Vienna, 1880; reprint Tel-Aviv, 1962-1963).

Braude, *Pesikta Rabbati*, trans. W. Braude (YJS 18; New Haven: Yale University, 1968), 2 volumes.

Friedmann, *Seder Eliahu rabba und Seder Eliahu zuta*, ed. M. Friedmann (Vienna, 1902-1904; reprint Jerusalem, 1969).

Braude and Kapstein, *Tanna debe Eliyyahu*, trans. W. Braude and I. Kapstein (Philadelphia: The Jewish Publication Society of America, 1981).

Buber, *Midrasch Samuel*, ed. S. Buber (Cracow: Fischer, 1893).

Wünsche, "Der Midrasch Samuel," German in A. Wünsche, *Aus Israels Lehrhallen*, V (Leipzig: Pfeiffer, 1910).

Buber, *Midrasch Tehillim*, ed. S. Buber (Vilna: Romm, 1891).

Braude, *The Midrash on Psalms*, trans. W. Braude (YJS 13, 1-2; New Haven: Yale University, 1959), 2 volumes.

Visotzky, *The Midrash on Proverbs*, trans. B. Visotzky (YJS 27; New Haven: Yale University, 1992).

Wünsche, "Der Midrasch Sprüche," German by A. Wünsche in *Bibliotheca Rabbinica* (Leipzig: Schulze, 1885) 4.1-77.

Eshkol, *Pirqe Rabbi Eliezer*, Eshkol edition (Jerusalem: Eshkol, 1973).

Friedlander, *Pirke de Rabbi Eliezer*, trans. G. Friedlander (New York: Hermon, 1970; original London, 1916).

Enelow, *The Mishnah of Rabbi Eliezer, or The Midrash of Thirty-Two Hermeneutical Rules*, ed. H. Enelow (New York: Bloch, 1933).

Milikowsky, *Seder Olam. A Rabbinic Chronography*, ed. and trans. Ch. Milikowsky (1981 Yale University Ph.D. dissertation).

VII. *Apocrypha, Pseudepigrapha, Philo and Josephus*

Apocrypha: see Rahlfs, *Septuaginta*.

OTP. The Old Testament Pseudepigrapha, ed. J. Charlesworth (Garden City, New York: Doubleday, 1983-1985), 2 volumes.

APOT, The Apocrypha and Pseudepigrapha of the Old Testament, II. Pseudepigrapha, ed. R. Charles (Oxford: Clarendon, 1913).

Harrington, *Les Antiquités Bibliques*, ed. D. Harrington, French by J. Cazeaux (SC 229-230; Paris: du Cerf, 1976), 2 volumes.

Saltman, *Pseudo-Jerome. Quaestiones on the Book of Samuel*, trans. A. Saltman (SPB 26; Leiden: Brill, 1975).

LCL, *Philo*, Greek and English translation by F. Colson, G. Whitaker, J. Earp and R. Marcus (Cambridge, Massachusetts: Harvard University, 1971), 10 volumes with 2 supplements.

LCL, *Josephus*, Greek and English translation by H. Thackeray, R. Marcus and A. Wikgren (Cambridge, Massachusetts: Harvard University, 1969), 9 volumes.

VIII. *Qumran*

Lohse, *Die Texte aus Qumran*, ed. with a German translation by E. Lohse (Darmstadt: Wissenschaftliche Buchgesellschaft, 1971).

Dupont-Sommer, *The Essene Writings from Qumran*, trans. A. Dupont-Sommer (Cleveland: The World, 1962).

Allegro, J., *Qumran Cave 4*, including "The Vision of Samuel," 4Q160 (DJD 5; Oxford: Clarendon, 1968).

Ulrich, Jr., E., *The Qumran Text of Samuel and Josephus* (HSM 19; Missoula, MT: Scholars, 1978).

Maier, *Die Tempelrolle vom Toten Meer*, German by J. Maier (Munich and Basel: Reinhardt, 1978).

Fitzmyer, J., *The Dead Sea Scrolls*. Major Publications and Tools for Study (SBLRBS 20; Atlanta: Scholars, 1990).

IX. *The Early Church*

Lake, *The Apostolic Fathers*, Greek and English translation by K. Lake (Cambridge, Massachusetts: Harvard University, 1959), 2 volumes.

Hennecke/Schneemelcher, *New Testament Apocrypha*, ed. E. Hennecke and W. Schneemelcher (Philadelphia: Westminster, 1963-1965), 2 volumes.

von Otto, *Iustini Philosophi et Martyris Opera*, ed. C. von Otto (Jena: Dufft, 1876-1881), 5 volumes.

The Ante-Nicene Fathers 1, trans. A. Roberts, J. Donaldson and A. Coxe (Grand Rapids, Michigan: Eerdmans, 1979).

Origène, *Homélies sur Samuel*, ed. with a French translation by P. and M.-T. Nautin (SC 328; Paris: du Cerf, 1986).

The Nag Hammadi Library, ed. J. Robinson (San Francisco: Harper & Row, 1977).

Migne, *Patrologia Graeca*, ed. with a Latin translation by J. Migne (Paris, 1857-1866), 167 volumes.

Migne, *Patrologia Latina*, ed. J. Migne (Paris, 1841-1864), 221 volumes.

X. *Pagan Authors*

Plutarch, *The Lives*, Greek text with an English translation by B. Perrin (LCL; Cambridge, Massachusetts: Harvard University, 1982), 11 volumes.

Dio Cassius, *Roman History*, Greek text with an English translation by E. Cary (LCL; Cambridge, Massachusetts: Harvard University, 1954), 9 volumes.

Ovid, *Metamorphoses*, Latin text with an English translation by F. Miller (LCL; Cambridge, Massachusetts: Harvard University, 1958-1960), 2 volumes.

XI. *Dictionaries and Reference Works*

BDB, *A Hebrew and English Lexicon of the Old Testament*, by F. Brown, S. Driver and C. Briggs (Oxford: Clarendon, 1962).

Jastrow, *A Dictionary of the Targumim, the Talmud Babli and Yerushalmi, and the Midrashic Literature*, by M. Jastrow (New York: Pardes, 1950), 2 volumes.

Levy, *Neuhebräisches und chaldäisches Wörterbuch über die Talmudim und Midraschim*, by J. Levi (Berlin and Vienna, 1924²), 4 volumes.

Segal, *A Grammar of Mishnaic Hebrew*, by M. Segal (Oxford: Clarendon, 1958).

Dalman, *Grammatik des jüdisch-palästinischen Aramäisch*, by G. Dalman (Leipzig: Hinrichs, 1927²).

Sokoloff, *A Dictionary of Jewish Palestinian Aramaic of the Byzantine Period*, by M. Sokoloff (Ramat-Gan: Bar Ilan University, 1990).

Krauss, *Griechische und Lateinische Lehnwörter in Talmud, Midrasch und Targum*, by S. Krauss (Berlin: Calvary, 1898-1899).

Eissfeldt, *The Old Testament. An Introduction*, by O. Eissfeldt (Oxford: Blackwell, 1966).

Nickelsburg, *Jewish Literature Between the Bible and the Mishnah*, by G. Nickelsburg (Philadelphia: Fortress, 1981).

Schürer, *The history of the Jewish people in the age of Jesus Christ (175 B.C. – A.D. 135)*, by E. Schürer, ed. G. Vermes, F. Millar and M. Black (Edinburgh: Clark, 1973-1986), 3 volumes.

Strack and Stemberger, *Introduction to the Talmud and Midrash*, by H. Strack and G. Stemberger (Minneapolis: Fortress, 1992). At times I refer to the German, *Einleitung in Talmud und Midrasch* (Munich: Beck, 1982⁷).

Kasher, *Encyclopedia of Biblical Interpretation*, ed. M. Kasher, trans. H. Freedman, Genesis III (New York: American Biblical Encyclopedia Society, 1957).

Ginzberg, *The Legends of the Jews*, by L. Ginzberg (Philadelphia: The Jewish Publication Society of America, 1968), 6 volumes and index.

JE, The Jewish Encyclopedia (New York: Funk and Wagnalls, 1905), 12 volumes.

Enc Jud, Encyclopaedia Judaica (Jerusalem: Keter, 1971), 16 volumes.

Volz, *Die Eschatologie der jüdischen Gemeinde,* by P. Volz (Tübingen: Mohr, 1934^2).

LSJ, *A Greek-English Lexicon,* by H. Liddell, R. Scott and H. Jones (Oxford: Clarendon, 1966^9).

BAGD, *A Greek-English Lexicon of the New Testament and Other Early Christian Literature,* by W. Bauer, W. Arndt, F. Gingrich and F. Danker (Chicago: University of Chicago, 1979^2).

BDF, *A Greek Grammar of the New Testament and Other Early Christian Literature,* ed. F. Blass, A. Debrunner and R. Funk (Chicago: University of Chicago, 1962).

TDNT, Theological Dictionary of the New Testament, ed. G. Kittel and G. Friedrich (Grand Rapids, Michigan: Eerdmans, 1964-1976), 9 volumes and index.

Kümmel, *Einleitung in das Neue Testament,* by P. Feine, J. Behm and W. Kümmel (Heidelberg: Quelle & Meyer, 1983^{21}).

Str-B, *Kommentar zum Neuen Testament aus Talmud und Midrasch,* by (H. Strack and) P. Billerbeck (Munich: Beck, 1924-1961), 6 volumes.

Wettstein, J., *Novum Testamentum Graecum* (Amsterdam: Dommerian, 1752).

IDB, The Interpreter's Dictionary of the Bible, ed. G. Buttrick et al. (New York and Nashville: Abingdon, 1962), 4 volumes. *Supplementary Volume,* ed. K. Crim et al., 1976.

PW, *Realencyclopädie der classischen Altertumswissenschaft,* ed. A. Pauly, G. Wissowa et al. (Stuttgart: Metzler, 1889-).

Index of Modern Authors

About the Author

Roger David Aus, b. 1940, studied English and German at St. Olaf College, and theology at Harvard Divinity School, Luther Theological Seminary, and Yale University, from which he received the Ph.D. degree in New Testament Studies in 1971. He is an ordained clergyman of the Evangelical Lutheran Church in America, currently serving the German-speaking Luthergemeinde in Berlin-Reinickendorf, Germany. The Protestant Church of West Berlin kir 'ly granted him a short study leave in Jerusalem, Israel, in 1981. His study of New Testament topics always reflects his great interest in, and deep appreciation of, the Jewish roots of the Christian faith.

South Florida Studies in the History of Judaism